THE REVOLUTIONA

FREDERI

Engels

Edited by **John Rees**

INTERNATIONAL SOCIALISM 65 ★ SPECIAL ISSUE

THE REVOLUTIONARY IDEAS OF FREDERICK ENGELS

by Lindsey German, John Rees, Chris Harman and Paul McGarr

Edited by John Rees

Issue 65 of International Socialism, quarterly journal of the
Socialist Workers Party (Britain)
Published December 1994
Copyright © International Socialism

Distribution/subscriptions: International Socialism,
PO Box 82, London E3.

American distribution: B de Boer, 113 East Center St, Nutley,
New Jersey 07110.

Subscriptions and back copies: PO Box 16085, Chicago, Illinois 60616

Editorial and production: 071-538 1626/071-538 0538

Sales and subscriptions: 071-538 5821

American sales: 312 666 7337

ISBN 0906-224993

Printed by BPC Wheatons Ltd, Exeter, England
Typeset by East End Offset, London E3

Cover design by Ian Goodyer

Subscription rates for one year (four issues) are:

Britain and overseas (surface):	individual	£14.00 ($30)
	institutional	£25.00
Air speeded supplement:	North America	nil
	Europe/South America	£2.00
	elsewhere	£4.00

Note to contributors

The deadline for articles intended for issue 67 of *International Socialism* is
1 February 1995.

All contributions should be double-spaced with wide margins. Please
submit two copies. If you write your contribution using a computer, please
also supply a disk, together with details of the computer and programme
used.

THE REVOLUTIONARY IDEAS OF

FREDERICK

Engels

CONTENTS

INTERNATIONAL SOCIALISM 65 ★ SPECIAL ISSUE

Frederick Engels: life of a revolutionary

LINDSEY GERMAN

Frederick Engels came from a privileged family but devoted his life to struggling for the poor and oppressed. He was a man of action but spent much of his time developing theoretical ideas. He worked in a job he hated to enable Karl Marx to concentrate on his studies which produced the three volumes of *Capital*. These were the two dominant features of Engels' life: his 50 year long commitment to revolutionary socialism and to working class struggle, and his equally strong personal commitment to Karl Marx, who he sustained politically, financially and with a deep friendship for 40 years until the relationship was broken by Marx's death in 1883.

Engels had no doubts on either count. He wrote to his mother in 1871, when he was criticised for supporting the first workers' government, the Paris Commune:

> *You know my views have not changed for nearly 30 years, and it cannot have come as a surprise to you that, when events compelled me, I should not only maintain them but also do my duty in other ways. You would have reason to be ashamed of me if I did not do so. If Marx was not here, if he did not exist at all, it would make no difference to that.*[1]

Commenting on his political and intellectual relationship with Marx, he wrote elsewhere that he was doing what he 'was meant for, to play second fiddle.'[2] Yet Engels was much more than a 'second fiddle'. He

was an independent revolutionary thinker, who was already in the
process of writing one of his finest books by the time he began his close
friendship with Marx in 1844. He combined an original mind with an
enthusiasm for revolution and struggle which never left him.

Early life

Frederick was born in Barmen (now Wuppertal) in the Ruhr region of
Germany on 28 November 1820. He was the eldest in the family of a
mill owner. The young Engels' politics, atheism and activity were a constant source of worry to, and disagreement with, his father. His home life
was comfortable and middle class, but he grew up in what was effectively becoming a factory district, since the adjoining town of Elberfeld
was experiencing its own industrial revolution, with the creation of a
growing working class. So, as his biographer Gustav Mayer has put it,
Engels knew from childhood the real nature of the factory system.[3]
    The defeat of Napoleon in 1815 led to the dominance of Prussian and
Austrian reaction in central Europe during Engels' youth. By the time he
was politically conscious, that had begun to change. The revolution of
July 1830 in France, which established a constitutional monarchy, gave
hope to liberals in Germany. There were the beginnings of movements
against the old tyranny. Germany at the time comprised a number of
sometimes tiny states with varying levels of economic and political
development dominated by Prussia which was by far the most important.
Many of the movements, particularly in the south German states, were
directed at Prussian autocracy.
    Engels was a supporter of these movements and ideas. He was also an
enthusiastic proponent of liberal German nationalism from a young age.
He was sent to work in the port of Bremen and did his military national
service for a year in Berlin where he mixed with others of similar views.
He wrote on literature and political issues under the name of Friedrich
Oswald, and discovered a proficiency in languages.
    He was attracted first to the Young Germany movement, whose liter-
ature and ideas expressed the youthful hopes of a new generation who
were trying to find the liberty they had read about in the French
Revolution of 1789 and its much paler shadow, the revolution of 1830.
The importance of philosophy in German intellectual life meant that
these ideas often expressed themselves in philosophical terms. The
Germans talked about what others did, as Marx put it, comparing the
Germans unfavourably with the English and French who had made their
bourgeois revolutions in the 17th and 18th centuries respectively. He saw
the predominance of philosophical thought in Germany as a sign of the
country's economic backwardness.

Engels and Marx were themselves products of this intellectual environment and therefore first developed an interest in philosophy. They were attracted to the ideas of the philosopher Hegel, the impact of whose teachings was revolutionary, since they stressed that the universe is in a constant process of development and change. This led many of his followers to believe that the struggle against existing institutions, for example the Prussian state and the monarchy, was an inevitable part of social development. Engels joined the Young Hegelians, and later became influenced by the ideas of communism, to which he was already attracted by the early 1840s.

So the young Frederick Engels had already developed left wing ideas when he was despatched to England at the end of 1842 to work in the family firm of Ermen and Engels, manufacturers of sewing thread in Manchester. His experience in England helped to create in Engels an understanding that the working class had the potential to put his communist ideas into practice. He arrived in England only weeks after the Chartist general strike of 1842 which, despite its eventual failure, had demonstrated the potential power of the workers. The strike's centre was in Manchester and the surrounding areas of Lancashire and Cheshire, the areas of textile production. England was by far the most advanced industrial economy in the world, having been the scene of the Industrial Revolution. It was already leading the world in the production of cotton, coal and iron. Its working class was also the most advanced in the world, organised through the Chartist movement.

Engels was horrified at the poverty and misery that he saw in Manchester. The city had grown up around the cotton industry and was a mass of filthy slums. Infant mortality, epidemic diseases and overcrowding were all facts of life. Up to a quarter of the city's population were immigrant Irish, driven there by even worse conditions in their own country. Poverty had existed in the old towns and rural areas—as it had done in Germany—but the growth of the big cities exacerbated and accentuated these conditions. The attitude of the capitalist class was brutal. Engels describes how:

> I once went into Manchester with such a bourgeois, and spoke to him of the bad, unwholesome method of building, the frightful condition of the working people's quarters, and asserted that I had never seen so ill-built a city. The man listened quietly to the end, and said at the corner where we parted: 'And yet there is a great deal of money made here; good morning, sir.'[4]

The effect of Manchester on the young man was electrifying. He came into contact with the Chartists and, in 1843, visited the Leeds office of the Chartist newspaper, the *Northern Star*. One of their leaders,

George Julian Harney, much later recorded this impression of Engels at that meeting: 'a slender young man with a look of almost immaturity, who spoke remarkably pure English, and said he was keenly interested in the Chartist movement'. Harney went on to say that Engels was as modest and retiring 50 years later as he was when a young man of 22 years old.[5]

Engels travelled round, spoke to workers and studied official statistics to produce his remarkable first book, *The Condition of the Working Class in England*. It documents not only how people lived, but also explains how this state of affairs could be—and needed to be—changed. Even today the book is cited by those quite hostile to Engels' politics for its accurate and sympathetic descriptions of working class life. However, the book is much more than reportage of the terrible conditions in which workers lived. Woven into it is the political analysis of capitalism which Marx and Engels later developed but which even at this stage was central to the book's analysis. Engels starts by looking at how the Industrial Revolution transformed the old ways of working to such an extent that it created a whole class of wage labourers, the proletariat. The introduction of machinery into the production of textiles, coal and iron turned the British economy into the most dynamic in the world, creating a mass of communications networks—iron bridges, railways, canals—which in turn led to more industrial development.

The new working class soon accounted for the mass of the population, as capitalist methods of manufacturing destroyed many of the old artisan or middle classes, turning the bulk of them or their children into workers. The needs of manufacturing industry led to the building of factories and mills and, moreover, 'population becomes centralised just as capital does.'[6] Industrial towns then developed into the great cities that Engels observed when he first visited England. He describes in great detail the condition of life in these cities, using a variety of contemporary press reports, official investigations and even diagrams of the back-to-back houses which formed the early Manchester slums. Nothing escapes Engels' eye, not even the workers' diet:

The better paid workers, especially those in whose families every member is able to earn something, have good food as long as this state of things lasts; meat daily and bacon and cheese for supper. Where wages are less, meat is used only two or three times a week, and the proportion of bread and potatoes increases. Descending gradually, we find the animal food reduced to a small piece of bacon cut up with the potatoes; lower still, even this disappears, and there remain only bread, cheese, porridge and potatoes, until on the lowest round of the ladder, among the Irish, potatoes form the sole food... But all this pre-supposes that the workman has work. When he has none, he is wholly at the mercy of accident, and eats what is given him, what he can beg or steal. And, if he gets nothing, he simply starves.[7]

At the heart of the misery Engels describes is the very nature of the capitalist system. The competition between capitalists leads them to pay their workers as little as possible, while trying to squeeze more and more work from them: 'If a manufacturer can force the nine hands to work an extra hour daily for the same wages by threatening to discharge them at a time when the demand for hands is not very great, he discharges the tenth and saves so much wages.'[8] This leads in turn to competition between workers for jobs, and to the creation of a pool of unemployed who can be pulled into the workforce when business is booming, and laid off again when it is slack. The existence of this reserve of unskilled and unemployed workers—especially among the immigrant Irish in the cities of the 1840s—holds down the level of wages and conditions for all workers.

The effects of this system are brutal. Engels describes the ill health and low life expectancy of workers compared with the bourgeoisie, the increasing tendency to suicide, the very widespread drunkenness and 'sexual licence'—'the bourgeoisie has left the working class only these two pleasures'[9]—and the very obvious class divisions, so that 'the working class has gradually become a race wholly apart from the English bourgeoisie...the workers speak other dialects, have other thoughts and ideals, other customs and moral principles, a different religion and other politics than those of the bourgeoisie'.[10]

Perhaps the most devastating aspect of this new society for Engels was that, far from resulting in increased prosperity for the workers, the development of capitalism had the inevitable result of producing great wealth for some and increased misery for many. Machinery which should have made lives easier in fact replaced jobs and drove down wages. To pay for their investment the capitalists introduced night working. Workers thrown out of work by the spread of machinery were reduced to selling oranges or shoelaces on the streets, or simply to begging for food. The factory owning class was castigated by Engels: 'I have never seen a class so deeply demoralised, so incurably debased by selfishness, so corroded within, so incapable of progress, as the English bourgeoisie... It knows no bliss save that of rapid gain, no pain save that of losing gold.'[11] The mass of beggars created by the system had at all costs to be hidden from view, and the bourgeoisie devised one of the most hated institutions ever just a few years before Engels visited Britain—the workhouse, into which poor, sick and destitute members of the working class were forced.

Yet the working class fought back in Britain in the 1830s and 1840s, through the great Chartist movement and in a whole number of skirmishes with the employers where they attempted to defend their living and working conditions. This movement helped Engels understand that as well as capitalism creating competition between workers it also led them to combine to organise against the employers. The attempts to form single unified unions and to withdraw their labour, which was the only weapon they possessed, was warmly applauded by Engels: 'As schools of war, the unions are unexcelled.'[12] He concluded the book enthusiastically:

> The war of the poor against the rich now carried on in detail and indirectly will become direct and universal. It is too late for a peaceful solution...soon a slight impulse will suffice to set the avalanche in motion. Then, indeed, will the war-cry resound through the land: 'War to the palaces, peace to the cottages!'—but then it will be too late for the rich to beware.[13]

Engels dedicated the book to 'the working classes of Great Britain' and it marked the start of his lifelong commitment to the working class as the agent of revolutionary change.[14] Writing towards the end of his life, Engels explained the importance of this in the development of his thought:

> While I was in Manchester, it was tangibly brought home to me that the economic facts, which have so far played no role or only a contemptible one in the writing of history, are, at least in the modern world, a decisive historical force; that they form the basis of the origination of the present-day class antagonisms; that these class antagonisms, in the countries where they have become fully developed, thanks to large-scale industry, hence especially in England, are in their turn the basis of the formation of political parties and of party struggles, and thus of all political history.[15]

On his way from Manchester in the summer of 1844, Engels stopped off in Paris, where he met Marx, and they embarked on their lifelong collaboration. The two had met briefly two years previously, but now they found they had a great deal in common politically, and that each could bring something to the relationship. Engels' biographer Gustav Mayer has summarised it like this:

> Marx...first showed him that politics and history are explicable only in terms of social relations—the principle which became the lever of their whole conception of history... Marx gave Engels both the final proof of his assumption that communism was the continuation and completion of German philosophical thought, and a convincing solution of the apparently irreconcilable conflict between mind and mass... Engels...taught him the technique he needed for the study of economic facts. Engels helped him to know the living realities: and Engels was the right man to do this, since

he had personal acquaintance with industry, commerce, and capital, and had been in personal contact with the modern proletariat.[16]

If anything this underestimates Engels' abilities and influence on Marx at the time. He had a much surer grasp of economics than Marx but also had a background in philosophy and communist politics which was comparable to that of Marx. In addition he had direct experience of the first mass workers' movement. As Franz Mehring wrote about the two men's early influences on one another:

The twenty-one months Engels then spent in England had the same significance for him as the year spent in Paris had for Marx. Both of them had gone through the German philosophic school and whilst abroad they came to the same conclusions, but while Marx arrived at an understanding of the struggles and the demands of the age on the basis of the French Revolution, Engels did so on the basis of English industry.[17]

Mehring also commented that, despite Engels' modest denials, with regard to economics 'the fact remains that in the beginning it was Engels who gave and Marx who received on that field on which in the last resort the decisive struggle must be fought out.'[18]

Engels went briefly back home to Barmen after this meeting. The town was buzzing with communist ideas—'in Barmen the police inspector is a communist', wrote Engels to Marx—and in early 1845 a communist meeting attracted 200, such was the level of discontent among even the factory owners and the middle classes.[19] But Engels never settled in Barmen. He railed against the place, against his bourgeois father and at having to work in the family firm:

Barmen is too beastly, the waste of time is too beastly and most beastly of all is the fact of being, not only a bourgeois, but actually a manufacturer, a bourgeois who actively takes sides against the proletariat. A few days in my old man's factory have sufficed to bring me face to face with this beastliness, which I had rather overlooked.[20]

His father was in turn horrified at his son's communism and by his illegal political activities in this small town in which Engels senior was such a respected citizen. Close interest from the police led Frederick to beat a retreat to Brussels, where Marx was already living. He moved in next door and 'never again did they work in such close contact as in those years before the revolution, when they were working out their final position both in philosophy and in practical politics'.[21]

The foundations of historical materialism

Marx and Engels' first written collaboration in 1844 was *The Holy Family*, or as they originally called it, *A Critique of Critical Criticism* (the final title was regarded as more punchy but worried Engels who thought it would offend his religious father). In 1846 they wrote *The German Ideology*, subtitled *Critique of modern German philosophy according to its representatives Feuerbach, Bruno Bauer and Stirner*. Its aim was to attack the ideas which dominated German philosophical and political thinking. These the two regarded as mystical and idealist, because they started from ideas in the abstract rather than a materialist analysis. The weight of Marx and Engels' argument was that an understanding of the world had to start, not from the ideas which existed in people's heads in any particular historical period, but from the real, material conditions in which these ideas arose. Their starting point was therefore an understanding of the historical development of class society and how people's ideas altered in this process of social change:

> We do not set out from what men say, imagine, conceive, nor from men as narrated, thought of, imagined, conceived, in order to arrive at men in the flesh. We set out from real, active men, and on the basis of their real life-process we demonstrate the development of the ideological reflexes and echoes of this life-process... Morality, religion, metaphysics, all the rest of ideology and all their corresponding forms of consciousness, thus no longer retain the semblance of independence. They have no history, no development; but men, developing their material production and their material intercourse, alter, along with this their real existence, their thinking and the products of their thinking. Life is not determined by consciousness, but consciousness by life.[22]

Nothing about the world could be understood without starting from an understanding of historical development. *The German Ideology* details some of this history and explains how the very development of society comes into conflict with the ideas, beliefs and structures of existing society. This clash between the two is represented in the struggles between the various classes which represent particular economic interests. It was impossible to develop a theory of socialism which ignored this development or ignored the material reality:

> It is only possible to achieve real liberation in the real world and by employing real means...slavery cannot be abolished without the steam engine and the mule and spinning-jenny, serfdom cannot be abolished without improved agriculture...in general, people cannot be liberated as long as they

are unable to obtain food and drink, housing and clothing in adequate quality and quantity. 'Liberation' is a historical and not a mental act.[23]

However, although the stress in *The German Ideology* is heavily weighted against the idealist philosophers, and their political counterparts the 'True Socialists', Marx and Engels did not make the mistake of believing that progress in history was inevitable or that socialists could ignore what human beings actually did to bring about change: 'circumstances make men just as much as men make circumstances'.[24] In any class society, they argue, the class which owns the wealth—the ruling class—also has a monopoly on the ideas of that society:

*The ideas of the ruling class are in every epoch the ruling ideas: ie, the class, which is the ruling **material** force of society, is at the same time its ruling **intellectual** force. The class which has the means of material production at its disposal, has control at the same time over the means of mental production.*[25]

In addition, 'for each new class which puts itself in the place of the one ruling before it, is compelled, merely in order to carry through its aim, to represent its interest as the common interest of all the members of society…it has to give its ideas the form of universality, and represent them as the only rational, universally valid ones.'[26]

So the ruling class controls both the means of producing wealth and the production of ideas which justified that control of wealth. The working class, on the other hand, was without property. Workers were also alienated from the products of their labour because they have no control over the productive process and because 'each man has a particular, exclusive sphere of activity, which is forced upon him and from which he cannot escape.'[27] The working class can only escape by making the revolution, by collectively seizing the means of production from which it is separated under capitalism. The description of this process is worth repeating for its clarity:

*A class is called forth, which has to bear all the burdens of society without enjoying its advantages, which, ousted from society, is forced into the most decided antagonism to all other classes; a class which forms the majority of all members of society, and from which emanates the consciousness and necessity of a fundamental revolution… In all revolutions up till now the mode of activity always remained unscathed and it was only a question of a different distribution of this activity, a new distribution of labour to other persons, whilst the communist revolution is directed against the preceding **mode** of activity, does away with **labour**, and abolishes the rule of all classes with the classes themselves, because it is carried through by the class which…is in itself the expression of the dissolution of all classes, nationali-*

*ties, etc, within present society… Both for the production on a mass scale of this communist consciousness, and for the success of the cause itself, the alteration of men on a mass scale is necessary, an alteration which can only take place in a practical movement, a **revolution**; this revolution is necessary, therefore, not only because the **ruling** class cannot be overthrown in any other way, but also because the class **overthrowing** it can only in a revolution succeed in ridding itself of all the muck of ages and become fitted to found society anew.*[28]

The proletariat is a revolutionary class, but it needs to make a revolution before it can control the wealth it produces. It is only in the process of making a revolution that it can fully come to revolutionary or 'communist consciousness'. Discussion of communist ideas led Marx and Engels to talk about organisation based on these ideas. Around this time they turned to trying to build such an organisation. They had formed the Communist Correspondence Committee in 1846, to keep in touch with those of like minded views. But Engels moved to Paris in August of that year (Marx was exiled from France) to organise among German artisans in the League of the Just, and to establish some contact with the French workers' movement.

He found it heavy going at first. The artisans' tradition of craft working, small family businesses and the like made them much less amenable to communist politics than the Manchester cotton workers. Trying to build among workers meant a sharp argument with other socialist tendencies inside the movement, including the 'True Socialists', followers of Karl Grun. Marx and Engels attacked the 'True Socialists' in their writings at the time, and saw them as a rival to communist ideas inside the emerging working class movement. The 'True Socialists' talked in very radical terms but Marx and Engels saw them as in fact the product of the retarded nature of Germany's economic and social development. The dominance of the petty bourgeoisie, of small businessmen, artisans and craftsmen, in German society meant that a socialism which played down the fundamental antagonism between the two major classes inside capitalism, and 'proclaims instead the universal love of mankind' could have a real appeal.[29]

A letter from Engels to the Communist Correspondence Committee describes a fraught meeting in Paris in October 1846 where Engels defined the aims of the communists off the cuff in response to the 'True Socialists' criticisms:

(1) to ensure that the interests of the proletariat prevail, as opposed to those of the bourgeoisie; (2) to do so by abolishing private property and replacing same with community of goods; (3) to recognise no means of attaining these aims other than democratic revolution by force.[30]

The form which the earliest communist organisation took was the Communist League. Marx and Engels joined the League of the Just, along with groups of exiled Germans and other nationalities of workers and artisans. Although Engels' direct experience led him to despair of the Paris League, Marx and Engels put their faith in the London branch. In late 1846 the leadership of the League moved from Paris to London. This group, led by Schapper, Moll and Bauer, was in the process of looking for new ideas and 'they turned to Marx, perhaps because the Marxian stress on economics and class warfare meant more to them, exposed as they were to the Chartist movement in the advanced industrial England'.[31]

At the League's London congress on June 1847 it changed its name to the Communist League and its slogan to 'Proletarians of all lands unite' from the previous, more 'True Socialist', 'All men are brothers'. At the London congress Marx and Engels were instructed to draft a platform— which became their most famous joint work and which remains one of the clearest statements of their politics—*The Communist Manifesto*. The first draft, known as *Principles of Communism*, was written by Engels. Marx worked on *Principles* to produce the final draft which was printed in German in early 1848.

Principles of Communism is a beautiful example of Engels' writing style: a very short, simple pamphlet written in question and answer form. He describes how capitalist society creates two major classes which stand in contradiction to one another:

> *Two new classes have come into being which are gradually swallowing up all others, namely:*
> *(I) The class of big capitalists, who in all civilised countries are already in almost exclusive possession of all the means of subsistence and of the raw materials and instruments (machines, factories) necessary for the production of the means of subsistence. This is the bourgeois class or the bourgeoisie.*
> *(II) The class of the wholly propertyless, who are obliged to sell their labour to the bourgeoisie in order to get in exchange the means of subsistence necessary for their support. This class is called the class of proletarians, or the proletariat.*[32]

The old ways of living were destroyed by the development of capitalism:

> *Free competition is necessary for the establishment of large-scale industry because it is the only state of society in which large-scale industry can make its way. Having destroyed the social power of the nobility and the guildmasters, the bourgeoisie also destroyed their political power.*[33]

Capitalism is a dynamic system, based on the accumulation of capital through commodity production. Competition between different capitalists leads to the constant search for greater profits and greater accumulation of capital. This means new investment in machinery, new ways of making workers work harder, new factories and industries.

But this revolutionary system is prone to crisis. The unplanned nature of capitalism and its drive to accumulate leads to overproduction, which in turn leads to factory closures and unemployment. Suddenly there is, as *The Communist Manifesto* puts it, 'too much civilisation, too much means of subsistence, too much industry, too much commerce...the conditions of bourgeois society are too narrow to comprise the wealth created by them.'[34] In the midst of such previously unheard of wealth there is misery and waste. The capitalist looks for ways out: destruction of some capital—so that the crisis leads to the collapse of individual capitalists to the benefit of their rivals—or the search for new markets and new investment. This search leads to greater investment, but there is less relative return on the investment. Both 'solutions' expand the system but eventually lead to further crises.

These means of escaping the crisis also deepen class antagonisms. Workers are forced to work harder and for longer hours. More workers are pulled into production, more of the old handicrafts and ways of working are destroyed. It is this new class which can make the communist revolution through the abolition of private property by socialised production. The revolution will,

> Have to take the running of industry and of all branches of production out of the hands of mutually competing individuals and instead institute a system in which all these branches of production are operated by society as a whole, that is, for the common account, according to a common plan and with the participation of all members of society. It will, in other words, abolish competition and replace it with association.[35]

Principles of Communism and then *The Communist Manifesto* were written in the expectation of imminent revolution. There were signs of worsening economic conditions and political discontent. The analysis of capitalism developed by Marx and Engels led them to assume that revolution would take place. As the capitalist mode of production developed and spread from England to Belgium, France, Germany and elsewhere in Europe, so it increasingly clashed with the old feudal regimes which still dominated Europe. The rise of capitalism brought with it the rise of the industrial bourgeoisie, whose interests were quite opposed to the old autocratic regimes. The production of capital and the development of a class of free wage labourers presupposed all sorts of legal freedoms, a limited suffrage to elect a democratic parliament, freedom of religion, and an end to the restraints on trade and business which characterised the old regimes.

In England in the 17th century and France in the 18th century the clash between these two classes brought about the great revolutionary movements which transformed property and social relations in those countries forever. Marx and Engels were convinced the same would happen elsewhere. In their native Germany, where the division of the country into 39 often very small states hampered the development of any sort of bourgeois democracy, they saw bourgeois revolution with national unification as essential for the development of capitalism and for progress in general. *The Communist Manifesto* began with the still famous phrase, 'A spectre is haunting Europe—the spectre of communism'.[36] Their prediction of revolution was accurate.

Revolution in Europe

The creation of the Communist League in 1847 took place against a background of growing social unrest. Economic depression had worsened living conditions. Famine and hunger were stalking Europe, most notoriously in Ireland where millions emigrated or starved, but also in continental Europe where bread riots occurred in many countries. 'The climax of the Hungry Forties in Europe came when the depression of 1847 brought business failures, unemployment and frequent reduction in wages. Every third family in Cologne received public relief'.[37] Among the middle classes there were growing liberal and nationalist protests in Germany, Austria and Italy—countries all under various forms of feudal rule.

Engels had returned to Paris in December 1847, after attending the second League congress in London in November and then staying with Marx in Brussels. He attempted to establish contact with the French socialist Louis Blanc, with some success. But by January 1848 he wrote to Marx in some despair, 'Things are going wretchedly with the League here'.[38] He was more optimistic about the state of the democratic movement and the impetus for bourgeois revolution in countries such as Germany and Austria, but at the end of January he was expelled from France just as revolution was about to break out. The government prohibited a big reform banquet in Paris, due to take place on 22 February. A number of such banquets had been held in the previous months as part of the growing mood for reform. Within two days there were barricades on the streets and the king abdicated. France was left with a provisional government which in turn proclaimed a republic. For the first time the government contained workers' representatives; Louis Blanc and the representative of the Parisian workers, called simply Albert. The government initially guaranteed a 'right to work' for all, with the creation of 'national workshops' for the jobless, to be paid for by increased taxation.

The movement spread throughout Europe in the following weeks: to Sicily, Vienna, Berlin, Milan. The Prussian regime was forced to allow political activity, and to endorse national unification. Engels wrote in March 1848 that, with the exception of Cologne, where some communists were arrested, 'otherwise the news from Germany is splendid. In Nassau a revolution completed, in Munich students, painters and workers in full revolt, in Kassel revolution on the doorstep, in Berlin unbounded fear and indecision, in the whole of western Germany freedom of the press and National Guard proclaimed'.[39] Two weeks later he wrote to Marx, 'In Germany things are going very well indeed, riots everywhere and the Prussians aren't giving way'.[40]

Marx and Engels returned to their native Germany in April—to Cologne, a city which was under Prussian rule but which had the liberal press laws inherited from French occupation under Napoleon. They launched their new daily paper as the 'organ of democracy'. The *Neue Rheinische Zeitung* appeared from June.

The historian Eric Hobsbawm has written of 1848, 'Within a matter of weeks no government was left standing in an area of Europe which is today occupied by all or part of ten states, not counting lesser repercussions in a number of others.' Yet 'within six months of its outbreak its universal defeat was safely predictable, within 18 months of its outbreak all but one of the regimes it overthrew had been restored, and the exception (the French Republic) was putting as much distance as it could between itself and the insurrection to which it owed its existence'.[41]

The 1848 revolutions were bourgeois, not workers' revolutions— which meant that in countries such as Germany the liberal capitalists and the middle classes such as doctors and lawyers, determined the course of the revolution, even though it was supported by the poorer classes of peasants, artisans and the emerging working class. That explains the nature of the revolution's early days when all classes united against the old order. Marx described February 1848 in France, symbolised by the poet Lamartine, as 'the beautiful revolution, the revolution of universal sympathy'.[42] Only seemingly small numbers of reactionaries were opposed to the revolutions.

But there was a crucial difference between 1848 and the earlier revolutions. When the English and French revolutions had taken place the working class was barely in existence. By 1848 it was a major and growing force in England, France and, increasingly, Germany. Marx and Engels had long been contemptuous of the German bourgeoisie, whom they viewed as too timid and 'philistine' to make a revolution. They regarded the Germans as wanting the fruits of revolution without being prepared to risk their property or lives. As the revolution took its course in the various states which made up Germany not only was this assessment proved accurate, but it also became increasingly clear that the German bourgeoisie was more frightened of the emerging working class than it was of the old order.

Engels wrote in early 1848 that the rule of the bourgeoisie would be short lived; they would taste the fruits of rule by making their revolution, but the proletariat was waiting in the wings:

> *Your reward shall be a brief time of rule. You shall dictate laws, you shall bask in the sun of your own majesty, you shall banquet in the royal halls and woo the king's daughter—but remember! The hangman's foot is on the threshold!*[43]

But what if the bourgeoisie shrank from this historic task because it would rather go into alliance with the old feudal order it so hated than side with the workers? This was, of course, exactly what happened in Germany. It took another 20 years before the project of national unification and untrammelled capitalist development was fully under way, and then it was under the leadership of Bismarck, one of the most frenzied reactionaries in 1848. The reason for the German bourgeoisie's timidity lay, above all, in their fear of what happened in France. There the hopes of the February revolution, which proclaimed the republic, increasingly gave way to fears that the class rule of the bourgeoisie was under threat from the workers. In particular the middle classes were infuriated by the increased taxes levied to pay for the national workshops.

The newly elected National Assembly moved against the workshops in June, enlisting the unmarried men into the army and moving various other people out of Paris, the hotbed of revolution. The day the Assembly met to consider closing the workshops, barricades were again thrown up, as they had been in February. But this time the fighting was *between* those who had made the February revolution. Although some 60,000 people fought behind the barricades, they were crushed after four days by the forces of General Cavaignac. This was how the ruling class dealt with the 'spectre of communism' and the liberal middle classes were well prepared to go along with such treatment rather than risk their property. Marx and Engels recognised the June days as the first big clash between the bourgeoisie and proletariat:

> *Fraternité, the brotherhood of opposing classes, one of which exploits the other, this 'fraternité' was proclaimed in February and written in capital letters on the brow of Paris, on every prison and every barracks. But its true,*

genuine, prosaic expression is **civil war** *in its most terrible form, the war between labour and capital. This fraternity flamed in front of all the windows of Paris on the evening of 25 June. The Paris of the bourgeoisie was illuminated, while the Paris of the proletariat burned, bled and moaned in its death agony.*[44]

Events in Paris influenced the revolution elsewhere in Europe and nowhere more so than in Germany. Here the revolutionary fervour was high. Despite concessions from the Prussian king, Frederick William IV, in March 1848—a Berlin parliament, an end to censorship and a unified Germany—barricades were thrown up in Berlin too. Shots had been fired at crowds celebrating their gains outside the royal palace. The crowds fought with the soldiers. The king called off the troops and was forced to pay his respects to the dead as they were carried past his balcony. By April the liberal leaders, Camphausen and Hansemann, were in key positions in the Prussian parliament and the transition towards a bourgeois democracy in Germany seemed inevitable.

The national Frankfurt parliament was established in May. It was moderate and stood for a constitutional monarchy, rather than the republic for which Marx and Engels hoped. They saw this form of national unification as a compromise with the old monarchy and aristocracy, rather than a break with them.

The liberal leaders in Germany gained the benefits of the February revolution in France, because Germany's rulers were frightened into making concessions without much resistance. But the liberals were also confirmed in their timidity by the June events which taught them that too many concessions to the masses would lead to 'anarchy'. They wanted stability and order in the new Germany. To this end they introduced various programmes of job creation and public works to buy off discontent.

The *Neue Rheinische Zeitung* appeared in this context at the beginning of June. Marx and Engels saw their place as being on the extreme left wing of the democracy movement, rather than cutting the communists off from the movement completely. They saw the major division as being between old reaction and the new democratic forces. So the first issue of their paper described the feudal reactionaries' victory over the revolution in Naples and Sicily and warned of the dangers of the military attacking the revolution in Germany.[45] Engels also attacked the Frankfurt parliament for its lack of drive and decisiveness.[46] The Prussian assembly came under even greater attack, especially when further street fighting loomed in the middle of June.

When the French June Days took place the German movement was split in its response. Marx and Engels and the *Neue Rheinische Zeitung* were fully behind the working class fighters, while the 'moderate' democrats opposed them and attacked the communists. The democrat and republican *Bonner Zeitung*'s attack had a now familiar ring when it stated 'we want freedom, but we also want order, without which no freedom can exist. Was the *Neue Rheinische Zeitung* truly defending democracy when it praised a wild insurrection which endangered the republic, the first fundamental basis for a democracy?'[47]

The fear of the June Days marked the turning point after which there was increased repression of the democratic and workers' organisations. The Camphausen ministry in Berlin was replaced by that of Hansemann which stressed constitutional monarchy and increased law and order. Yet the revolutionary mood remained, heightened in the summer by the Frankfurt parliament's capitulation over the Danish annexation of the northern Schleswig-Holstein province. By September the situation had reached boiling point. The class forces were polarising: the military, monarchy and aristocracy towards further repression and a showdown with the Prussian assembly, the democrats by demonstrating against the Hansemann ministry and against the attacks by reactionaries on the Democratic Society. The assembly's attempts to control the army were blocked by Hansemann, who in turn faced demonstrations and protests.

In Cologne the communist influence was growing and in early September a Committee of Public Safety was formed to defend the revolution. Members of the committee, which was openly elected at a mass meeting, included Marx, Engels and their fellow communists Schapper, Moll and Wolff. A meeting held in the town of Worringen just up the river from Cologne attracted thousands and many of the barges travelling to it carried red flags. Engels spoke, among others. The 'Demands of the Communist Party' were distributed at the meeting. This was the high point of communist organisation in the revolution. Less than a fortnight later the Prussians declared a state of siege in Cologne and several of the most prominent speakers and organisers were arrested. Engels had left home by the time the police called. The *Neue Rheinische Zeitung* was banned. Engels escaped via Barmen to Belgium and then into France. Meanwhile a wanted poster was put out for him.

Engels spent the closing months of the year walking through eastern France to Switzerland, where he stayed for a couple of months until things had died down in Germany. While there he wrote a large number of articles for the *Neue Rheinische Zeitung* (only briefly prevented from publication) on Swiss politics and what was happening to the revolution elsewhere in Europe, especially in the Austrian empire, where the Hungarians led by Louis Kossuth were fighting for independence. Engels' views on the various national struggles have long proved controversial, since he distinguished between certain national groups who he believed had a future as independent nations within Europe—especially the Germans, the Italians, the Poles and the Hungarians—and those, in particular the small groups of Slavic peoples, whose national movements Engels regarded as sometimes little more than a cover for reactionary Russian despotism. So Engels wrote in 1849 that 'the revolution of 1848 compelled all the European peoples to declare for it or against it. In one month all the peoples which were ripe for revolution had made their revolution, all the unripe peoples had formed an alliance against the revolution.'[48] He saw the development of the revolution, especially in the Austrian empire, as clearly divided into 'two huge armed camps: on one side, the side of revolution, were the Germans, Poles and Magyars; on the other side, the side of counter-revolution, were the others, ie all the Slavs with the exception of the Poles, plus the Romanians and the Saxons of Transylvania'.[49]

He saw the counter-revolutionary nature of the South Slavs in particular as connected with their lack of economic and social development, which not only led them to ally with the Russian Tsar, but also meant that their future as nations in an emerging capitalist Europe was in doubt. He compared them to groups such as the Scottish Highlanders who supported the reactionary Stuarts from 1640 to 1745, or the Bretons in France who supported the old Bourbon monarchy during the French Revolution. Mehring describes the political background which justified these views:

> In the Slav question also the interests of the revolution were paramount in determining the attitude of Marx and Engels. The Austrian Slavs—with the exception of the Poles—had sided with the reaction in the struggle of the Vienna government against the revolutionary Germans and against Hungary. They had taken revolutionary Vienna by storm and handed it over to the merciless vengeance of the 'Royal and Imperial' authorities.'

Mehring continues, 'Their struggle for national independence made them the willing tools of Tsarism, and not all the well-meaning self-deceptions of the democratic Pan-Slavs could alter this fact'.[50]

Engels' view of the future of the Slav nationalities has come under attack for seeming to favour particular national groups while attacking others, and for being wrong about whether all the Slav peoples had a future as nation states.[51] But he always approached the question from the point of view of European politics: that national independence in Germany, Italy, Poland and Hungary would represent progress over the patchwork of nations held together by reactionary autocratic empires which dominated central and eastern Europe. His judgement on particular peoples was based on how far they supported such advances, and also whether they supported the arch reactionary empire, that of Russia.

In both instances the record of most of the South Slavs was appalling. As one not particularly sympathetic biographer has put it:

> *Engels' judgements on whole peoples reflected the real struggles and hard choices of the time, when democratic rights were difficult to achieve and easy to lose. In those circumstances he felt obliged to identify potential enemies to the cause of constitutionalism—though he may not have been correct in his allegations—because actual enemies were causing numerous deaths amongst the democrats whom he was supporting.*[52]

It was this which motivated his views on the national question.

Engels was active in the workers' movement in Switzerland and was appointed a delegate to a workers' congress while there, but he wanted to get back to Germany and managed to do so by the end of January 1849, when he heard that there would be no charges against him. The revolutionary wave which had erupted a year before was by no means over, but its impact was fading. Vienna was once again in the hands of the feudal reactionaries, but the Hungarians were still fighting under Louis Kossuth. Engels still hoped for a new French revolution, and Germany itself was still seemingly bound for unification. He wanted the Frankfurt parliament to declare for unification against Prussia and so open up a revolutionary civil war.

Tension in the Rhineland mounted in early May 1849, as the hopes of the people clashed with the military might of Prussia, encamped in occupation of the region. The government's mobilisation of the militia to thwart democratic revolt brought matters to a head and barricades were thrown up in Engels' home town of Elberfeld, where a Committee of Public Safety was appointed. Engels threw himself into the struggle with his usual gusto, despite attempts by the local bourgeoisie to drive this dangerous red from their town.

But the uprising was defeated, the *Neue Rheinische Zeitung* suppressed and the end of the German Revolution was in sight. While Marx went to Paris, Engels stayed in the Palatinate, last bastion of revolution. When the Prussians invaded, Engels joined in the ensuing war, fighting in the army as assistant to the 'True Socialist' Willich, and was the veteran of four battles before he once again retreated to Switzerland. This time, however, his exile was anything but temporary.

Exile

Marx made his way to London in the summer of 1849. Engels joined him that autumn, travelling via Genoa by sea to avoid problems in France. They were both young men and could not have dreamt that their

exile would last for the rest of their lives. For one thing, they expected
the failed revolution to rise again very rapidly, as was clear from a letter
Marx wrote to Engels that summer.[53] They spent much time analysing the
revolution and what had gone wrong, and further developed the analysis
which they held for the rest of their lives: the bourgeoisie wanted revolution, but was too cowardly to really fight for it once the working class
was an active force on the political scene. The democrats and various
supporters of the bourgeoisie were therefore half hearted revolutionaries
who would pull back from the final confrontation in favour of compromise with the old order.

In their writings therefore Marx and Engels put a lot of emphasis on
workers needing to follow a bourgeois revolution with their own
workers' revolution and increasingly talked about the need for a 'permanent revolution' until workers' power was achieved. Their address to the
Communist League written in 1850 said:

> *[the workers] themselves must contribute most to their final victory, by*
> *informing themselves of their own class interests, by taking up their indepen-*
> *dent political position as soon as possible, by not allowing themselves to be*
> *misled by the hypocritical phrases of the democratic petty bourgeoisie into*
> *doubting for one minute the necessity of an independently organised party of*
> *the proletariat. Their battle-cry must be: The Permanent Revolution.*[54]

The Russian revolutionary Leon Trotsky was to extend the analysis
half a century later to explain how it was that Russian workers in backward semi-feudal Russia had to jump over the heads of the extremely
weak and vacillating bourgeoisie in order to make the revolution.[55]

Hopes of immediate revival of revolution soon faded, however, and
the exiled revolutionaries had to seriously assess what they should do.
Attempts to publish a German paper from London were short lived, and
the two quickly became disillusioned with emigre politics. They broke
with the habits and petty squabbles of the other European exiles, and the
Communist League split. They also had strategic differences with other
socialists, especially the Blanquists who believed that if only the revolutionary vanguard acted alone it could somehow make the revolution,
despite unfavourable objective conditions. Marx and Engels came to see
that capitalism had stabilised itself politically following the revolutionary
wave, and was poised for great economic expansion into corners of the
globe which had previously been untouched.

In 1850 Engels made a decision which meant great personal sacrifice
to him; he agreed to work once again in the family firm of Ermen and
Engels in Manchester. He did so to ensure that he received a decent
income from his father, who wanted a member of the family keeping an

eye on the Ermen side of the partnership while he himself stayed in Germany. Engels' income went in large part to sustain Marx and his family—a task which Engels took upon himself from 1850 until Marx's death over 40 years later. He did so out of personal and political regard for Marx, whose family were suffering terrible poverty.

Marx's wife, Jenny, endured many pregnancies but only three children survived into adulthood—Jenny Caroline, Jenny Laura and Jenny Eleanor. Marx wrote to Engels in 1850 on the death of his baby son Heinrich Guido that his wife was in a state of exhaustion and that the baby had died as a 'victim of bourgeois *misère*'.[56] The family had to endure much travelling, police persecution and above all poverty. They lived in miserable lodgings in London's Soho and were constantly beset with problems of ill health and unpaid bills.

Engels saved the Marx family from this destitution and allowed Marx to develop his theoretical studies which culminated in *Capital,* the first volume of which appeared in 1867. Engels' help eventually enabled the family to move to a house in north London, ensured that Christmas was always celebrated, paid for holidays and made sure the girls got an education. He was also totally uncomplaining about it. He detested work at Ermen and Engels, and thought initially he would be there for just a short time. Eleanor Marx described the day, nearly 20 years later, when he was able to finally leave, having secured enough money to keep himself and the Marx family in some comfort :

> *I was with Engels when he reached the end of this forced labour and I saw what he must have gone through all those years. I shall never forget the triumph with which he exclaimed 'for the last time' as he put on his boots in the morning to go to his office. A few hours later we were standing at the gate waiting for him. We saw him coming over the little field opposite the house where we lived. He was swinging his stick in the air and singing, his face beaming. Then we set the table for a celebration and drank champagne and were happy.*[57]

That Engels agreed to work in Manchester was a sign of his dedication to the Marx family, but his situation was also eased by his personal relations with the Burns sisters, Mary and Lizzie. Engels is assumed to have met Mary when he first visited Manchester in the early 1840s, and she certainly accompanied him to continental Europe in 1845. Mary was Irish and working class. She and Engels never married but he lived much of the time at the house he provided for her and Lizzie in Ardwick (although he maintained separate lodgings). Engels was distraught at her death at the age of 41 in 1863. As he wrote to Marx, 'I felt as though with her I was burying the last vestige of my youth'.[58]

Mary Burns's death was the occasion of almost the only sharp interchange between the two friends. Marx received a letter from Engels telling him of the death and Engels, not unnaturally, expected his old friend to extend great sympathy. Instead, Marx's reply mostly dwelt on the problems of finance and health which were yet again besetting his family. Engels did not reply for a week and then wrote a fairly reproachful letter, to which Marx then wrote a deeply apologetic reply. Engels finally came round, although obviously still hurt:

> *I tell you, your letter stuck in my head for a whole week, I couldn't forget it. Never mind, your last letter made it quits: and I am glad that when I lost Mary I did not also lose my oldest and best friend.*[59]

So the threatened rift between the two was mended. Why did Marx respond in this way? We can only conjecture, but it would seem to be a combination of obsession with his own problems (he and Jenny had decided to get the two older daughters posts as governesses and move into a lodging house with their youngest daughter—although Engels eventually came to their rescue on this, as on so much else) plus, possibly, a lack of understanding of Engels' feelings for Mary. Their relationship was unconventional. Mary and Engels never married and lived apart, at least formally. The great class differences between them were much harder to overcome in the 19th century than they would be today. Culturally they must have seemed very far apart—Mary was probably illiterate, for example, and did not share the same friends as Engels.

When Engels eventually started a relationship with Mary's sister Lydia, known as Lizzie, Marx and Jenny appear to have been careful not to make the same mistake again. They became friendly with Lizzie (she and Jenny Marx would holiday together in later years) and Eleanor visited Manchester to stay at the Engels-Burns household. She also accompanied them on a trip to Ireland.

Much is made of Engels' unconventional relationships with the Burns sisters (he only married Lizzie on her deathbed in 1878). It is often implied that their relationship must have been unequal and so fits closely the image of the well off bourgeois man with his working class mistresses who are kept out of the way of respectable society. Terrell Carver's remark that, 'in love Engels does not seem to have gone searching for his intellectual equal' is fairly typical.[60] It is impossible at this distance to know whether the Burns sisters were his 'intellectual equal'. But we do know that they were political, sympathetic to communism and to the cause of Irish nationalism. Eleanor Marx learnt about Irish oppression from Lizzie Burns who also showed her the haunts of the Fenian Manchester Martyrs.[61] When Engels met the young Mary

Burns in 1840s Manchester she was almost certainly involved in the Chartist politics of the time, as were so many Irish textile workers. There is no sign that the relationships were ever regarded by any of the participants as one sided or oppressive. There is, however, some evidence that Engels gained a great deal from living with these women, and that their personalities were at one with his own. Engels wrote to the German socialist August Bebel's wife in 1878 after Lizzie's death, 'She was of genuine Irish proletarian stock and her passionate, innate feeling for her class was of far greater value to me and stood me in better stead at moments of crisis than all the refinement and culture of your educated and aesthetic young ladies.'[62] The 14 year old Eleanor Marx wrote home in 1869 with a description of the Burns household:

> *On Saturday it was so warm that we, that is Auntie* [Lizzie] *and myself and Sarah, lay down on the floor the whole day drinking beer, claret, etc… In the evening when Uncle* [Engels] *came home he found Auntie, me and Ellen* [Lizzie's niece], *who was telling us Irish tales, all lying our full length on the floor, with no stays, no boots, and one petticoat and a cotton dress on, and that was all.*[63]

His role as a respectable businessman was one reason why Engels had to keep his private life separate from his work, and so it was only when he left Ermen and Engels and moved to London that he could live openly with Lizzie.

The period which opened up before Marx and Engels in the 1850s was quite difficult for political agitation. Reaction was triumphant in much of Europe. In France, Louis Napoleon established a dictatorship which lasted until the Franco-Prussian War nearly 20 years later. In Germany an alliance of the Prussian monarchy with the statesman Bismarck, representative of the reactionary noble Junker caste, ushered in the move towards a centralised and industrialised capitalist state, with eventual unification under Prussian dominance. Britain and its empire were going through an unprecedented period of domestic and overseas expansion, and its once militant working class was entering a long period of social peace and relative prosperity. Left wing politics, as so often in times of reaction and working class defeat, were dominated by inward looking, sectarian squabbling.

The 1848 revolutionaries, the men of action, now found themselves in a very different situation. Marx worked on his studies for *Capital*, and both men spent much of their time commenting, in their correspondence and in various pieces of journalism and other writings, on events about which they could do little. They wrote on the Crimean War, the American Civil War and the economic depression of 1857. Marx was hired to write regular articles for the *New York Daily Tribune* on a variety of topics. Often they were written by Engels, especially where they concerned military matters or questions of international diplomacy. Engels himself found it impossible to get full time journalistic work because of his political views, as his attempt to become military correspondent of the *Daily News* demonstrated.[64]

Although the class struggle remained at a low ebb in Britain, there were two events in the early 1860s which Marx and Engels considered to be important: the emancipation of the serfs in Russia in 1861 and the Civil War in America, which began in the same year and was eventually to complete the bourgeois revolution started against English colonialism in 1776. Marx wrote in 1860, 'In my opinion, the biggest things that are happening in the world today are on the one hand the movement of the slaves in America, started by the death of John Brown, and on the other the movement of the slaves in Russia'.[65]

The American Civil War was a struggle between the Southern Confederacy of slave owning states and the Northern states under Lincoln, who wanted to stop the extension of slavery to any new states. The British ruling class tended to support the Southern Confederacy, from whom it bought the cotton so central to the British economy. The British ruling class also saw the emerging United States as a major threat to its world dominance. British workers, on the other hand, overwhelmingly opposed slavery and demonstrated in favour of victory for the North. Marx and Engels were enthusiastic supporters of the Northern Union side. The Union represented the more industrialised, democratic and progressive society. But Marx and Engels were very impatient at the failure of the Northern armies to score rapid and decisive victories against the supposedly inferior South. Engels wrote to Marx in November 1862, 'I must say I cannot work up any enthusiasm for a nation which on such a colossal issue allows itself to be continually beaten by a fourth of its own population, and which after eighteen months of war has achieved nothing more than the discovery that all its generals are asses and all its officials rascals and traitors'.[66]

He and Marx had already debated whether the North was likely to win. The superior tactics of the South, under General Lee, led Engels at times to despair of the North's victory. On purely military grounds he had good reason, since the North conducted the first two years of war in a shambolic and half hearted way. Most importantly, its leaders and military men refused to mobilise the radical sentiments of the mass of Northerners and its natural supporters in the Southern states—the slaves themselves. Marx wrote in August 1862 that 'the North will finally make war seriously, adopt revolutionary methods and throw over the domination of the border slave statesmen. A single Negro regiment would have a remarkable effect on Southern nerves'.[67]

This is in fact what happened. Crucial to the North's fortunes were, firstly, Lincoln's Emancipation Proclamation to free the slaves and, secondly, the bringing into play of the superior industrial strength of Northern industrial capitalism over the slave system of the South. Engels recognised the mark the Civil War would make on future development in what was to become the United States. He wrote to his old friend Joseph Weydemeyer, now living in St Louis, that:

> [the war's] *outcome will doubtless determine the future course of America as a whole for hundreds of years. As soon as slavery—that greatest of obstacles to the political and social development of the United States—has been smashed, the country will experience a boom that will very soon assure it an altogether different place in the history of the world, and the army and navy created during the war will then soon find employment.*[68]

The First International

Solidarity among British workers with the Northern side in the American Civil War, the massive sympathy for Garibaldi's attempt at Italian unification in 1861, and support for the democratic struggle in Poland, all contributed to a sense of internationalism among the British working class and also formed the backdrop for Marx and Engels' decision to involve themselves directly in working class organisation for the first time since the collapse of the 1848 revolutions. The International Working Men's Association, known as the First International, was set up in 1864 and held its first Congress in 1865. Marx was absolutely central to its political development and to the fact that it held together as an organisation over the ensuing years.

The International was an amalgam of very different politics, drawn from its two main national components, the English and French. Its main English support stemmed from the London Trades Council, a body which was beginning to feel its industrial strength after years when the working class had remained quiescent. But it represented only a minority of the working class, the skilled trade unionists, and its leaders—men like the shoemaker George Odger, the cabinet maker Robert Applegarth and the carpenter William Cremer—held politics a fairly long way from Marx's. One of their main aims in establishing the International was to stop foreign scab labour from undermining trade unions in Britain, although they were also keen on developing solidarity with movements for democracy in other countries. The French were followers of

Proudhon, and therefore adhered to some form of artisan socialism which criticised capitalism from the point of view of returning to small scale production. Consequently they were hostile to the state and were also opposed to strikes and revolution.

Marx drew up the inaugural address and rules for the General Council of the International which was based in London, where he tried to steer a course between his own politics and those of the various components of the International, in order to ensure that the organisation got off the ground and made some advances in organising across national boundaries. Marx wrote enthusiastically to Engels on 1 May 1865:

> *The great success of the International Association is this: the Reform League* [based on agitation for the suffrage] *is our work... We have baffled all attempts of the middle class to mislead the working class... If we succeed in re-electrifying the political movement of the English working class, our Association...will have done more for the working class of Europe than has been possible in any other way.*[69]

Again in 1866 he wrote, 'The workers' demonstrations in London, which are marvellous compared with anything we have seen in England since 1849, are purely the work of the International'.[70]

Marx's other great achievement in the mid-1860s was the publication of the first volume of *Capital* in 1867. Marx was well aware of the debt he owed Engels both in terms of financial support and of the constant collaboration which had enabled him to test his ideas and theories with his oldest friend:

> *So this volume is finished. It was thanks to you alone that this became possible. Without your self-sacrifice for me I could never possibly have done the enormous work for the three volumes. I embrace you, full of thanks!*[71]

Engels, being in Manchester, was clearly not involved in the day to day work of the International but he followed the politics and the international situation closely. When war broke out between Austria and Prussia in 1866, Engels wrote a series of articles on the conflict and, unusually, quite wrongly predicted the defeat of Prussia. However, he also saw that the Prussian victory would lead inevitably to German unification on Prussia's terms and the falling out between Bismarck and his erstwhile ally, Louis Napoleon.

Engels also maintained a strong interest in the situation in Ireland, which reached crisis point in the late 1860s. The Fenian movement of Irish nationalists organised a series of armed protests against the British state and so brought home the struggle against Irish colonial oppression to the British ruling class. The huge Irish immigrant population in cities like Manchester and London supported their struggle. The reprisals against the Fenians by the British ruling class were vicious and there was an outcry when the 'Manchester Martyrs' were hanged in 1867. There was, however, just as in more recent times, a backlash against the Irish nationalists among English workers, especially when a bombing in Clerkenwell killed ordinary people.

Engels wanted to write a history of Ireland and visited the country with Lizzie and Eleanor Marx in 1869, after he had left Ermen and Engels. He wanted to explain the economic reasons why Ireland was kept in subordination, but why also this subordination had not—despite the best efforts of the English rulers—wiped out Irish identity, culture and nationalism. He wrote to Marx on his return, 'Irish history shows one how disastrous it is for a nation to have subjected another nation...things would have taken another turn in England too, if it had not been necessary to rule in Ireland by military means and to create a new aristocracy there.'[72]

However, the book did not materialise. Some sections were found in Engels' papers after his death, but it seems that much of it was never completed. Perhaps the reason for this was the turn in political events and, to a lesser extent, in Engels' personal circumstances. He and Lizzie moved to London in the autumn of 1870, to a house in Regent's Park Road, since he now had the financial independence to work full time at politics.

The political situation in Europe was then in flux. When war broke out between the two major continental European powers, France and Germany, in the autumn of 1870, Engels backed Germany at first, seeing its expansion as the means of defeating the French emperor on the one hand, and of curtailing the power of reactionary Russia on the other. It was only after Napoleon III's defeat at the battle of Sedan that he saw the main threat to European workers as German expansionism. The annexation of Alsace-Lorraine (the provinces on France's eastern borders) by Germany, Marx and Engels predicted, would only lead to further war between France and Germany.

Events in France were of central political importance in 1870 and 1871. They also brought out the political differences in the International, which could be smoothed over in periods of relative social calm but could not hold together when there were fundamental questions at stake. Such was the situation which Marx and Engels now faced.

The overthrow of Napoleon III led to political turmoil in France between September 1870, when the French army was defeated, through to the end of May 1871, when the Paris Commune was finally defeated and the reactionaries took control. A republic was proclaimed in

September 1870, but very soon there were differences over what sort of republic it was to be. Should it continue to govern in the interests of large scale capital, as the Second Empire had done, or should there be a government which represented the workers and small shopkeepers? The collapse of the Second Empire led to various localised attempts at insurrection. They failed but in Paris the possibility of revolutionary government was on the agenda.

Paris was under siege from October by occupying Prussian troops. This led to a radicalisation within the city, which was greatly strengthened in the new year when the existing government made peace with the Prussians in return for the siege being lifted. The French government refused to return to Paris, staying in Versailles until the militant population was disarmed. This led to the revolution on 18 March which established the Paris Commune.

The Commune was the first ever attempt at working class revolutionary government and was therefore of critical importance to Marx and Engels. They saw it as a model for a workers' state: representatives were elected and accountable, the whole working population was involved in politics and decision making, and perhaps most importantly there were attempts to set up a form of state power or armed rule in opposition to the army and police of the old capitalist state. The Commune was real democracy in action.

Its life span was short. Just two months after its inception the Commune was once again besieged, this time by the Versailles government's army. The Commune was put down after over a week of the bloodiest fighting imaginable: thousands were killed by counter-revolutionaries and many more were exiled or deported.

During the Commune's closing days Marx set about writing one of his best known works, *The Civil War in France*, which was commissioned by the General Council of the International. It was delivered verbally to the General Council meeting on 30 May and then printed as a pamphlet.

Here Marx spelt out his ideas on the capitalist state and how the crushing of the Commune represented the most basic class instincts not just of the French bourgeoisie, but of its counterparts elsewhere: 'Class rule is no longer able to disguise itself in a national uniform; the national governments are *one* as against the proletariat!'[73] The Commune was a new form of democracy, 'a working, not a parliamentary, body, executive and legislative at the same time'.[74] Education was open to all and free from religious or state interference. Public functionaries were paid workmen's wages. Judges and magistrates were accountable and elected. The army and conscription were abolished, replaced by a National Guard made up of all citizens. Elections were by universal male suffrage.

The crucial lesson of the Commune for Marx was that 'the working class cannot simply lay hold of the ready-made state machinery, and wield it for its own purposes'.[75] Instead revolutionaries had to be prepared to smash the old capitalist state, which was there to protect the capitalist class and its property, and to establish in its place a workers' state, based on the most complete form of democracy and on new forms of power: a workers' militia which could protect the gains of the revolution and ensure that the capitalists did not regain power. This, Engels said, was what he and Marx meant by 'the dictatorship of the proletariat'.[76]

The need for a completely new form of state was vindicated by the terrible events with which the Commune met its end. The attempt to storm heaven by the Communards was destroyed in the most bloody way by the men—and women—of property. It became the habit of fashionable women to go and watch the execution of many thousands of Communards in the days following its defeat.

There were demonstrations of solidarity with the Commune among workers in many different countries. The workers' movement internationally saw the Commune's defeat as a blow to them all. Conversely, the rulers of all the capitalist powers took heart from the smashing of this first workers' government, and themselves launched a witch hunt against the International. In 1872 membership of the International became a punishable offence in France. Similarly repressive measures were considered elsewhere, and Bismarck proposed a European alliance against the International.[77]

The backlash led to the fracturing of the International. The English trade union leaders Odger and Lucraft left the organisation which they had helped to found because they objected to *The Civil War in France*. In fact, they were out of sympathy with the whole experience of the Commune, which was far too revolutionary for their cautious reformist politics. On the other hand, Marx and Engels now found a full scale battle on their hands with the Russian anarchist Bakunin, who they suspected of having joined the International in order to wreck its organisation.

Marx and Engels therefore spent the remainder of 1871 and much of 1872 on two tasks: organising relief work and political solidarity with the refugees from the Commune, many of whom fled to London, and fighting against the influence of Bakunin and his followers in the International.

To this end they held a closed conference in September 1871, which Marx and his supporters were able to dominate because so few of their opponents turned up. They argued strongly for a centralised organisation against the decentralising tendencies of Bakunin. In the months that followed the debates continued, with Engels—responsible for corresponding with Italy and Spain—spending a great deal of time trying to win more influence for his and Marx's ideas in areas where Bakunin and his supporters were relatively strong.

Things came to a head at the Hague conference in 1872, which Engels was largely responsible for organising and where he still pushed for strengthening the General Council so that it could, if necessary, discipline or control the various sections, and so that it could provide some impetus to the formation of independent working class parties throughout Europe which were firmly committed to revolutionary upheaval.

Opposition to Marx and Engels again came from two sources: the English trade union leaders did not want a tight revolutionary disciplined organisation because this cut across their pragmatic and timid politics, and they did not want to be tied to a political line. The anarchists on the other hand also wanted decentralisation because it gave them more influence, and also because it fitted better with their denial of the state and its importance. At the Hague conference the English trade union leaders preferred to back the anarchists.

But despite the trade union leaders' attitude Engels realised that the majority of delegates would vote with him and Marx. He argued that Bakunin was in fact organising a centralised secret conspiracy, quite against the interests and spirit of the International. Engels then pushed the question of Bakunin's secret organisation into a subcommittee, managed to win the expulsion of Bakunin and his ally Guillaume, and then proposed the removal of the General Council to New York. From America it was unable to influence events in Europe and was much less prey to internal intrigue.

The last days of the First International, like any infighting on the left, are not its best testament. Engels and Marx did what they thought necessary because they saw no way of salvaging the International. The course of the class struggle had been on the rise in the latter half of the 1860s. The bloody reaction which followed the defeat of the Commune left the revolutionaries much as they had been after 1848. Left wing circles were dominated by internal squabbles and had less and less contact with reality. Marx and Engels were under attack from all sides. All that they could see to do was to allow the First International to die a natural death and wait for a new rise in class struggle which would enable international socialist organisation to be rebuilt. This time it would take nearly 20 years and Engels would be undertaking the task without Marx, and with a new generation of socialists.

The end of an era

Engels now lived in London, and so was able to collaborate much more closely with Marx, as his increased intervention in the International between 1870 and 1872 demonstrated. He continued his military writing and interests, and was given the nickname of 'the General' by the Marx family because of his skill and enthusiasm in military matters.

He also began a number of other works. He started work on his book *The Dialectics of Nature* in 1873, although he continued to write notes for it over a number of years and it was never completed. It represented an attempt to apply his philosophical ideas to the study of science.[78] But perhaps his most important writing in these years was a polemic against the ideas of one man who was becoming increasingly influential inside the German socialist movement and whom Engels and Marx regarded as a dangerous miseducator of even some of the most experienced socialists.

The background to the argument was the Franco-Prussian War and the collapse of the Commune. This was a watershed in European politics. Germany replaced France as the pivotal continental European power. This had its impact on the workers' movements in various countries. They tended to develop stable nationally based parties, often oriented to the parliamentary structures which had also emerged at this time. This was true above all in Germany, where two socialist groups— those influenced by Marx and those influenced by the ideas of Lasalle—merged in the 1870s to form what became the Social Democratic Party (SPD), the most powerful socialist party in the world. The party participated from its inception in the new parliament created as a result of German unification.

Marx and Engels were extremely critical of the German socialists. The party's unity programme, moved at the Gotha conference in 1875, was subject to a critique by Marx because it accepted a number of non-Marxist concepts, such as the idea that all other classes apart from the working class were 'one reactionary mass'. In the *Critique of the Gotha Programme* Marx argued that socialists should not dismiss all other classes as incapable of struggling against the system.[79] At various points in their lives Marx and Engels were prepared to ally with even bourgeois parties against reactionary feudalism, and very often with various petty bourgeois organisations and tendencies.

The 'one reactionary mass' formulation came from the supporters of the socialist Lasalle, who despite his rhetoric against all other classes, had in practice favoured alliance with the Bismarckian monarchy against the bourgeois opposition.

Hal Draper has described how, for Marx and Engels, the petty bourgeoisie had to be viewed as capable of both reactionary and progressive political action. They considered that the programme of the German party would lead to sectarianism. Both the petty bourgeoisie and the peasantry (the urban and rural sectors of the class) are 'classes that are on the decline and *reactionary* in relation to the proletariat as soon as they aspire to maintain themselves artificially', wrote Engels:

> *But they are not reactionary under all social conditions; not all sectors of the class are equally reactionary under the same conditions; different sectors and groups might vary widely on different issues; and last but not least, the difference must always be borne in mind between parties and groups based on this class and the possibilities of recruiting the rank and file of the class or of parts of it, in a fight against their own parties. In other words, we enter the realm of intelligent political leadership of a broad revolutionary movement that is striving to reach out, without compromising its own politics, as against the wooden drill of a self-pickling sect.* [80]

The tendency to reformism, to accommodation with the German state, was apparent to Marx and Engels from the Gotha programme. However it is also clear that the theoretical level of the German party was low. In the early 1870s it attracted all sorts of people and the party did not always have a clear understanding of how to win them to revolutionary politics. Marx's best known biographer, from the next generation of German socialists, Franz Mehring, has written of the party in the mid-1870s:

> *It was the rapid growth of its practical successes which made the new party indifferent to theory, and even that is saying too much. They were not indifferent to theory as such, but rather to what, in their vigorous advance, they regarded as theoretical hair-splitting. Unappreciated inventors and misunderstood reformers, anti-vaccinationists, nature healers and similar cranks flocked to the standards of the new party because they hoped to find in the active ranks of the working class the recognition which had been denied them in the bourgeois world. Whoever showed good-will and offered some remedy for the sick body politic was sure of a welcome, particularly those who came from academic circles and whose presence promised to seal the alliance between the proletariat and science. A university professor who befriended or seemed to befriend socialism in one or the other of its manifold interpretations, had no need to fear any very strict criticism of his intellectual stock in trade.* [81]

Engels's *Anti-Dühring*, a critique of the ideas of Dr Eugen Dühring, has to be seen against this background. He and Marx were extremely perturbed at the influence Dühring had on even the intellectuals of the party such as the young Eduard Bernstein. *Anti-Dühring* started as a series of articles in the German party's publication *Vorwärts* in 1877. The articles came under attack from within the party itself. The tone of Engels' articles and their content were regarded by some as 'objectionable' and they were relegated to the paper's scientific supplement.[82]

However, Engels persevered, and this polemic became central to turning the ideas of Marx into reality for a new generation of socialists who held Marx and Engels in great esteem but who knew little of their theoretical ideas. Although it was soon banned in Germany, a section of the book was published as a popular pamphlet, *Socialism, Utopian and Scientific,* which was translated into various European languages and sold widely. It was and remains one of the best and most easily understood introductions to Marxist ideas.

Engels describes how the great Utopian socialists, Saint-Simon, Fourier and Owen, derived their ideas from the rationalist thinking of the Enlightenment, which culminated in the great French Revolution. They expressed the disappointment felt at the political and social institutions which came out of the revolution. According to Engels, 'Society presented nothing but wrongs; to remove these was the task of reason.'[83] He describes how this sort of socialism dominated the earliest socialist thinkers:

> *To all these socialism is the expression of absolute truth, reason and justice, and has only to be discovered to conquer all the world by virtue of its own power. And as absolute truth is independent of time, space, and of the historical development of man, it is a mere accident when and where it is discovered.*[84]

Yet socialist thought had to move beyond moral outrage with capitalism and exhortations for change to an understanding of how that change could be brought about. Socialism became a science, according to Engels, with the development of the materialist conception of history and with the understanding that the basis of capitalist accumulation is the exploitation of workers:

> *The socialism of earlier days certainly criticised the existing capitalistic mode of production and its consequences. But it could not explain them, and, therefore, could not get the mastery of them. It could only simply reject them as bad.*

With the ideas of Marx, 'socialism was no longer an accidental discovery of this or that ingenious brain, but the necessary outcome of the struggle between two historically developed classes—the proletariat and the bourgeoisie'.[85] A system which should have been able to make life easier for all of humanity instead made it far more wretched for many, while a minority benefited:

> *Machinery, the most powerful instrument for shortening labour time, becomes the most unfailing means for placing every moment of the labourer's time and that of his family at the disposal of the capitalist...the overwork of some becomes the preliminary condition for the idleness of others... Accumulation of wealth at one pole is...accumulation of misery at the other pole.*[86]

Moreover, the constant development of newer and more powerful machinery, which is central to the accumulation of capital, produces great wealth but leads eventually to crisis: 'markets are glutted, products accumulate...hard cash disappears, credit vanishes, factories are closed, and the mass of workers are in want of the means of subsistence, because they have produced too much of the means of subsistence.'[87]

The only way out of this crisis is the socialisation of the means of production, a solution which, says Engels, even the capitalist system half recognises, with its increased attempts to regulate the free market by monopoly, nationalisation and state intervention. But genuine socialism can only come about when the working class seizes control of the means of production.[88]

The success of *Socialism, Utopian and Scientific* helped to establish Marx and Engels' reputation among a new generation of socialists internationally. However, the political problems which Marx and Engels encountered in their dealings with the German party did not disappear. In 1879 the Anti-Socialist Law was passed by Bismarck in response to the growing strength of the party. In fact, the law did not harm the party's growth, but its leaders responded to restrictions on their activity in the most compromising and mealy mouthed way. Its parliamentary group followed a policy of adaptation, and its leader, Wilhelm Liebknecht, declared in the *Reichstag* (parliament) that the SPD would obey the law. Marx said of the parliamentary group of socialists that 'they are already so far affected by parliamentary idiotism that they think they are *above criticism*'.[89]

Engels in particular was angry with the leadership of the German party at the time. He felt attacked unjustifiably over *Anti-Dühring* and also believed that residual 'Lassalleanism' kept showing through in the party's politics. He considered that the advice that he and Marx had given was not readily accepted by the German party and that this often led it to opportunist and even reformist tendencies, as over the Anti-Socialist Law. Although a visit to London by August Bebel in 1880 helped allay his fears, the German party remained a source of worry to Engels for the rest of his life.

Lizzie Burns had died in 1878, and had become Engels' wife on her deathbed. Three years later Marx's wife, Jenny, also died, to be followed just over a year later by her eldest daughter, Jenny. Marx had long been in bad health, as his correspondence frequently testified, but these deaths had a terrible effect on him. His health deteriorated further, despite convalescent trips to Algeria and the Isle of Wight. He developed a tumour on the lung and died on 14 March 1883, just two months after his eldest daughter and a few days before his grandson, the four year old Harry Longuet, who is buried in Marx's grave.

Engels was there at the time of death and wrote the next day to their old friend in America, Frederick Adolph Sorge, 'Mankind is shorter by a head, and that the greatest head of our time'.[90] He spoke at Marx's graveside where he stated that 'just as Darwin discovered the law of development of organic nature, so Marx discovered the law of development of human history'. He went on to reaffirm their revolutionary commitment:

> *'For Marx was above all else a revolutionist. His real mission in life was to contribute, in one way or another, to the overthrow of capitalist society and of the state institutions which it had brought into being... Fighting was his element... And, consequently, Marx was the best hated and most calumniated man of his time.*[91]

After Marx

The void in Engels' life following the death of Marx must have been great, but he was not the sort of person to allow it to prevent him from carrying on the work to which the two men had always devoted their energies. Therefore Engels' final years—he was to live another 12 years after Marx—were as full and demanding as any in his younger life. His life in those years was devoted to arguing for, explaining and clarifying Marx's ideas; working on the remaining volumes of *Capital* which would probably never have seen the light of day if it were not for Engels; looking after the Marx daughters, Laura and Eleanor; and advising those trying to build organisations in various countries, especially in Germany and Britain.

Engels' theoretical production never diminished. Indeed in 1884 he published one of his best known books, *The Origin of the Family, Private Property and the State,* which drew on anthropological writings to trace the course of women's oppression throughout class society. This was a pathbreaking book in more ways than one. Not only did it tie the development of family forms and structures to the rise of private property held by a particular class in society, it also demonstrated a completely egalitarian attitude towards women. Throughout his life Engels saw women's oppression as an unnatural product of property relations which would disappear once those property relations disappeared. He therefore developed a view which set him well in advance of even liberal commentators in Victorian England, who all too often saw women as weak beings who had to be protected, rather than as equals.[92]

Much of volume II of *Capital* had been completed before Marx's death, and Engels was able to write an introduction to it by 1885. He was only able to publish the final volume nearly ten years later, just before he died in 1895, and much of that had to be written from scratch. His task was made harder since much of the data on which it was based was ten or 15 years old.

The desire to finish *Capital* may be one reason that Engels stayed in England, rather than return to his native Germany or to German speaking Switzerland. He often stressed that he felt able to continue his theoretical studies better in London than in Germany or Switzerland. He was also much less directly involved in the workers' movement in Britain than he would have been in Germany. Indeed, Engels was fairly isolated from the working class movement—in contrast to his youth when he was involved with the Chartists, the Communist League and later with the International. In part this reflected what had happened to the working class movement over the intervening two decades—although the passivity and lack of struggle among English workers began to change in the last years of Engels' life.

He also had a number of strong personal commitments in England: to Helene Demuth, the lifelong friend and servant of the Marx family, and like them a committed socialist—she spent the last years of her life as housekeeper to Engels in Regent's Park Road; to 'Pumps' (Mary Ellen) Burns, niece of Mary and Lizzie, who with her husband and family was also ensconced there much of the time; and to the Marx daughters. Laura lived with her husband the French socialist Paul Lafargue in Paris, but Eleanor lived in London, in a relationship with the socialist Edward Aveling from 1883.

Engels treated them with the utmost affection and generosity, tact and sympathy, and smoothed many problems, such as Laura's unhappiness that Eleanor, not she, was one of her father's executors. Right up until his death, he provided them with money and left them both enough in his will to provide for them for the rest of their lives. Engels took all this as a matter of course, just as he had supported Marx throughout his life. He also defended them from attack—an impulse which he generously extended to Edward Aveling, who had a bad personal reputation but whom Engels always regarded as one of the most able socialists in Britain.

Rebirth of the English socialist movement

When Engels had first come to England in the early 1840s, his enthusiasm for the English working class movement knew no bounds. The Chartist movement was the most advanced in Europe. But the defeat of Chartism after 1848 and the ensuing dominance inside the working class movement of a layer of skilled trade union leaders led him to change his views. The experience of the First International reinforced these later views that the English working class movement—or at least its leaders—were narrow, parochial and all too willing to do deals with the bourgeois Liberal Party, rather than form their own independent workers' party. So Engels could write to Eduard Bernstein in 1879 :

> *The workers are divided politically into Conservatives and Liberal Radicals, into supporters of the Disraeli Cabinet and supporters of the Gladstone Cabinet. One can therefore speak of a labour movement only in so far as strikes take place here, which, whether they are won or not, do not get the movement one step further.*[93]

He wrote in even more scathing vein to the German socialist Karl Kautsky:

> *You ask me what the English workers think about colonial policy. Well, exactly the same as they think about politics in general: the same as the bourgeois think. There is no workers' party here, you see, there are only Conservatives and Liberal-Radicals...*[94]

Things began to change around the time of Marx's death. Engels himself had started to write articles in the London Trades Council paper the *Labour Standard* in 1881, in which he called for the establishment of a workers' political party rather than just trade union organisation—a call which led to his departure from the paper.[95] Soon afterwards came the establishment of tenuous socialist organisation in Britain. The Democratic Federation, led by H M Hyndman, was a coming together of various radical organisations. It developed in a socialist—as opposed to Liberal—direction. In 1884 it renamed itself the Social Democratic Federation, with a socialist programme and widespread support, especially among young trade unionists who were to become famous later in the decade for their role in leading strikes.

But the SDF soon split. Its departing members cited Hyndman's opportunism coupled with his authoritarian behaviour—and set up the Socialist League in the beginning of 1885. The signatories to its founding statement included some of the best known names of English socialism such as Eleanor Marx, Edward Aveling, William Morris,

Belfort Bax and John Lincoln Mahon. Their quarrel with Hyndman was understandable: he had irritated Marx with his frequent visits during the last years of his life, and irritated Engels as somebody who although he had read *Capital* did not grasp the essentials of Marxism. Neither had he broken fully from his own bourgeois background and ideas, in particular suffering from a degree of national chauvinism which coloured his socialism, and so was indeed capable of the opportunism of which he was accused. The SDF concentrated on abstract propaganda, did not see the relevance of strikes and was incapable of grasping many of the opportunities which came its way. Engels regarded it as a sect: 'It has not understood how to take the lead of the working class movement generally, and to direct it towards socialism. It has turned Marxism into an orthodoxy'.[96] But the SDF did attempt to popularise Marx's ideas, in however distorted a way, to a new generation of socialists. Hyndman's book *England for All* was an attempt to put forward Marx's ideas (although without crediting them).

The Socialist League, despite high hopes, did not really fare any better. Its reaction to opportunism was to stress abstract propaganda for socialism still further and just wait for the revolution. It was distrustful of 'palliatives' which could in any way improve the condition of workers under capitalism. The League was therefore unable to combine its vision of socialism with a support for the day to day struggles which could enable it to win workers to its broader vision, unable to combine its theory with any practice. Those who did engage in activity found themselves doing so as individuals, not as part of a supportive organisation. So Eleanor Marx and Aveling were heavily involved in free speech and assembly activity in the East End of London from the mid-1880s, but increasingly felt estranged from the League and eventually left it. The League became more influenced by anarchism than Marxism.

A third group of socialists came into being in the mid-1880s: the Fabians. Unlike the other groups the Fabians exclusively attracted the educated middle classes, not workers. At first some of its members were sympathetic to left wing ideas, but the increasing class conflict in evidence in the second half of the 1880s, especially the unemployed riots in 1886 and the fighting in Trafalgar Square in 1887, led their leaders to move consciously away from any flirtation with revolutionary change and towards the theory of gradualism which eventually influenced the Labour Party.

Engels kept fairly aloof from these movements, although he was far from aloof from the activities which took place in these years. He did not play an active role himself, but worked closely with Eleanor and Aveling, and can be assumed to have agreed with the thrust of their politics in the various disputes which took place. He was sceptical about the fortunes of the early British socialists, as his comments in 1886 demonstrate:

> Here the lack of any competition, on the one hand, and the government's stupidity, on the other, have enabled the gentlemen of the Social Democratic Federation to occupy a position which they did not dare to dream of three months ago... The labour movement is beginning here and no mistake, and if the SDF is the first to reap the harvest that is the result of the cowardice of the radicals and the stupidity of the Socialist League, which is squabbling with the anarchists and cannot get rid of them, and hence has no time to concern itself with the living movement that is taking place outside under its very nose. Incidentally, how long Hyndman and Co will persist in their present comparatively rational mode of action is uncertain. Anyhow I expect that they will soon commit colossal blunders again; they're in too much of a hurry'.[97]

Engels still had much more contact with socialists from abroad than from England, and his regular Sunday dinners were a gathering place for German socialists in London.[98] But he became increasingly enthusiastic about the class struggle in Britain as the decade came to an end. The movement of the New Unions began in 1888 and spread like wildfire for the next three years. It was a movement from below, led by the supposedly unorganisable: the women, the unskilled, the Irish. All had been excluded from the existing unions by the skilled craftsmen who dominated them. These union leaders were timid and conservative. In 1886 Tom Mann, a socialist engineer who went on to lead the dockers' strike which was so central to the New Unionism, wrote this of the old unions:

> None of the important societies have any policy other than that of endeavouring to keep wages from falling. The true unionist policy of **aggression** seems entirely lost sight of; in fact the average unionist of today is a man with a fossilised intellect, either hopelessly apathetic, or supporting a policy that plays directly into the hands of the capitalist exploiter... I take my share of the work of the trade union to which I belong; but I candidly confess that unless it shows more vigour at the present time, I shall be compelled to take the view—against my will—that to continue to spend time over the ordinary squabble-investigating, do-nothing policy will be an unjustifiable waste of one's energies. I am sure there are thousands of others in my state of mind.[99]

The misery caused by economic depression, the increasing attacks by the police on demonstrators and campaigners for civil liberties in 1886 and 1887, the lack of any political or economic voice for the bulk of the working class suddenly exploded. The match girls' strike at the Bryant and May factory in east London, following an exposé of their terrible conditions by the radical Annie Besant in the *Link* newspaper, was a terrible shock to respectable opinion, and was widely supported throughout the working class. The match girls won their demands.

The women's strike was followed by that of the gas workers, led by Will Thorne (whom Eleanor Marx taught to read and write) and then by the London dockers' strike for their 'tanner' increase, led by the socialists John Burns and Tom Mann. Other strikes followed in all the sweated, unskilled trades—shops, transport, food industries. They also affected the unionised sections of the working class, who themselves became more militant.

The New Unionism was notable for a number of features: it started in the East End of London, the poorest and most politically backward slum in Britain; the strikes were frequently led by socialists who had agitated in the East End and elsewhere in small numbers in the years before struggle broke out; and the level of political generalisation was high. Engels made all these points in a letter sent to his old friend Sorge at the end of 1889:

> *The people are...drawing far greater masses into the struggle, shaking up society far more profoundly, and putting forward much more far reaching demands: the eight hour day, a general federation of all organisations and complete solidarity. Through Tussy [Eleanor Marx], the Gas Workers' and General Labourers' Union has got women's branches for the first time. Moreover, the people regard their immediate demands as only provisional, although they themselves do not yet know toward what final goal they are working. But this vague notion has a strong enough hold on them to make them elect as leaders only downright Socialists'.[100]*

The success of the agitation was shown in the mass May Day demonstration organised around the theme of the Eight Hour Day in 1890. Despite sectarian opposition from some of the old union leaders around the London Trades Council, hundreds of thousands went to Hyde Park—organised through a committee including the Avelings. Engels was on one of the speakers' platforms and was full of enthusiasm for the event, which he saw as symbolising the reawakening of the working class.[101]

There were moves afoot for a political voice for labour, motivated especially by the Scottish socialist Keir Hardie. The Liberal Party had always been supposed to represent working people in parliament but when the great disputes of the New Unionism blew up, they were often in opposition to Liberal employers or their supporters: such were the owners of Bryant and May, the shipowners and the bosses of Manningham Mill who broke their workers' strike in 1891. As the strike movement subsided and the employers' offensive grew in the early

1890s, so the appeal of the Independent Labour Party grew. It was an appeal which Engels initially welcomed, because it was based on working people, it was oriented away from the sectarian squabbles of the old left and it seemed to have the chance to develop into a mass socialist party. However, it never really involved all the different socialist groupings, was racked with divisions and did fairly badly electorally in its early years. Most importantly, it was completely unclear theoretically and politically, rejecting Marxism and putting its emphasis on educating workers towards socialism rather than on struggle. By the mid-1890s the ILP became much closer to the gradualist Fabians:

> Thus, when the great upsurge of the late 'eighties and early 'nineties began to die away, the old ideas of bourgeois Liberal reformism reasserted themselves in a form more suitable to the level which the movement, both political and industrial, had now reached.[102]

The final years

Engels was 70 years old in 1890. Eleanor Marx, writing on his 70th birthday for a Viennese socialist paper, said:

> He carries his six foot odd so lightly…and although Engels looks young he is even younger than he looks. He is really the youngest man I know. As far as I can remember he has not grown any older in the last 20 hard years.[103]

At the birthday celebration guests were 'all regaled with claret and champagne until half past three in the morning, when twelve dozen oysters were consumed'.[104] Among the guests were the German socialists Liebknecht, Bebel and Singer. The international links between the socialists were growing by now, given a boost by the founding of the Second International, the first congress of which took place in Paris in 1889, on the hundredth anniversary of the storming of the Bastille.

Engels was instrumental in ensuring that the Congress took place. Before its very inception there was such division amongst the left that two international conferences were planned in Paris for the same time. His attempts to ensure that the Congress was an open public conference and that it was a means of launching a campaign for an eight hour day internationally were all important, and he worked very closely with Eleanor Marx, who was central to its organisation, although he did not attend himself.

The growth of socialist organisations, often under the influence of at least some form of Marxism, meant that Engels' advice was much in

demand. He became close friends with Victor Adler, a leader of the
Austrian Social Democratic Party, who visited him in London, and also
corresponded with socialists in countries as far apart as Russia and
Portugal. The leaders of the emerging movement looked to him as the
embodiment of a revolutionary tradition stretching back before 1848—
and as one of the last survivors of his generation.

A sign of this recognition came at the Zurich International Socialist
conference in 1893. Yet again this was one of two conferences—the
other called by the English trade unions in London, which Engels saw as
a political challenge to the more advanced continental socialists. Engels
managed to get the English conference cancelled by urging the German,
Austrian and French trade unions to pass resolutions demanding one
conference. Engels used the occasion to revisit Germany after many
years and turned up only near the end of the Congress. He was feted by
the international delegates and made the closing speech to the Congress.
Engels' lifelong modesty was evident here as elsewhere:

> *The unexpectedly magnificent welcome you have given me and which I could
> not but receive with deep emotion, I accept not in my personal capacity but as
> the collaborator of the great man whose portrait you have here. It is just 50
> years ago that Marx and I came into the movement, when we wrote the first
> socialist articles for the **Deutsche-Französiche Jahrbücher**. From the small
> sects of the time, socialism has since developed into a powerful party making
> the officials of the whole world tremble. Marx has died, but were he still alive
> there would be no one in Europe and America who could look back upon his
> life's work with such justifiable pride.*[105]

But Engels found that despite the growth of these parties there was a
danger within them—that their very success could hide theoretical and
political problems. His concern was always that they should develop into
proper mass workers' parties, as opposed to the sects with no real roots
in the class struggle which had so often dominated the left. He was therefore always extremely critical of anarchist tendencies, and took the side
of the German party when it was faced with an anarchist splinter in the
1890s. But the stress that he put, quite rightly, on the need to work
through the unions and parliament, the need to build up a mass base,
could easily lead the German party to an opportunist accommodation
with the system.

The arguments that broke out after Engels' death in favour of
'revisionism'—led by the theoretician Eduard Bernstein—had their seed
in the years before. The idea that the system would simply expand
without contradiction and would therefore yield up the fruits of socialism
almost as a matter of course were there, in Engels' view, in the revised

programme put to the German party's 1891 conference. Engels had always been very bitter about the suppression by Liebknecht of Marx's *Critique of the Gotha Programme*. He was even more furious when that programme came to be revised after the repeal of the Anti-Socialist Law that no acknowledgement of past mistakes, or of Marx's critique, was made by the party's leaders.

He therefore took it upon himself to publish the *Critique* so that young comrades in Germany and elsewhere could see what Marxism was really supposed to mean in practice. In the process he attacked the tendencies towards opportunism in parts of the socialist press. His fears were well grounded since opportunism later became a dominant tendency inside the party. Even while Engels was still alive, his writing was subject to censorship by the party, when party leaders deleted references that he had written to the violent overthrow of society.[106]

In Engels' final years he found no respite from the demands for theoretical clarification which had dominated his life. 'In the last five years of his life Engels had some 135 works of greater or lesser importance to his credit'. He read seven daily papers (three German, two English, one Austrian and one Italian) and 19 weeklies in a variety of languages.[107] His most important work in these years was volume III of *Capital* which he wrote largely from scratch.

But he was also concerned to keep up with current debates and politics and to try to understand a very rapidly changing world. Sometimes he succeeded admirably. Engels was always very clear, for example, about the role that nationalisation played in the modern capitalist economy. He saw that state control of railways, the postal system and other means of communication was vital to the efficient accumulation of capital by the ruling class. He was scathing about those who equated such state control with some form of socialism.[108]

He also had a very good picture of the course and level of class struggle in a whole number of countries. But he was sometimes less accurate on changed conditions in other matters, particularly where he had taken a certain position in his youth. For example, he still thought that a defensive war by Germany against the Russian Empire might be necessary. In the 1840s Germany was an emerging nation which was fighting for unification and national identity. Russia was regarded as the most reactionary bastion of feudalism in Europe, which did its utmost to foster national divisions and to prevent revolution.

But the balance of forces changed after the Franco-Prussian War, when Germany became the fastest growing industrial and imperial power, gradually rivalling even Britain. Whereas German socialists would earlier have supported war against Russia, by the 1890s this meant siding with their own imperialist ruling class. Yet Engels still clung to the idea that in certain circumstances there could be a justified defensive war, for which German socialists would have to vote war credits. His 'argument was to be parroted with disastrous effect in 1914 by the same party leaders who censored Engels' other writings when the German socialists supported their ruling class in the imperialist First World War and, indeed, voted them war credits.'[109]

However, the fact that Engels said or wrote things that could later be turned against revolutionary socialists can in no way diminish his record as a revolutionary. His activity spanned a huge period from the Chartists through to the birth of the modern trade unions. He lived through some of the biggest changes in the development of capitalism, nowhere more so than in Germany. He left his imprint on the socialist movement in both Europe and America. Despite his desire to always take a back seat, he was a man of huge talents. He never became a mere commentator, or a fossilised armchair socialist but was always inspired and enthused by the activities of workers and the oppressed. His writings on a range of subjects demonstrate his tremendous knowledge and interest in science, the military and, perhaps most importantly, history. Engels' historical writings show a real grasp of the subject and a style which makes them widely accessible.

He made his last public speech at the Zurich conference. He continued his activity and writing but became ill at the beginning of 1895, with cancer of the throat. He died on 5 August. Engels was cremated at a funeral attended by the leaders of the German, Austrian and French parties, by the Russian revolutionary Vera Zasulich and the English gas workers' leader Will Thorne. His ashes were scattered in the sea six miles out from Eastbourne by Eleanor Marx. The attendance at his funeral shows how Engels was able to carry the spirit of the founders of revolutionary socialism and of the 1848 revolutions to the next generation of socialists.

Engels' Marxism

JOHN REES

A strange thing has happened to the reputation of Frederick Engels in the 100 years since his death. For the vast majority of that time both Engels' allies and his enemies agreed that he was Marx's *alter ego*. Indeed, the very expression 'alter ego' was Marx's own description of his relationship to Engels. Most commentators and virtually all Marxists thought that a lifetime of common work, the undeniable and almost undisturbed years of close personal and political co-operation, spoke for themselves.[1]

But by the 1960s that easy certainty was faced with a sustained challenge. The first cracks in the Cold War consensus were beginning to appear. The growth of CND, the rise of the New Left and, later, opposition to the Vietnam War inevitably produced an enormous increase in interest in radical ideas in general and Marxist ideas, or what passed for Marxist ideas, in particular. This process necessarily led to a reaction against the stifling conformity of reformism and the oppressive legacy of Stalinism. Much of what was said and written marked a rebirth of interest in the genuine Marxist tradition and delivered a long-delayed blow to the reformist and Stalinist traditions.

Yet the reaction against Stalinism was also shaped by Stalinism, in two senses. Firstly, some of those reacting to Stalinism got no further than adopting another variant of Stalinism, either Maoism, or Third Worldism or the 'reform Communism' that came to dominate the Western European Communist Parties. Secondly, even those who broke completely with Stalinism tended to confuse elements of the genuine

Marxist tradition with the economic determinism characteristic of Stalinism.

All this led to altered perceptions of the Marxist inheritance. Perhaps inevitably, critics began to search the writings of the founders of Marxism for the seeds of Stalinism and failures of reformism. Many of these developments particularly affected students and so fuelled the expansion of academic Marxism. They also coincided with the wider availability of Marx's early 'humanist' writings. A new consensus emerged, both in academic circles and among many on the left, about the nature of Engels' thought.

The critics of Engels

One of the first studies to systematically assert a cleavage between Marx's ideas and those of Engels was George Lichtheim's *Marxism: an Historical and Critical Study*, first published in 1961.[2] Lichtheim insisted that in Marx's vision 'critical thought was validated by revolutionary action', but in Engels' scheme 'there now appeared a cast-iron system of "laws" from which the inevitability of socialism could be deduced with almost mathematical certainty...the "goal" was transferred from the here-and-now of conscious activity to a horizon so distant as to be almost invisible.'[3]

For Marx, Lichtheim claims, 'the only nature relevant to the understanding of history was human nature.' Engels therefore broke with Marx when he argued that 'historical evolution is an aspect of general (natural) evolution and basically subject to the same "laws".'[4] This meant that Engels had appropriated Hegel's heritage quite differently to Marx. Marx had taken from Hegel the importance of self conscious activity in the making of history. In contrast 'what really fascinates' Engels 'is Hegel's determinism: his ability to make it appear that nature (and history) follow a pre-ordained course'.[5] Such a drastic recasting of Marxism inevitably had political consequences:

> ...determinism in thought making for dogmatism in action. The cast-iron certainty which Engels imported into Marxist thinking found its counterpart at the political level in an unshakable conviction that the stars in their courses were promoting the victory of socialism.[6]

Consequently, Engels, Kautsky—the leading thinker of the Second International—'and the orthodox school in general' transformed Marxism 'from the vision of a unique breakthrough into a doctrine of a casually determined process analogous to the scheme of Darwinian evolution'.[7]

Lichtheim's book rehearses many of the themes that were to become so familiar in other work published over the following 20 years: that Engels replaced Marx's notion of conscious activity with an empricist notion of science, that he mistakenly extended Marxism so that it covered the natural as well as the social world, that this inevitably drew him into deterministic and reductionist formulations and that these in turn led him at the end of his life to endorse a reformist political practice on the part of the German Social Democratic Party. And not for the last time the revolutionary, humanist Marx was counterposed to the reformist, determinist Engels by a writer such as Lichtheim who was an opponent of Marxism in theory and a convinced reformist in practice.

After Lichtheim the deluge. Alfred Schmidt's otherwise more careful and interesting book, *The Concept of Nature in Marx*, first published in German in 1962, argued that 'where Engels passed beyond Marx's conception of the relation between nature and social history, he relapsed into a dogmatic metaphysic'.[8] Schmidt also saw a departure from the concerns of the early Marx: 'For Engels, nature and man are not united primarily through historical practice; man appears only as a product of evolution and a passive reflection of the process of nature, not however as a productive force'.[9] By adopting this approach Engels also abandoned Marx's view of how consciousness is formed:

> *The movement of thought in Marx is by no means limited to a mere mirroring of the factual. The uncritical reproduction of existing relationships in consciousness has precisely an ideological character for Marx.*[10]

So Schmidt believed that where Marx saw ideas formed in interaction with the material world Engels saw only a crude reflection of the outside world in the brains of human beings, a vulgar 'copy theory' of consciousness. By 1969 Lucio Colletti could question, almost in passing:

> *how far this distortion of Marx's thought by Kautsky and Plekhanov...was already prepared, if only in embryo, in some aspects of Engels's work; and how in general the search for the most general laws of development in nature and history made these attempts a preconstitution of the contamination with Hegelianism and Darwinism.*[11]

He went on to argue that Engels' influence on the leaders of the Second International was partly a result of 'the place given in Engels' work to philosophical-cosmological development, "the philosophy of nature", in other words, the "extension" of historical materialism into "dialectical materialism".'[12]

In books as diverse as John Lewis's *The Marxism of Marx* (1972),

Shlomo Avineri's widely read textbook *The Social and Political Thought of Karl Marx* (1970) and Leszek Kolakowski's sophisticated and profoundly anti-Marxist *Main Currents of Marxism* (1978) it became an article of faith that Engels had distorted Marx.[13]

Even authors Paul Walton and Andrew Gamble, who were sympathetic to Marxism at the time they wrote *From Alienation to Surplus Value* (1972), could conclude that:

> [Engels] *seems debarred from understanding the real premises of Marx's method because he seeks to make Marxism an objective science on the model of the natural sciences...he tries to establish the truth of historical materialism by treating human interaction as analogous to the interaction of chemical particles.*[14]

For Gareth Stedman Jones, influenced by Louis Althusser's structuralism, it was Engels' 'inability adequately to think through the novelty of historical materialism as a science' which 'led him to an understandable attempt to fill in the gaps with philosophy—the Hegelian philosophy of his youth'. This not only led to a 'lack of any theory of the political instance of social formations' but to Engels embracing 'a dangerous implication of the Hegelian theory of knowledge—that everything in reality is, in principle at least, already known'. Thus Engels 'unintentionally converted the infant science of historical materialism into the appearance of a finished system, a corpus of absolute knowledge which encompassed the whole of empirical reality'.[15]

By the early 1970s the pattern was fully established—Engels was the villain. And it did not seem to matter what political or theoretical position a writer set out from—the neo-Kantianism of Colletti, the humanism of Avineri or Schmidt, the Althusserianism of *New Left Review* contributors—the destination was always the same: Engels was at the root of whatever was wrong with Marxism. With few exceptions,[16] the argument against Engels had now become a virtual orthodoxy, perhaps best summarised in Norman Levine's *The Tragic Deception: Marx contra Engels* (1975) and Terrell Carver's *Marx and Engels, the Intellectual Relationship* (1983). Levine states the anti-Engels orthodoxy in its bare essentials:

> *Engels' materialism...was a cold, unremitting, and remorseless system. Men had little impact on fashioning the course of development of history and nature. Rather than being the subject of history, men were basically the passive objects of unrelenting external forces... Engels' materialism was mechanistic.*[17]

Naturally, for Levine, it followed that 'Engels continuously affirmed the copy theory of knowledge...there was absolutely no variance, no difference between our comprehension of the external world and the external world itself'.[18]

Engels' grave error lay in 'making the laws of nature themselves dialectical...something which Marx himself never attempted'.[19] Engels 'was a unilinear evolutionist'[20] for whom 'causality...meant additive sequence'[21] and from whose thought 'the notion of human praxis was absent'. Consequently:

> *Engels' thought moved from a mechanistic materialist view of the universe to a deterministic view of human history...it was Engels, not Marx, who was the originator of economic determinism.*[22]

Carver's work is more qualified and careful in its argument, but it arrives at similar conclusions.[23] Engels was led to 'incorporating the causal laws of physical science and taking them as a model for a covertly academic study of history, "thought" and, somewhat implausibly, current politics'.[24]

There are many more writers who have argued that Engels was responsible for transforming Marxism into a crude, deterministic philosophy of nature which led to the reformism of the Second International and even Stalinism. To those already quoted could be added Richard Gunn in *Marxism Today*, Jeff Coulter in *Socialist Register*, Frederick Bender's *The Betrayal of Marx*, Z A Jordan's *The Evolution of Dialectical Materialism* and many others.[25] These authors combine different elements of the argument in different ways, and few agree on all the arguments used against Engels, but they say little new.

There are two ways of examining these claims. One is to look at the record of Marx and Engels' partnership. The second is to study the works in which, both jointly and separately, they elaborated their ideas.

The unity of Marx and Engels' thought

The most remarkable aspect of the view that there was a fundamental divergence between Marx's theory and Engels' thought is that it ignores the evidence of their lifelong partnership. Some considerable intellectual contortion is necessary to overcome the elementary biographical facts of Marx and Engels' lives. For Terrell Carver 'the intellectual relationship between the two living men, however, was very much the story of what they accomplished independently'. These accomplishments 'were by no means theoretically coincident'. After Marx's death 'Engels moved into an all-powerful role' in which he 'invented dialectics and reconstructed

Marx's life and works accordingly'.[26] Nor is Carver alone in this kind of assertion. It is common coin among Engels' critics to insist that he codified Marxism as a rigid dialectical philosophy either without Marx's explicit approval or after his death. Norman Levine argues:

> The height of Engels' career corresponded with the termination of Marx's life. It is, therefore, entirely consistent that five of Engels' major works were published in the years closely preceding Marx's death, or after the termination of Marx's life. **Anti-Dühring** appeared in 1878, **Socialism: Scientific and Utopian** [sic] in 1882, **The Origin of the Family, Private Property and the State** in 1884, and **Ludwig Feuerbach and the End of Classical German Philosophy** in 1888. **The Dialectics of Nature** was first published in 1927 by Riazanov, although the manuscript itself appears to have been completed by 1882.[27]

Levine makes a more extraordinary claim when he attempts to answer the obvious question of 'why basic intellectual differences between the two men did not come to the surface as tangible and real, articulated and acknowledged dispute'. This is a question to which no convincing reply is easily available. Levine's answer takes us into the ghost world of 'the psychological meaning the friendship had for each'. In this realm 'Engels chose to tie himself' to Marx because Marx 'would also build a place of fame and renown in time for him'; and Marx needed Engels because 'Marx did not find the professional and emotional support he needed from his wife'.[28] But if we leave the territory of Mills and Boon and return to the world of Marx and Engels a very different picture reveals itself.

The first and most striking point about Marx and Engels' relationship is the strength of the foundations on which it rested. In the 1840s both men arrived at what would later be known as the historical materialist view of the world. But it is by no means the case that Engels simply followed where Marx led. On the vitally important strategic question of the attitude which the pair took to the trade unions it was Engels who blazed the trail. And the entire content of Marx and Engels' joint work, *The Communist Manifesto*, was first outlined by Engels alone in *Principles of Communism*.

On economic questions Engels led the way, even though Marx's later work in *Capital* was the decisive contribution. Marx was still extracting himself from the coils of Hegelian philosophy when Engels wrote his *Outlines of a Critique of Political Economy*. Not only was this the spur to Marx's own 40 year immersion in economic analysis, it was also the immediate inspiration for Marx's own transition to a fully materialist class analysis, a process recorded in his *Economic and Philosophical*

Manuscripts of 1844. Indeed, Marx thought Engels' work 'brilliant' and *Capital* itself carries the subtitle 'A Critique of Political Economy'. Even Carver admits that 'Marx's manuscript notes on Engels' essay prefigured the course of his lifework' and that 'Marx's *Capital* was in effect a much elaborated specification of the contradiction discussed by Engels in his *Outlines*'.[29]

Having arrived at a common outlook, Marx and Engels jointly authored two key works which elaborated their views, *The Holy Family* and *The German Ideology*. They struggled together to win the organisation they were both involved in, the League of the Just, to their ideas, transforming it into the Communist League. *The Communist Manifesto* was issued in its name. They went on to fight together in the 1848 revolutions—in Engels' case literally revolver in hand, on the barricades. This then was the foundation of Marx and Engels' partnership, forged by intense, common intellectual and practical, political work.

The start of Marx's exile in England and Engels' life in Manchester unavoidably altered the pattern of their joint work, but it did not end it. Partly, Marx and Engels chose to specialise in different areas. Partly also this differentiation was forced on them by the economic circumstance of Marx's poverty and Engels' decision to support his friend while Marx worked on what became *Capital*. But these new circumstances did not break the intellectual and political trust between them. When Marx had to write articles for newspapers in order to earn some money he never hesitated to put his name to articles which were, in fact, written by Engels.

In the long gestation of *Capital* Engels was Marx's constant adviser, either in their almost daily exchange of letters or in conversation when they paid each other visits. Marx consulted Engels on everything from the correct German translation for 'gigs' to rent theory, constant and variable capital, surplus value and exploitation. In August 1862 Marx implored Engels to visit him:

> *I have overthrown so many old views in my critique* [ie **Capital**] *that I would at least like to consult you over a few points. Writing about the rubbish is tedious for you and me.*[30]

Constant collaboration continued at every stage of the writing of *Capital* up to and including the reading of the proofs, which Marx largely entrusted to Engels. Even the presentation of *Capital* bears Engels' mark. Looking at the proofs, Engels advised Marx that the dialectical points might be made more historically and that Marx had made 'a great mistake' in not following the pattern of Hegel's *Encyclopedia* with its short sections and many sub-headings.[31] Marx followed this advice, but ignored other suggestions, 'to proceed dialectically in this regard also', as he joked to Engels in reply. Nevertheless, he insisted, 'your satisfaction up to now is more important to me than anything the rest of the world may say of it'.[32] At the end of it all Marx was in no doubt about his debt to Engels. He wrote:

> *Without you, I would never have been able to bring the work to completion, and I assure you, it has always weighed on my conscience like an Alp that you have dissipated your splendid energy and let it rust on commercial matters, principally on my account, and into the bargain, still had to participate vicariously in all my minor troubles.*[33]

In this Marx was undoubtedly right, and not just about his debt to Engels. He was right in his assessment of the terrible cost to Engels' intellectual output during the years in which he worked in Manchester. Although he never complained, Engels knew it too—as is confirmed by the image left to us by Marx's daughter of Engels joyously coming home from the factory after his last day's work. When Engels was able to retire he could once again publish major works.

Levine argues that Marx's death left Engels free to publish his distorted version of Marxism. But even the chronology of publication which Levine gives undermines his own argument. *Anti-Dühring* was not only published during Marx's lifetime, the whole project was Marx's idea. Moreover, Engels read the entire manuscript to Marx and Marx himself wrote one of the chapters on economics. The idea behind the book was to give a defence of Marx's ideas, so it is hardly likely that such an obviously programmatic statement of his views would have been published without his complete agreement. As Engels noted, 'it was self-understood between us that this exposition of mine should not be issued without his knowledge'.[34] *Socialism, Utopian and Scientific* was extracted from *Anti-Dühring* and also published before Marx's death. *The Origin of the Family, Private Property and the State* appeared after Marx's death, but was composed by Engels using the ethnographical notebooks which Marx had written. *Ludwig Feuerbach* was also published after Marx died but, as if to stress the continuity of the ideas expressed in it with the views of Marx and Engels' first writings, Engels published Marx's newly discovered *Theses on Feuerbach* as an appendix. Engels obviously saw no contradiction between the 'humanist' young Marx and the 'determinist' older Engels, otherwise he would scarcely have risked such a course, going so far as to describe the *Theses* as 'the brilliant germ' of historical materialism.

Finally, *The Dialectics of Nature*, which is often used to support distortions of Engels' work, was never intended for publication and actually bore the inscription, 'All this to be revised', almost as if it were a warning to those who were to take every last word as a finished, polished formulation. Nevertheless, the broad sweep of Engels' intention was clear from *Anti-Dühring*, which was written at the same time.

On the key issue of whether Marx endorsed the idea of a dialectic in nature there can be little doubt. In *Anti-Dühring* Engels specifically quoted Marx's *Capital* to this effect: 'Here, as in natural science, is shown the correctness of the law discovered by Hegel in his *Logic,* that merely quantitative changes beyond a certain point pass into qualitative differences.'[35] And Marx goes on to say in a footnote that: 'the molecular theory of modern chemistry...rests on no other law'.[36] Marx himself had earlier drawn Engels' attention to these passages in *Capital*, explicitly stating his belief that dialectical laws were in evidence in natural science: '*in that text* I quote Hegel's discovery regarding the *law that merely quantitative changes turn into qualitative changes* and state that it holds good alike in history and natural science'.[37] Also in *Capital* Marx described exchange relations as operating like 'a determining law of nature'. And, despite Carver's claim that Engels' admiration for Darwin is evidence of his inclination toward the model of natural science, Marx shared Engels' assessment: 'Darwin's book is very important and it suits me well that it supports the class struggle in history from the point of view of natural science'.[38]

So the idea that Marx and Engels developed along separate theoretical paths finds little support in the biographical evidence. Naturally, the rough division of labour which they evolved led to different emphases. Equally naturally, they stressed different aspects of the theory depending on whether they were arguing against empiricists or idealists, system builders or vulgar economists, anarchists or reformists. But in all essentials they were at one. Perhaps nothing conveys this fact as forcefully as the testimony of Laura Marx's husband, Paul Lafargue:

Engels was, so to speak, a member of the Marx family. Marx's daughters called him their second father. He was Marx's alter ego...

...From their youth they developed together and parallel to each other, lived in intimate fellowship of ideas and feelings and shared the same revolutionary agitation: as long as they lived together they worked in common... But after the defeat of the 1848 Revolution Engels had to go to Manchester, while Marx was to remain in London. Even so, they continued their common intellectual life by writing to each other almost daily... As soon as Engels was able to free himself from his work he hurried from Manchester to London, where he set up his home only ten minutes away from his dear Marx. From 1870 to the death of his friend, not a day went by but the two men saw each other, sometimes at one's house, sometimes at the other's...

> *Marx appreciated Engels' opinion more than anybody else's, for Engels was the man he considered capable of being his collaborator. For him Engels was his whole audience. No effort could have been too great for Marx to convince Engels and win him over to his idea. For instance, I have seen him read whole volumes over and over to find the fact which he needed to change Engels' opinion on some secondary point... It was a triumph for Marx to bring Engels round to his opinion.*
>
> *Marx was proud of Engels. He took pleasure in enumerating to me all his moral and intellectual qualities... He admired the versatility of his knowledge and was alarmed that the slightest thing should befall him...*[39]

Marx and Engels were inevitably prey to the limitations of their age. They could not foresee all that natural science would achieve or the problems that would arise in the course of the next century of class struggle. But it is their joint legacy, as the content of their work also demonstrates, on which modern socialism rests.

Human history and natural history

For Marx and Engels human beings remain part of the natural world from which they have evolved. The human hand, the human brain, the development of language and consciousness have all taken place as part of the processes which dominate the natural world. From their very earliest collaborations Marx and Engels were insistent that no rigid and absolute distinction could be drawn between human history and natural history.

The book in which they first systematically worked out the principles of their approach was *The German Ideology*. In it Marx and Engels were unambiguous in asserting that human biology and the physical constitution of nature were essential starting points in any attempt to understand the world:

> *The premises from which we begin are not arbitrary ones, not dogmas, but real premises... They are the real individuals, their activity and the material conditions of their life, both those which they find already existing and those produced by their activity...*
>
> *... Thus the first fact to be established is the physical organisation of these individuals and their consequent relation to the rest of nature.*[40]

And, while they elaborate these factors at length, Marx and Engels did spell out that they included 'the actual physical nature of man' and 'the natural conditions in which man finds himself—geological, oro-hydrological, climatic and so on.' They argued that 'all historical writing must start out from these natural bases and their modification in the course of history through the action of men'.[41]

Marx and Engels castigate one of their philosophical opponents for going 'so far as to speak of "the antithesis in nature and history" as if these were two separate "things" and man did not always have before him an historical nature and a natural history'.[42]

More than 30 years later Engels returned to the same argument in *Anti-Dühring*, his broadside against Eugen Dühring, an academic who was gaining a hearing among Marx and Engels' supporters in Germany. Engels criticises Dühring for 'accepting "consciousness", "thought", quite naturalistically, as something given, something opposed from the outset to being, to nature'. And he continues:

If that were so it must seem extremely strange that consciousness and nature, thinking and being, the laws of thought and the laws of nature, should correspond so closely. But if the further question is raised what thought and consciousness really are and where they come from, it becomes apparent that they are products of the human brain and that man himself is a product of nature, which has developed in and along with its environment; hence it is self-evident that the products of the human brain, being in the last analysis also products of nature, do not contradict the rest of nature's interconnections but are in correspondence with them.[43]

But the idea that human beings form part of the natural world does not exhaust Marx and Engels' views on this issue. In the first place, it was the process of development in nature which gave rise to conscious human beings who, from that point on, formed a quite *distinct part of nature*. This consciousness has material preconditions, and when it has emerged, its further development cannot be separated from the development of the material base on which it rests. In *The German Ideology*, Marx and Engels outline the preconditions for the emergence of human consciousness:

We must begin by stating the first premise of all human existence and, therefore, of all history, namely, that men must be in a position to live in order to be able to 'make history.' But life involves before everything else eating and drinking, housing, clothing and various other things. The first historical act is thus the production of the means to satisfy these needs, the production of material life itself.[44]

The second prerequisite is 'that with the satisfaction of the first need, the action of satisfying and the instrument of satisfaction which has been acquired, leads to new needs; and this creation of new needs is the first historical act.'[45] The third precondition is that 'men who daily re-create their own life, begin to make other men, to propagate their kind: the relation between man and woman, parents and children, the *family*.'[46]

Once these elements have developed, and not before, Marx and Engels see the development of a human consciousness which distinguishes human beings from the animal world:

> *Only now...do we find that man possesses 'consciousness'. But even from the outset this is not 'pure' consciousness. The 'mind' is from the outset afflicted with the curse of being 'burdened' with matter, which here makes its appearance in the form of agitated layers of air, sounds, in short, of language. Language is as old as consciousness, language **is** practical, real consciousness that exists for other men as well, and only therefore does it exist for me; language, like consciousness, only arises from the need, the necessity, of intercourse with other men. Where it exists it exists for me: the animal does not '**relate**' itself to anything, it does not '**relate**' itself at all. For the animal its relation to others does not exist as a relation. Consciousness is, therefore, from the very beginning a social product, and remains so as long as men exist at all.*[47]

And not only is consciousness social, it is also historical. Just as consciousness developed *from* a long historical process, so its further development is *part of* a historical process—it develops over time. The consciousness of our very earliest ancestors was only narrowly distinguishable from the instincts of the apes from which they had evolved. It is only with the accumulation of productive forces that human consciousness really becomes distinct from, but not ever separate from or independent of, the natural world.

Neither is this the end of Marx and Engels' view of the relationship between human history and nature. There is more at stake in this relationship than a historical account of the way in which human history emerges from the history of 'raw nature'. Indeed, for Marx and Engels, there is no longer any such thing as 'raw nature': 'nature, the nature that preceded human history...is nature which today no longer exists anywhere (except perhaps on a few Australian coral islands of recent origin).'[48]

The nature which does actually exist is one which has been moulded by human beings. The unity of human beings and nature 'has always existed in industry and has existed in various forms in every epoch according to the lesser or greater development of industry, and so has the "struggle" of man with nature'. So it is that 'in Manchester, for instance', there are 'only factories and machines, where a hundred years ago only spinning wheels and weaving looms were to be seen, or in the Campagna di Roma...only pasture and swamps, where in the time of Augustus…nothing but the vine-yards and villas of Roman capitalists'.[49]

Here, then, are Marx and Engels' early views on the relationship between human beings and the natural world. They stressed the essential unity of human beings and the natural world *and* the difference between the two *and* the historical development of this relationship. It was a bril-liantly dialectical analysis, a presentation of an internally differentiated totality, a unity of opposites, in which human labour's interaction with its natural, material environment is the basis of the transformation of both the natural and the human world over time.

As a result of adopting this starting point, Marx and Engels were able to resist the temptation to make a rigid separation between the human sciences and the natural sciences, since materialism is the basis of both, but also to see that human history contained a vital distinguishing feature, *conscious* labour, which required a distinct approach.

Did Engels depart from this early vision in later life, as his critics insist? Did he abandon the view that conscious human labour was what distinguished human history from natural history? Did he simply revert to a natural science model which he then imported into the received version of Marxism? The quotation from *Anti-Dühring*, above, indicates that his general attitude had not altered. But in *The Part Played by Labour in the Transition from Ape to Man*, written in 1876, we can also see that Engels' approach remained identical. This manuscript, unfin-ished and unpublished in Engels' lifetime, forms part of the much derided *Dialectics of Nature*. Yet the account of the relationship between human beings and the rest of nature reproduces in all essentials the account which Marx and Engels gave in their earliest writings.

The account of evolution, for instance, although much more detailed in the light of the publication of Darwin's work, still stressed the devel-opment of human capacities which resulted from the necessity of meeting the most elementary material needs. Engels' magnificent account of the development of the human hand, the first human tool, stressed not only the strictly natural, evolutionary development but also the role played by labour in the development of the hand:

> *Thus the hand is not only the organ of labour, **it is also the product of labour**. Only by labour, by adaptation to ever new operations, through inheritance of muscles, ligaments, and, over long periods of time, bones that had undergone special development and the ever-renewed employment of this inherited finesse in new, more and more complicated operations, have given the human hand the high degree of perfection required to conjure into being the pictures of a Raphael, the statues of a Thorwaldsen, the music of Paganini.[50]*

But this labour and the power of speech which developed from it 'were the two most essential stimuli under the influence of which the brain of the ape gradually changed into that of man'. Yet even now this 'was not labour in the proper sense'.[51] Labour begins, according to Engels, with the making of tools. But even then the fundamental distinction between humans and animals has not yet been made. Animals, says Engels, 'change the environment by their activities in the same way, even if not to the same extent, as man does, and these changes...react upon and change those who made them'.[52] It is not hard to see here the kind of dialectical process of natural development which Engels thought united the natural with the human world. Nevertheless, he was far from seeing this as a one sided identity. There was, just as in Marx and Engels' early writings, not only an identity but also a difference between natural and human history. This is why Engels goes on to insist:

> But animals exert a lasting effect on the environment unintentionally and, as far as the animals themselves are concerned, accidentally. The further removed men are from animals, however, the more their effect on nature assumes the character of premeditated, planned action directed towards definite preconceived ends.[53]

And he summarised his attitude in absolutely unambiguous terms:

> In short, the animal merely **uses** its environment, and brings about changes in it simply by its presence; man by his changes makes it serve his ends, **masters** it. This is the final, essential distinction between man and other animals, and once again it is labour that brings about this distinction.[54]

This conclusion was not, however, designed to make a final and irrevocable separation between human beings and nature. It was merely a distinction, albeit a vital distinction, within the unity of man and nature. Engels goes on to say that we should not 'flatter ourselves overmuch on account of our human victories over nature' since although our conscious designs are often realised in the first place they later bring about results which have unforseen effects. And so:

> ...at every step we are reminded that we by no means rule over nature like a conqueror over a foreign people, like someone standing outside nature—but that we, with flesh, blood and brain, belong to nature, and exist in its midst, and that all our mastery of it consists in the fact that we have the advantage over all other creatures of being able to learn its laws and apply them correctly.[55]

And just in case the final phrases of this quotation should make it seem as if Engels' critics are in the right when they argue that he had a technocratic approach to social change, one in which science simply paves the way for a better life, Engels concludes:

> This regulation [of the natural world] requires something more than mere knowledge. It requires a complete revolution in our hitherto existing mode of production, and simultaneously a revolution in our whole contemporary social order.[56]

From this account of Marx and Engels' view of the relationship between human beings and the rest of the natural world it is clear that: (i) at the close of his life Engels held the same general attitude that he held in his early writings, (ii) that this attitude was the same as Marx's, (iii) that it was not a view which sought to either force human history into the same pattern as natural history or to insist on a rigid separation of the two, and, (iv) that it did try, concretely and empirically, to spell out both what unites human society with, and distinguishes it from, its natural environment.

The dialectic

It was on the basis of their new materialist conception of history that Marx and Engels generalised to produce a dialectical approach to human and natural change. 'The dialectic' is often said to be obscure and difficult to understand. Yet its fundamental approach is not hard to grasp, especially against the background of natural evolution and social change outlined in the previous section.

The first basic principle on which the dialectic rests is that the world is in a process of change. Society and nature are not static, neither do they 'move in an eternally uniform and perpetually recurring circle', as Engels says. Instead they undergo a 'genuine historical evolution'.[57] Yet static views of society are still very common today. Through all the hurly-burly of society certain values and institutions are seen as virtually eternal—the family, the market, nationalism, religion, parliamentary democracy and, above all, 'human nature'. A dialetical view would recognise that all these ideologies and institutions have a history, that in the past they came into being and in the future they will cease to exist. Marx and Engels developed their own views in criticism of the ideas of the great German philosopher Hegel. But one of Hegel's great virtues was that he saw 'the whole world, natural, historical, intellectual...as a process, ie, as in constant motion, change, transformation, development'.[58] Rejecting static views of the world is, however, only the first step. Trying to understand the way in which this process of change unfolds is the next step.

Here the key is to see all the different aspects of society and nature as interconnected. They are not separate, discrete processes which develop in isolation from each other. Mainstream sociological and scientific thought 'has bequeathed us the habit of observing natural objects and processes in isolation, detached from the general context'.[59] Much of our schooling today still follows this pattern—the development of the arts is separated from that of the sciences, and 'technical' subjects are separated from languages, history and geography. Our newspapers and TV news programmes divide the world up in the same artificial way—poverty levels and stock exchange news, wars and company profit figures, strikes and government policy, suicide statistics and the unemployment rate are all reported in their own little compartments as if they are only distantly related, if at all. A dialectical analysis tries to re-establish the real connections between these elements, 'to show internal connections'. It tries, in the jargon of dialectics, to see the world as 'a totality', 'a unity'.

To see society and nature as an interconnected totality which is in a process of constant change still leaves one vital question unanswered. What makes this whole process develop? *Why* does it change? There are any number of religious and philosophical theories which try to answer this question by insisting that the motor of change lies outside the historical process—with god, or in the unchanging pattern of human nature or in the eternal features of the human soul. Marx and Engels rejected these approaches as mystical and, literally, supernatural. They insisted that the processes which drove the development of nature and society forward must be *internal contradictions*, not supersensible entities like god, the soul or, as Hegel had argued, the general essence of human consciousness existing somewhere in the ether beyond the consciousness of actual living human beings.

The relationship between nature and the conscious labour of human beings is, as we have seen, one example of a contradictory totality in a process of change. Since the rise of class society, the struggle between the exploited (the slaves, peasants and wage labourers of ancient Greece and Rome; the peasants and craftsmen of feudal society; the modern working class) and the exploiters (slave owners, landlords and capitalists) provides another example of a series of class contradictions which have led to changes in the totality of the social structure as one great mode of production rises, falls and gives birth to another. In all these cases it is the relationships, the contradictions, between the different parts of the totality which give rise to change. Engels argues:

> *So long as we consider things as at rest and lifeless, each one by itself, alongside and after each other, we do not run up against any contradictions in them.*[60]

But as soon as we look for the cause of change we are confronted with contradictions—'as soon as contradiction ceases, life, too, comes to an end, and death steps in.'[61]

These then are the basic terms of the dialectic—contradiction, totality and change. The 'three laws' of the dialectic described by Engels cannot be understood without this larger context, since they are ways of specifying how this process of change takes place. Engels' simplified codification has sometimes led both his followers and his critics to try and isolate the 'three laws' from the more general principles of the dialectic. This is a mistake, as the following brief account of those laws makes clear:

i) The unity of opposites. This is simply another way of describing a totality composed of contradictory elements. The totality of capitalist society, for instance, develops in response to the contradiction between the two major classes contained within it, workers and capitalists. The natural and human worlds form, as we have seen, a unity of opposites. Nature and humanity are united, but not identical. It is the relationship between them which shapes the development of each.

ii) The transformation of quantity into quality. This is the process by which small changes of degree eventually result in changes of type. For example, an *economic* strike in one factory or industry might spread to others until the point is reached where they become a *political* strike against all employers and the government. Or the working class may suffer a series of individual defeats at the end of which an entirely different *type* of period in working class history has opened up.

iii) The negation of the negation. This phrase is designed to show how two contradictory (but not necessarily equal) forces react on one another in such a way that the situation which results from their clash both preserves and completely alters them at the same time. Engels follows Marx's example from *Capital*. Marx had explained how the change from feudal society to capitalist society had dispossessed peasants and craftsmen of their individual private property, pushing the peasants off the land and depriving craftsmen of the means of production, and consolidated it in the hands of the capitalist class. Capitalism thus expropriated, or negated, individual private property as it had existed under feudalism. A socialist society would 'expropriate the expropriators'. It would put means of production in the hands of society collectively and extend 'individual ownership to the products, that is, the articles of consumption.' Thus the original negation, of feudal property by capitalist property, is negated once more by a socialist form of ownership.[62]

Engels immediately recognised that this process, the negation of the negation, might be interpreted in a fatalistic fashion—it might be read as if socialism were inevitable. He insisted that the negation of the negation was not 'a mere proof producing instrument'. He went on:

> *Thus, by characterising the process as the negation of the negation, Marx does not intend to prove that the process was historically necessary. On the contrary: only after he has proved from history that in fact the process has partially occurred, and partially must occur in the future, he in addition characterises it as a process which develops in accordance with a definite dialectical law.*[63]

This was a point which Marx and Engels were to make again and again with regard to the whole dialectical approach, not just the negation of the negation. It was not, they insisted, a substitute for studying the real world, not an equation into which the facts merely had to be slotted, or a pattern into which historical events had to be forced. Each aspect of society had to be studied empirically and in detail. Only then might the unique dialectical pattern be discovered. In each circumstance it could be expected to contain particular features: 'Every kind of thing therefore has a peculiar way of being negated in such a way that it gives rise to development, and it is just the same with every kind of conception or idea.' Just playing with dialectical phrases without studying real, empirical developments could only result in 'the silliness of the person who adopts such a tedious procedure'.[64]

Engels approached the distinction between natural and human history in this way. He looked, as we have seen, not just for what unified the two, but also for what made them distinct. Not surprisingly, the distinction between natural evolution and human history reappeared in Engels' attitude to the dialectic. In *The Dialectics of Nature* Engels makes an important distinction between the dialectic in human history and that in nature:

> *In history, motion through opposites is most markedly exhibited in all critical epochs of the foremost peoples. At such moments a people has only the choice between two horns of a dilemma: 'either-or!' and indeed the question is always put in a way quite different from that in which the philistines, who dabble in politics in every age, would have liked it put.*[65]

And he goes on to give an example from the 1848 revolutions when 'even the German philistine...found himself in 1849, suddenly, unexpectedly, and against his will confronted with the question: a return to the old reaction in an intensified form, or the continuation of the revolution...' But on the same page Engels outlines a significantly different pattern of dialectical change in the natural world:

> **Hard and fast lines** *are incompatible with the theory of evolution... 'Either-or' becomes more and more inadequate... For a stage in the outlook on nature where all differences become merged in intermediate steps, and all opposites pass into one another through intermediate links, the old metaphysical method of thought no longer suffices. Dialectics, which likewise knows no hard and fast lines, no unconditional, universally valid 'either-or' and which bridges the fixed metaphysical differences, and besides 'either-or' recognises also in the right place 'both this-and that' and reconciles opposites, is the sole method of thought appropriate in the highest degree to this stage.*[66]

In an important passage in *Ludwig Feuerbach and the End of Classical German Philosophy* Engels wrote that 'dialectics was...the science of the general laws of motion, both of the external world and of human thought' and that they were 'two sets of laws which are identical in substance'. But he explained that the laws were necessarily 'different in their expression insofar as the human mind can apply them consciously, while in nature...these laws assert themselves unconsciously, in the form of external necessity...'[67] He also added that, so long as human beings are prevented from consciously controlling the social world it will continue to resemble the natural world in that its laws will operate beyond the will of human beings.

A few pages later Engels returns to and elaborates this point. He notes that human beings do not, in class society, have collective conscious control of their destiny and so 'that which is willed happens but rarely'. Consequently, social laws become analogous to those prevailing 'in the realm of unconscious nature.' Nevertheless, Engels insists:

> *In one point, however, the history of the development of society proves to be essentially different from that of nature. In nature—insofar as we ignore man's reaction on nature—there are only blind, unconscious agencies acting on one another, out of whose interplay the general law comes into operation. Whatever happens...does not happen as a consciously desired aim. On the other hand, in the history of society the actors are all endowed with consciousness, are men acting with deliberation or passion, working towards definite goals; nothing happens without conscious purpose, without intended aim.*[68]

Such a complex and dialectical approach has only one weakness: it makes it easy for critics to isolate one side of the analysis and then adopt superior airs by correcting Marx and Engels' supposed shortcomings by presenting the complementary side of the analysis as if it were their own invention.

An arrogant theory?

Engels, like Marx, believed that the natural and social worlds should not be rigidly separated and, therefore, that similar if distinct patterns could be discerned in both. But does this not make Engels guilty of having devised an all embracing theory which prescribes the findings of science? Certainly Gareth Stedman Jones argues that Engels embraced the idea that 'everything in reality is, in principle at least, already known', and that he invented 'a finished system, a corpus of absolute knowledge which encompassed the whole of empirical reality'.

In fact, Engels repeatedly insisted that any such 'system building' was completely foreign to historical materialism. Indeed, the whole of one of his major works, *Anti-Dühring*, is specifically designed to combat such a system. So it is that Engels writes, 'To me there could be no question of building the laws of dialectics into nature, but of discovering them in it and evolving them from it.'[69] It was not only in relation to natural science that it was important not to impose dialectical laws from the outside. Both Marx and Engels often made precisely the same point about the study of history, insisting that their method was a guide to studying history, not an excuse for not studying history.

Any general statements had first to be proven in detailed empirical and historical study, not simply asserted as universal laws. Engels insisted taht 'a system of natural and historical knowledge, embracing everything, and final for all time, is a contradiction to the fundamental laws of dialectic reasoning'. But why did Engels believe that a finished, all embracing system of knowledge was an illusion? One of the fundamental tenets of the dialectic is that the world is in a state of continuous change. Any finished system would necessarily imply that this process had halted, which is why Engels describes such notions as in conflict with the fundamental laws of dialectical reasoning. He elaborates:

> *If at any time in the development of mankind such a final, conclusive system of interconnections within the world—physical as well as mental and historical—were to be brought about, this would mean that human knowledge had reached its limit, and, from the moment when society had been brought into accord with that system, further historical development would be cut short—which would be an absurd idea, sheer nonsense.*[70]

It is not surprising that Marx and Engels were hostile to any kind of universal system—their own ideas had been developed as a critique of the grandest of all universal systems, that developed by Hegel.[71] But Marx and Engels' ideas were not *only* a critique of Hegel's idealist system. They were also a critique of the mechanical materialism of the Enlightenment and of the similarly one sided materialism of the post-Hegelian philosopher Ludwig Feuerbach. So it was, on the face of it, unlikely that Engels would simply recoil from Hegel's idealism into the arms of a crude, empirical materialism. Indeed, part of Marx and Engels' critique of existing philosophy was that the two undialectical extremes, idealism and crude materialism, often collapsed into one another in a completely uncritical (and unacknowledged) way.

Marx and Engels frequently make the point that Hegel was forced to simply incorporate, in an ad hoc manner, economic facts and the discoveries of the physical sciences into his philosophical system. And the empiricists suffer the same fate from the opposite starting point: they find great, undigested lumps of theorising appearing willy-nilly in what they assume to be a mere recitation of 'the facts':

> *It is the old story. First of all one makes sensuous things into abstractions and then one wants to know them through the senses, to see time and smell space. The empiricist becomes so steeped in the habit of empirical experience, that he believes that he is still in the field of sensuous experience when he is operating with abstractions.*[72]

So Engels was far from being an empiricist inclined system builder. His thought was constitutionally opposed to all-embracing abstract models of thought, whether they issued from the expected direction of idealism or from the less usual route of abstract empiricism. Engels' own method was once again more dialectical. It involved a conscious recognition *both* of the theoretical elements in any empirical study *and* the necessary empirical basis on which any theoretical generalisation must stand. And once again Engels' critics largely rely on removing one side or the other of his approach; they then insist that what remains proves that he was either a Hegelian intent on pushing the natural world into the preconceived forms of the dialectic, or a positivist who had abandoned the key terms of Marx's dialectic.

An economic determinism?

The charge most commonly levelled at Engels is that he was a determinist intent on maintaining that every aspect of society could only be explained by its direct causal relationship with the economic structure. For example, George Lichtheim believes Engels' thought was 'hardly different from the fashionable materialist evolutionism of the epoch'.[73] In Norman

Levine's view, 'by making economics the primary causal agent...Engels remained in the camp of positivism'.[74]

The grain of truth on which this mountain of speculation rests is that Engels, like Marx, believed that the material circumstances in which human beings find themselves shape their thoughts and actions. These material circumstances do contain an important economic element, although we should be careful about translating the current academically constricted notions of 'economics' into the days when Marx and Engels wrote. These see economics as a quantative science restricted to predicting human behaviour on the basis of supply and demand curves. In this sense modern bourgeois economics is overwhelmingly more determinist than anything Marx and Engels, or for that matter the bourgeois economists of their day, could have imagined.

Indeed, the discipline which Marx and Engels knew was called 'political economy', not 'economics'. Its remit covered much territory now known as sociology and political science. Consequently, the notion of 'economics' is much wider in Marx and Engels than many superficial observers comprehend. As we have seen, they considered human beings' relationships with nature, their family relationships and the social relationships they formed with other human beings to be some of the most important constituents of a materialist analysis of any particular epoch. Marx's mature economic theory insisted that both means of production (tools, machines, factories, offices and so on) and the relations of production (above all, the class relations) were, together, what constituted the mode of production. And it was upon this basis, the 'production and reproduction of real life' as Engels put it, that they sought to understand the development of social institutions, political parties, ideologies, religions, philosophies and so on.

At no point, however, did either Marx or Engels argue that this was a deterministic relationship. They never suggested that the various political institutions, parties and ideologies had no effect on the course of history. One of the most trenchant statements of this attitude was written by Engels, although it is often attributed to Marx, in one of the sections which he contributed to their joint early work, *The German Ideology*:

> **History** does **nothing**, it 'possesses **no** immense wealth', it 'wages no battles'. It is **man**, real, living man who does all that, who possesses and fights; 'history' is not, as it were, a person apart, using man as a means to achieve **its own** aims; history is **nothing but** the activity of man pursuing his aims.[75]

A lifetime later Engels' attitude had not altered. Towards the end of his life he wrote a series of letters, as well as general statements in his published work, designed to clarify exactly this point. In September 1890, for instance, in a letter to Joseph Bloch, Engels wrote:

> *Marx and I are ourselves partly to blame for the fact that the younger people sometimes lay more stress on the economic side than is due to it. We had to emphasise the main principle vis-a-vis our adversaries, who denied it, and we had not always the time, the place or the opportunity to give their due to the other factors involved in the interaction. But when it came to presenting a section of history, that is, to applying the theory in practice, it was a different matter and there no error was permissible.*[76]

Engels recommends, as 'a most excellent example' of dealing with a particular historical event, Marx's *The Eighteenth Brumaire of Louis Bonaparte*. This work contains Marx's famous formulation of the relationship between material conditions and human action in the making of history: 'Men make their own history, but...not under circumstances they themselves have chosen but under the given and inherited circumstances with which they are directly confronted'.[77] Engels clearly had this formulation in mind when he wrote his letter to Bloch:

> *We make our history ourselves, but, in the first place, under very definite antecedents and conditions. Among these the economic are ultimately decisive.*[78]

And he went on to argue that 'it is hardly possible, without making oneself ridiculous, to explain in terms of economics the existence of every small state in Germany, past and present'. The next month, October 1890, saw Engels return to the same theme in terms strikingly reminiscent of those which he used in *The German Ideology*. He complained bitterly that one of his 'supporters' had written 'as if, according to Marx, history makes itself quite automatically, without the co-operation of human beings (who after all are making it!), and as if these human beings were simply played like mere chessmen by the economic conditions (which are the work of men themselves!)'. Engels was quick to point out that this was a repetition of the *corruption of Marx* peddled by Dühring. He concluded in an exasperated tone, 'A man who is capable of confusing the distortion of Marxist theory by an opponent such as Dühring with this theory itself must turn elsewhere for help—I give up'.[79]

Later the same month Engels was again recommending Marx's *Eighteenth Brumaire*, this time to Conrad Schmidt, as a model of non-deterministic analysis because:

> [It] *deals almost exclusively with the **particular** part played by political struggles and events, of course within their **general** dependence on economic*

*conditions. Or **Capital**, the section on the working day, for instance, where legislation, which is surely a political act, has such a drastic effect.*

And he concludes, 'And why do we fight for the political dictatorship of the proletariat if political power is economically impotent? Force (that is, state power) is also an economic power!'[80]

But Engels' letters did far more than simply make general statements to the effect that historical materialism was not a crude economistic interpretation of history. They went on to spell out how Marxists set about relating various political institutions to the economic structure of society.

Engels argued that state power generally can have one of three effects on the economic development of a society. It can accelerate economic change, retard economic change or alter the course of economic development and 'prevent economic development from proceeding along certain lines, and prescribe other lines'.[81] The state can gain this *relative* independence because it is based on the development of the division of labour. Engels explains:

*Society gives rise to certain common functions which it cannot dispense with. The persons appointed for this purpose form a new branch of the division of labour **within society**. This gives them particular interests, distinct, too, from those of their mandator; they make themselves independent of the latter and— the state is in being...the new independent power, while having in the main to follow the movement of production, reacts in turn, by virtue of its inherent relative independence—that is relative independence once transferred to it and gradually further developed—upon the course and conditions of production.[82]*

And, as each new area of political and social development opens up, there arise institutional structures and networks of social relations which, while ultimately related to the economic structure, develop a certain independent power of their own. Engels uses the example of the legal structure:

As soon as the new division of labour which creates professional lawyers becomes necessary, another new and independent sphere is opened up which, for all its general dependence on production and trade, has also a specific capacity for reacting on these spheres.[83]

More than this, the very nature of the law means that it *cannot be a direct reflection of the economic conditions which gave rise to it*. This is for three reasons. Firstly, the law, although fundamentally an expression of the ruling class's control of property, cannot simply be a 'blunt, unmitigated, unadulterated expression of the domination of a class', otherwise it would fail to be effective as an arbiter of the class struggle. It must have, at least, the *appearance* of independence from the ruling class.

Secondly, although based on a contradictory economic system, the law itself has to be seen to be internally coherent, to be rational in its judgments. But 'in order to achieve this, the faithful reflection of economic conditions suffers increasingly'.[84] Finally, and as a result of these two factors, 'the jurist imagines he is operating with *a priori* propositions, whereas they are really only economic reflections; everything is therefore upside down'.[85] So this *necessarily* independent sphere 'influences the economic base and may, within certain limits, modify it.' Indeed, Engels adds, laws like those governing inheritance can 'exert a very considerable effect on the economic sphere, because they influence the distribution of property.'[86]

None of this, however, was meant to deny the materialism of Marx and Engels' approach, merely to spell out that they were not *mechanical* materialists or economic *determinists*:

> *It is the interaction of two unequal forces: on the one hand, the economic movement, on the other, the new political power, which strives for as much independence as possible, and which, having once been set up, is endowed with a movement of its own. On the whole, the economic movement prevails, but it has also to endure reactions from the political movement which it itself set up and endowed with relative independence, from the movement of state power, on the one hand, and of the opposition simultaneously engendered, on the other.*[87]

Here once again the key elements of a dialectical analysis are in place: the whole of society is shown to be based on a fundamental economic contradiction which gives rise to a state structure which is related to, but distinct from, its economic base. Either completely separating the economic and the political, or completely dissolving either side into the other, destroys the real pattern of relations. It is, in dialectical terminology, a contradictory totality, a unity of opposites. As Engels wrote of his contemporary critics:

> *What these gentlemen all lack is dialectics. They always see only cause here, effect there. That this is an empty abstraction, that such metaphysical polar opposites exist in the real world only during crises, and that the whole vast process goes on in the form of interaction—though of very unequal forces, the economic being by far the strongest, the primary and the most decisive and that in this context everything is relative and nothing absolute—they cannot grasp at all. As far as they are concerned Hegel never existed.*[88]

So even in Engels' day it was not new for critics to be ignorant of what is involved in a dialectical materialist analysis of society, and allow one side of the analysis to be abstracted, so they could condemn Engels as a determinist.

A copy theory of knowledge?

Engels' did not believe that human society simply reproduced relations found in the natural world, or that the political life of society simply reflected its economic preconditions. Therefore it would be surprising if he held a copy theory of knowledge—a theory which holds that our ideas are simply a mirror of the world around us. But since Engels frequently uses the term 'reflection' to indicate the relationship between ideas and reality, this issue requires some further examination.

When Marx and Engels describe thought as a 'reflection' of the material world they are usually talking in the most general terms and they are often arguing against idealists, for whom the material world is the creation of thought. So it is, for instance, in a passage from *Ludwig Feuerbach and the End of Classical German Philosophy* which seems particularly to irritate Engels' critics. Here, as part of a paragraph in which Engels is polemising against the Hegelian notion that thought is 'the actual living soul of the whole existing world', he writes, 'We comprehend the ideas in our heads materialistically again—as reflections of real things instead of regarding the real things as reflections of this or that stage of the absolute idea'.[89]

But the moment Engels moves beyond such aphoristic formulations he makes it quite obvious that the relationship between thought and its material conditions cannot be reduced to simple reflection. Thus later in *Ludwig Feuerbach*, where Engels discusses philosophy and religion, he insists that these 'higher ideologies…are still further removed from the material base' and that 'the connection between ideas and their material conditions of existence becomes more and more complicated and more and more obscured by the intermediate links.'[90] And he goes on to elaborate:

> Once it has arisen…every ideology develops in conjunction with the given conceptual material and elaborates on it; otherwise it would not be an ideology, that is, dealing with ideas as autonomous entities which develop independently and are subject to their own laws.[91]

So ideologies develop their own internal coherence and, therefore, have their own relatively independent modes of development (as we saw in the previous section with regard to the law). But there are two more reasons for believing that Engels did not hold a crude copy theory of knowledge.

Firstly, such a theory would have contradicted a fact which Engels regarded as fundamental to his understanding of the dialectic: the natural and the social world are in a never ceasing process of change and development. Any idea, but particularly any widely accepted ideological system, is both relatively abstract and relatively stable in comparison to the diversity and change which is present in the real world. It follows that concepts are necessarily an inexact representation of reality. Sometimes such inexactitude is a virtue—it helps isolate the essential from the inessential—but it always results in a disjunction between thought and reality.

There is a related problem raised by the comparatively static nature of concepts. To analyse certain elements of material reality it is often important to extract them deliberately from the constant passage of time, and then treat them as fixed and unchanging. But this also introduces a necessary inaccuracy into our concepts. Engels elaborated these points in a letter to Conrad Schmidt:

> *The concept of a thing and its reality, run side by side like two asymptotes, always approaching each other yet never meeting. The difference between the two is the very difference which prevents the concept from being directly and immediately reality and reality from being immediately its own concept…the concept…does not therefore prima facie directly coincide with reality, from which it had to be abstracted in the first place, it is nevertheless more than a fiction, unless you declare that all the results of thought are fictions because reality only corresponds to them only very circuitously, and even then approaching it only asympomatically.*[92]

But these difficulties are only half the problem:

> *…or are the concepts which prevail in the natural sciences fictions because they by no means always coincide with reality? From the moment we accept the theory of evolution all our concepts of organic life correspond only approximately to reality. Otherwise there would be no change. On the day when concepts and reality completely coincide in the organic world development comes to an end. The concept fish includes life in water and breathing through gills: how are you going to get from fish to amphibian without breaking through this concept?*[93]

Indeed, for Marx and Engels, one of the main virtues of dialectical thought was that it developed a number of concepts which more accurately corresponded to the changing nature of reality than the more static and abstract categories of either empiricism or idealism. But precisely because such enormous theoretical effort was necessary in order to correctly apprehend the nature of reality, it was inconceivable that either Marx or Engels would have subscribed to the idea that reality was immediately reflected in the mind in any simplistic or automatic manner.

One final argument against the view that Engels held a reductionist explanation of the relationship between society and ideology rests on Marx and Engels' theory of alienation. This argued that in a society where human beings could not control either their natural environment or the social and economic mechanism it was inevitable that they would fail to be able to easily comprehend the nature of their world. This was true of all class societies, at least to some degree. But it was most true of capitalist society, since capitalism is a society in which the economic exploitation of the working class is masked by the legal equality of all its members. Everyone, capitalist or worker, is subject to the same laws, at least in theory. Everyone, factory owner or wage earner, has the same right to vote. The surface appearance of society is thus very different from its actual workings.

This results in the illusion that the political structure shapes the economic structure—the basis of, among others, the reformist ideology —rather than the reverse. The fact that the ruling class really does use the state to protect its economic power lends weight to this appearance, helping to further obscure the capitalists' fundamental dependence on its economic power:

> *The traditional conception...saw in the state the determining element... Appearances correspond to this...so all the needs of civil society—whichever class happens to be the ruling one—must pass through the will of the state to obtain general validity in the form of laws. That is the formal aspect of the matter, which is self-evident. But the question now arises, what is the content of this merely formal will...? If we look into this, we discover that in modern history the will of the state is by and large determined by the changing needs of civil society, by the supremacy of this or that class, in the last resort, by the development of the productive forces and the relations of exchange.*[94]

Here, once again, a simple reflection of appearances in the minds of human beings does *not* accord with reality but with a mistaken image of reality. It would be impossible, on this understanding, for Engels to hold a copy theory of knowledge. If thought mirrored reality it would simply be reflecting the ideological appearance, not the scientifically uncovered reality. Marx made this point in his criticism of the vulgar economists, whose fault lay precisely in the fact that they did simply reflect the appearance (or 'phenomenal form', as Marx calls it) not the underlying reality. Engels is unlikely to have missed this point since it was made in a letter to him:

*The philistine's and vulgar economist's **way of looking at things** arises,
namely, because it is only the immediate phenomenal **form** of these relations
that is reflected in their brains and not their **inner connection**, Incidently, if
the latter were the case what need would there be of **science**?*[95]

Moreover, not only would there be no need for science if the reality of
things were immediately obvious from their appearance, there would be
no need for, or possibility of, working class consciousness changing in the
course of class struggle. Either the real nature of capitalist society would
be obvious and workers would reject it, in which case a revolution would
be automatic; or the appearance of capitalism would be taken as true and
workers would accept it, in which case a revolution would be impossible.
It is because, in the course the struggle, workers move from a consciousness which partly accepts the system at face value to a rejection of the
system based on a truer comprehension of its real nature that a revolution
is both possible and the culmination of a historical process. So, contrary
to assertions by Kolakowski, Schmidt and others, Marx *and* Engels'
theory requires a rejection of a copy theory of consciousness, both as a
method of analysis and as an explanation of working class consciousness.

The self emancipation of the working class

Marx is sometimes acquitted of the charge that he saw socialism as
inevitable on the grounds that the commitment to the self emancipation
of the working class is unmistakable in his writings, particularly his early
writings. Such judgments rarely extend to Engels. Engels, as we have
seen, is accused, in Lichtheim's words, of transferring 'the here-and-now
of conscious activity to a horizon so distant as to be almost invisible,' or
else of propagating a version of Marxism in which 'the notion of human
praxis was absent'. Supposedly Marx is the humanist whose vision
incorporated the struggle of real workers, Engels the determinist whose
scientific framework had no room for human intervention.

Despite being well established this view has little basis in fact. Much
of what was said in refutation of Engels' alleged determinism is also relevant here. But to avoid straying into the area of general principles again,
some of Engels' remarks about the class struggle should suffice.

Interestingly, even when Engels is deploying some of his most deterministic formulations in response to Dühring's contention that 'political
conditions are the decisive cause of the economic situation', even when
he is arguing that capitalism is being driven forward 'as if necessitated
by a law of nature', Engels still insists that there is not one pre-deter-
mined outcome. He argues that the class struggle can *either* result in
'ruin *or* revolution'. Which possibility actually materialises is clearly
dependent on the course of the class struggle. In this respect Engels'

thought reproduced towards the end of his life exactly the patterns which he and Marx had first described in the *Communist Manifesto* in their youth. There the fate of capitalism is described as *either* proletarian revolution *or* 'the common ruin of the contending classes'. History, for Engels, was no more independent of the course of the class struggle in the 1880s than it had been in the 1840s. Indeed, in those early days it was Engels as much as Marx who took the lead in asserting the centrality of the self activity of the working class.

It was Engels, for instance, who in the face of the whole of accepted opinion on the left at that time, insisted on the importance of trade unions precisely because they were organisations in which workers taught themselves to fight and in which they could learn the real nature of the capitalist system:

> *What gives these Unions and the strikes arising from them their real importance is this, that they are the first attempt of the workers to abolish competition. They imply the recognition of the fact that the supremacy of the bourgeoisie is based wholly upon the competition of the workers among themselves; ie upon their want of cohesion. And precisely because the Unions direct themselves against the vital nerve of the present social order, however one-sidedly, in however narrow a way, are they so dangerous to this social order.*[96]

Consciousness and organisation are seen as going hand in hand. And the further development of the struggle is seen as promoting the possibility of going beyond the limits of trade union consciousness and organisation:

> *If the competition of workers among themselves is destroyed, if all determine not to be further exploited by the bourgeoisie, the rule of property is at an end... The moment the workers resolve to be bought and sold no longer, they take the part of men possessed of a will as well as of a working power, at that moment the whole Political Economy of today is at an end.*[97]

And it was in Marx and Engels' joint work, *The German Ideology*, that this famous statement of revolution as the act of the working class was made:

> *Both for the production on a mass scale of this communist consciousness and for the success of the cause itself, the alteration of men on a mass scale is necessary, an alteration which can only take place in a practical movement, a* **revolution***; the revolution is necessary, therefore, not only because the* **ruling** *class cannot be overthrown in any other way, but also because the class* **over-**

throwing *it can only in a revolution succeed in ridding itself of all the muck of ages and become fitted to found itself anew.*[98]

And it was Engels alone who reported a few years later on the practical experience of living through one such moment in the revolutionary Berlin of 1848. And, as he did so, he forged one of the most striking formulations of necessity of the self emancipation of the working class:

*The people that fought and won on the barricades is an altogether different people from the one that assembled before the castle on 18 March to be enlightened about the meaning of the concessions obtained, by the attacks of the dragoons. It is capable of altogether different things, it has an altogether different stance with relation to the government. The most important conquest of the revolution is **the revolution itself**.*[99]

Engels' commitment to the idea of working class self emancipation remained undimmed in later life. In 1888, for instance, he wrote to Margaret Harkness criticising her novel *City Girl* because she failed to highlight this aspect of working class life:

*In the **City Girl** the working class figures appear as a passive mass, unable to help itself and not even showing (making) any attempt at striving to help itself. All attempts to drag it out of its torpid misery come from without, from above. Now if this was a correct description about 1800 or 1810...it cannot appear so in 1887 to a man who for nearly 50 years has had the honour of sharing in most of the fights of the militant proletariat. The rebellious reaction of the working class against the oppressive medium which surrounds them, their attempts—convulsive, half-conscious or conscious—at recovering their status as human beings, belong to history and must therefore lay claim to a place in the domain of realism.*[100]

In every aspect of Engels' thought—whether it be the stress on consciousness as the element which which makes human beings a distinct part of nature, or the centrality of the class struggle, or the complaint that a novel does not accurately portray the self activity of workers—he is careful to avoid mechanical materialism. It does not seem, therefore, that any honest reading of Engels' works can accuse him of neglecting the role of working people in the struggle for their own liberation.

Engels and reformism

Another common accusation is that Engels invented a mechanical Marxism which resulted in the reformist strategy which increasingly came to dominate the German SPD and the Second International of which it was a part. This view involves a series of falsifications.

This first falsification is, as we have seen, that Engels' approach was mechanical to start with. Even Engels' least guarded formulation of historical materialism was qualitatively different from the kind of fatalism which marked, for instance, the thought of the leading theoretician of the Second International, Karl Kautsky. The future, wrote Kautsky:

> *Is certain and inevitable in the sense that it is inevitable that inventors improve technique, that capitalists in their greed revolutionise the economic life...that it is inevitable that wage-earners aspire to shorter working hours and higher wages, that they organise themselves and struggle against the class of capitalists and the power of the state... That it is inevitable that they aspire to political power and the abolition of the capitalist domination. Socialism is inevitable because the class struggle and the victory of the proletariat are so too.*[101]

There is clearly an intellectual continuity between this kind of general formulation and the passive reformism, the rejection of revolution, that became the hallmark of the leaders of the Second International. If socialism is inevitable, after all, why endanger its progress by revolutionary adventures? Why not wait for its inevitable progress to register in a parliamentary majority for the SPD?

Equally clearly, Engels' work does not contain anything remotely resembling this kind of formulation. So, for it to be made into an intellectual justification for reformism, selective quotation and distortion must be used. Whereas in Kautsky's case the general theoretical approach *did* result in reformist political formulations, there is no evidence that Engels' supposed mechanical materialism actually resulted in him endorsing a reformist political strategy.

This last assertion requires justification since it is sometimes argued that in his last years Engels did endorse the first signs of reformism as they emerged in the SPD. Indeed, it is even argued that Marx first raised the issue in a speech he gave in Amsterdam in 1872 following the Hague conference of the First International where he said that it might be possible, in England for instance, that 'workers can achieve their goals through peaceful means.' This interpretation is, however, only possible on the basis of highly selective quotation. Not only does it neglect Marx's general statements in his writings on the Paris Commune, where he insisted that workers must 'smash the state machine', it also ignores Engels' explicit and specific elaboration of Marx's remark about England. In 1886, in his preface to the first English translation of *Capital*, Engels returned to Marx's remark that 'in Europe at least, England is the only country where the inevitable social revolution might be effected by peaceful and legal means.' Engels goes on to add a crucial qualification: 'He [Marx] certainly never forgot to add that he hardly expected the English ruling classes to submit, without a "pro-slavery rebellion" to the peaceful and legal revolution'.[102]

The gravity of this remark can be understood by recalling the event to which Engels is referring when he uses the phrase 'pro-slavery rebellion'. This was the term used to describe the revolt of the Southern states of America against the Federal government—its result was the American Civil War. The full meaning of Engels' statement is, therefore, that, even if the working class in England were to attain power peacefully, they would then have to defend it by means of a revolutionary civil war. It is, consequently, difficult to see the embryo of reformism in Engels' formulations or—on Engels' testimony—in Marx's statement either.

This is not, however, the end of Engels' alleged reformism. In the very last year of his life Engels wrote an introduction to Marx's *The Class Struggles in France* which is said to have pointed towards a reformist strategy. It is certainly true that Engels insists on the importance of 'slow propaganda work and parliamentary activity'. But this insistence was born of two considerations.

Firstly, the leaders of the SPD, in whose paper, *Vorwärts*, the introduction was to appear, were worried that the anti-socialist laws then before the German parliament would be passed and therefore begged Engels to tone down the more revolutionary of his formulations. This he did only in part and then with the greatest reluctance. Engels wrote to Richard Fischer of the SPD executive:

> *I have yielded to your serious misgivings as much as possible, although with the best will I cannot understand about half of the concerns. I still cannot accept that you intend to pledge yourselves body and soul to absolute legality, legality under all circumstances, legality even in the face of laws broken by their authors—in short the politics of proffering the left cheek to whoever has struck you on the right... I'm of the opinion that you win nothing when you preach the absolute renunciation of striking hard...and no party anywhere goes so far as to renounce armed opposition to illegality.*[103]

The second consideration behind some of Engels' formulations was a *tactical* desire to instruct his readers on when a revolutionary uprising was possible, and what tactics were appropriate at which stage of an insurrection. Engels explains, for instance, that a premature putsch which does not enjoy the support of the majority of workers can be counterproductive, handing the ruling class a chance to recover its confidence and go over to the offensive. This was not a rejection of revolution, it was a rejection of coups carried out by elites:

The time of surprise attacks, of revolutions carried through by small conscious minorities at the head of masses lacking consciousness is past. Where it is a question of a complete transformation of the social organisation, the masses themselves must be in on it, must themselves already have grasped what is at stake, what they are fighting for, body and soul.[104]

Engels also discussed another, entirely minor, tactical question: when and where it was appropriate to build street barricades. It is possible that Engels' military interests led him to spend too much time on this issue, but his concerns were not meant to deny the possibility of revolution. His point about street barricades was simply that developments since the 1848 revolutions made these a much more dangerous proposition than they once were. The forces of the state were better armed and trained than in 1848, for instance. Even so, Engels did not completely renounce the use of barricades. He concluded his lengthy overview of the changed conditions since 1848 with the sentence, 'This is the key point to keep in mind in analysing any future possibilities for street fighting', clearly indicating the provisional and conditional nature of his judgments.[105] Later he posed point blank the question of whether street fighting would be debarred from future use. His reply: 'Absolutely not'. These sentences, however, were removed from the printed copy in *Vorwärts*. These and other alterations made Engels' piece seem much more reformist than he had ever intended.

Engels wrote a bitter letter of protest to Karl Kautsky, then editor of another SPD paper, *Neue Zeit*:

*To my astonishment I see today in **Vorwärts** an extract from my 'Introduction', **printed without my knowledge** and trimmed in such a way as to make me appear a peace-loving worshipper of legality at any price. So much the better that the whole thing is to appear now in **Neue Zeit** so that this disgraceful impression will be wiped out.*[106]

Engels also wrote to Paul Lafargue complaining of the 'trick' that had been played on him by the editor of *Vorwarts* so that 'everything could serve him to support that tactics of *peace at any price and of opposition to force and violence*, which it has pleased him for some time now to preach, especially at present when coercive laws are being prepared in Berlin'. Engels insisted that he supported these tactics only 'today' and only in Germany. And even so they 'may become inapplicable tomorrow'.[107]

All this is of a piece with an earlier letter to Lafargue where Engels argued that the great virtue of legal political work was that it showed 'with absolute exactitude that day on which one must take up arms for the revolution'.[108]

There is, perhaps, some excuse for those who only had the censored text of Engels' introduction before them to believe that, in some of his last printed words, he had given ground to reformist ideas. For those who have to hand the full text, and Engels' subsequent correspondence, such a judgement can only be based on malice or misunderstanding.

Engels' legacy

If Engels' ideas are not a theoretical precursor of either reformism or Stalinism, why is it that so many theorists have attempted to prove that they are? The answer to this question lies in the theoretical weakness which haunted the New Left in the 1960s and 1970s and which, in different ways, affected many of those who looked at the history of Marxism, whether or not they regarded themselves as radicals.

The dominant tone emphasised philosophical and cultural analysis, often in reaction to what was rightly perceived as the reductionism of the Stalinist tradition and the anti-theoretical nature of reformism. But such an approach was fundamentally flawed when it came to understanding the roots of just those two traditions.

It is one thing to say that Stalinism was a form of economic reductionism and that reformism has a pragmatic distrust of theory. But it is quite another to say that reductionism in theory leads to, much less *causes*, Stalinism; or that pragmatism in theory *causes* reformism in practice. The New Left's concern with culture and theory tilted over into a kind of idealism where the emphasis in explaining any historical event rests on inadequacies of theory. And once this logic is accepted it is not long before the intellectual lines of inheritance are scoured to find the thinker who first introduced such erroneous ideas into the movement. The search for original sin has begun.

Right wingers would, of course, have no difficulty here. For them Engels and Marx are *both* guilty of determinism and of being the precursors of Stalinism. But those radicalised in the 1960s and 1970s were formed by a rejection of this kind of Cold War mentality. They knew too much about the methods of right wing academia, and too much about Marxism, to accept the right wing argument—but most of them did not know enough to reject the argument against Engels.

What was necessary was a *materialist* explanation of the rise of reformism and the roots of Stalinism. Kautsky's revisionism was ultimately the product of the relative stability which accompanied the epoch of classical imperialism (1870-1914), the rise of mass reformist parties and the trade union bureaucracy. Adapting to these material circumstances, the leaders of the Second International were forced to distort the revolutionary essence of Marxism while attempting to preserve its form.

Likewise the isolation of the Russian Revolution led to the rise of the Stalinist bureaucracy and then to its abandonment of Marxism, while simultaneously retaining the phrases of the revolutionary tradition as an ideological tie between itself and the mass of the population.

This kind of materialist account was adopted by some of those radicalised in the 1960s and 1970s, but the weakness of the Trotskyist movement which carried this analysis limited the numbers it could influence. For those not influenced by this approach the difficulties of surviving a period when the struggle ebbed were enormously increased. Under the pressure of defeat those who started out trying to establish Marxism without Engels tended to end up at Marxism without Marx.

Those who understood the materialist causes of Stalinism and reformism were better equipped to separate the Stalinist and reformist distortions of Engels from what Engels himself intended. This, in turn, left them with a Marxism better able to meet the demands of the coming decades. And this is the real point of rescuing Engels from the hands of his critics. Understanding Engels' ideas makes it more likely, though far from inevitable, that in the struggles which lie ahead we will avoid defeat and ensure victory.

When Engels spoke the words, 'Before all else, he was a revolutionist,' over Marx's grave, it was an epitaph as fitting for the speaker as for his dead friend. And, because they were more than just active revolutionaries themsleves, Marx and Engels developed an analysis which, while it could not possibly forecast the struggles of the 20th century, provided the basis for understanding that century. And so it is Marx *and Engels'* thought which provides socialists today with the best chance of meeting the challenges with which the development of the natural sciences and the capitalist system are confronting us as the millennium approaches.

Engels and the origins of human society

CHRIS HARMAN

Arguments for socialism are always intertwined with arguments about the origins of human beings and social institutions. Socialists see the exploitation of some people by others, the existence of an oppressive state and the subordination of women to men in the nuclear family as products of human history. Our opponents see them as the result of human nature.

That was why when Marx and Engels first formulated their ideas, they did so by developing a completely new understanding of the how human beings relate to the world around them. This involved rejecting the two dominant ways of seeing this relationship: *idealism* which sees human beings as semi-divine, subject to God's will and completely separate from the animal world; and *crude materialism* which hold humans to be no more than machines or animals, either simply reacting to stimuli from the external world (today generally labelled 'behavourism'), or as biologically programmed to perform in certain ways (today, called 'sociobiology').[1]

Marx and Engels first presented their own view in *The German Ideology* and the *Theses on Feuerbach* of 1845-6. They saw human beings as products of the natural, biological world, and history as part of natural history. But they also saw the specific character of humans as lying in their ability to react back on the circumstances that had created them, changing both those circumstances and themselves in the process.

Knowledge of both natural history and human history was still very

limited when Marx and Engels first formulated their ideas: the first discovery of early human remains (of Neanderthals) was not until 1856;
Darwin's *Origin of Species* was not published until 1859 and his *Descent
of Man* until 1871; and the American Lewis Henry Morgan did not
publish his pioneering account of the evolution of the family and state,
Ancient Society, until 1877.

Engels relied on these scientific advances to enlarge on his and
Marx's earlier insights. This he did in two important works, *The Part
Played by Labour in the Transition from Ape to Man* (written in 1876)[2],
and *The Origin of the Family, Private Property and the State* (published
in 1884)[3]. They contain the most extensive account by the founders of
historical materialism of how human beings came to live as they do in
modern times—of where 'human nature' and human institutions come
from. For this reason attacks on the validity of Marxism and on Engels'
reputation have often concentrated on them—especially on *The Origin of
the Family*. Scientific advance over the last century has, of course, dated
some of Engels material: he was writing before the discovery of the
Mendelian theory of genetics[4], before the earliest hominid remains were
found in Africa and at a time when investigation into preliterate societies
was in its infancy. Yet his writings still retain enormous relevance. He
applies a method which is materialist without being mechanical—and
which continues to challenge both idealism and the terrible twins of
behaviourism and sociobiology.

That is why it is worthwhile looking at Engels' arguments in these
two works and to defend what is valid in them while sifting out what is
dated. This I attempt to do, looking first at his account of human evolution in *The Part Played by Labour*, then at his explanation of the rise of
classes and the state in *The Origin of the Family*, and then, finally at the
same work's explanation for women's oppression. In each case I will
attempt to deal with gaps and discrepancies in Engels' arguments by discussing some of the most important more recent material on these
questions.

I The argument on human origins

Engels outlined his account of human origins in a few paragraphs which
are worth reproducing here with only slight editing:

> *Many hundreds of thousands of years ago, during an epoch not yet definitely
> determinable...a race of anthropoid* [ie human-like] *apes lived in the tropical
> zone...they lived in bands in the trees...*
>
> *These apes began to the lose the habit of using their hands to walk and
> adopted a more and more erect posture. This was **the first decisive step in the***

transition from ape to man.

Other diverse functions must, have devolved upon the hands. The first operations for which our ancestors gradually learned to adapt their hands...could have been only very simple ones...But the decisive step had been taken, the hand had become free and could henceforth attain ever greater dexterity...

Using the hand for labour had other effects:

Our simian ancestors were gregarious...the development of labour necessarily helped to bring the members of society together by increasing the cases of mutual support and joint activity, and by making clear the advantages of this joint activity to every individual.

*Men-in-the-making arrived at the point where **they had something to say** to each other. Necessity created the organ; the undeveloped larynx of the ape was slowly but surely transformed by modulation to produce constantly more developed modulation, and the organs of the mouth gradually learned to pronounce one articulate sound after another.*

Parallel with this there was a necessary development of the brain: 'The reaction of labour and speech on the development of the brain and its attendant senses, of the increasing clarity of consciousness, power of abstraction and of conclusion, gave both labour and speech an ever renewed impulse to further development.' Overall:

*Hundreds of thousands of years certainly elapsed before human society arose out of troop of tree climbing monkeys. Yet it did finally appear. And what do we find once more as the characteristic difference between the troupe of monkeys and human society? **Labour**.*

Engels' position, then, sees human evolution as going through a number of interlinked stages: two-legged walking, tool making and use, development of the hand, sociability, brain and speech development, more control over nature, more sociability, more brain and speech development. His account of this was dependent on Darwin's prior work, and each of these elements is mentioned by Darwin. But Engels alters the order of the stages in a significant way.

Darwin assumed that the growth in brain size and intellect occurred *before* the transition to two-legged walking and the use of hands to make tools. Engels argued the sequence of events was the other way round. It was the freeing of the hands that made co-operative labour possible on a scale unimaginable among apes, and from this flowed the development of the brain. As the archaeologist Bruce Trigger tells:

Darwin was...constrained by reluctance to challenge the primacy which the idealistic religious and philosophical thinking of his time accorded to rational thought as a motor in bringing about cultural change. Hence in discussing human evolution...it was the development of the brain that in turn resulted in tool use.[5]

By contrast:

Engels argued that an increasingly terrestrial life-style had encouraged... increasing use of tools. This caused natural selection in favour of bipedalism and manual dexterity as well as...a more complex division of labour. Tool making and the development of a capacity for language the better to co-ordinate productive activities led to the gradual transformation of the brain of an ape into the that of a modern human being...

Darwin's view of the sequence of stages dominated research on human origins for the best part of a century, leading to the belief that any 'missing link' between apes and humans had a large brain but an ape-like posture and throwing the whole study of our evolution askew. It encouraged acceptance for some 50 years of one of the great scientific frauds of all time—the Piltdown affair, in which the skull of a man and the jaw of an ape were presented as the remains of one of our earliest ancestors. And it led to the refusal for 30 years to take seriously a genuine find, the discovery in South Africa by Raymond Dart of the remains of an ape-like creature which had adopted two legged walking. It was not until the discovery by Donald Johanson in 1974 of a complete three and half million year old skeleton with an ape sized brain and a erect posture that Darwin's sequence was finally abandoned.[6] Only then could archaeologists begin to explain the evolution of one set of skeletons from another.[7]

Assessing Engels' argument today

But if Engels was, amazingly, right in this respect as against Darwin, how does the rest of his account hold together? We have much more knowledge today than in Engels' time. But there are still enormous problems in fitting it together.

Most physical knowledge of our ape and early human ancestors rests on findings of odd fragments of bone, occasional teeth, and small bits of rock which may or may not once have been tools. Using such evidence, students of human origins have to try to guess what whole skeletons were like, the nature of the nerves and muscles that once encased them, the intellectual capacities of the creatures to which they belonged, how they fed themselves and the social context in which they lived. As one of Britain's leading archaeologists, Chris Stringer, has put it:

The field of human evolution is littered with abandoned ancestors and the theories that went with them… Failure to realise the complexities involved in trying to interpret a few fossils scattered sparsely through space and time has characterised the approach of even the most competent workers, resulting in naive interpretations… Consequently, whole evolutionary edifices would collapse, complete with attached ancestors and descendants, with each development in theory, investigation of an underlying assumption or new discovery.[8]

So, for instance, until the late 1970s it was assumed there had been four ice ages in the last 800,000 years. Now it is believed there were at least eight.[9] Again, until 20 years ago it was commonly accepted that the separation of our ancestors from those of great apes occurred with an ape known as Ramapithecus, 15 million years ago. Now it is usually held the separation took place with the evolution of the 'Southern Apes', Australopithecus, that lived in east and south Africa 3 or 4 million years ago.[10]

The sparsity of reliable information makes it very easy for people to make elaborate, unsubstantiated conjectures about what might have happened, with no facts to confirm or deny them—the modern version of the 'Just So' stories Rudyard Kipling wrote for children nearly a century ago. All sorts of writers on human evolution make hypotheses of the form, 'And, so, perhaps, we can explain the descent of certain apes from the trees by their need to do X'. Within a couple of paragraphs, the 'perhaps' has gone, and X becomes the origin of humanity.

This method is the special hallmark of sociobiologists,[11] but there are also some very good theorists who fall into it occasions.[12] It is a method Marxists have to reject. We are not interested in story telling for the sake of story telling. So I will try to concentrate on what we know for certain.

The established record: our relatives

It is generally accepted that our nearest relatives are the chimps, the pygmy chimps (or bonobos)[13] and the gorillas[14]. Studies of genetic material suggest that we shared a common ancestor some 4 to 7 million years ago and that even today, after evolving in different directions, we still have some 97.5 percent of genes in common with the chimpanzees. Genetically, 'man and chimpanzee are more closely related than horse and donkey, cat and lion, or dog and fox'.[15]

This is still an uncomfortable fact for idealists of all sorts, and confirms Marx's view that human history is part of natural history. But it is often seised on by modern mechanical materialists who claim that we are simply 'naked apes' and that all the faults of society can be blamed on our inherited mammalian genetic make up. As one popular account of human origins put it:

Hierarchy is an institution among all social animals and the drive to dominate one's fellows an instinct three or four million years old… The human drive to acquire possessions is the simple expression of an animal instinct many hundreds of years older than the human race itself… The roots of nationalism are dug firmly in the social territory of almost every species of our related primate family… Status seekers are responding to animal instincts equally characteristic of baboons, jackdaws, rock cod and men.[16]

Even an allegedly more sophisticated socio-biological text that claims to take into account the effects of cultural as well as genetic evolution concludes that 'bigotry' and 'group aggression' stem from genetic determination—'the fear of strangers response, the proneness to associate with groups of the early stages of social play and the intellectual tendency to dichotomise continua into in-groups and out-groups'.[17]

From such standpoints, Marxism rests on a terrible error—the 'romantic fallacy' of failing to see the genetic basis for the horrors of modern society and instead blaming them on 'the social environment'[18], Marxism's ' key error' being to 'conceive of human nature as relatively unstructured and largely or wholly the product of external socio-economic forces'.[19]

But the fallacy in fact lies in any 'naked ape' claim that we can read off from ape behaviour some inbuilt genetic basis of human behaviour. It ignores a most important feature of the human genetic make-up which separates us from both our closest cousins. They are genetically programmed in narrow ways that provide them with the behaviour appropriate to a limited range of environments, while we are characterised precisely by an immense flexibility in our behaviour that enables us, virtually alone in the animal world, to thrive on any part of the globe. This is a fundamental difference between us and the existing apes. So gorillas are not to be found outside tropical rain forests, chimps outside wooded regions in sub-saharan Africa, gibbons outside the tree tops of south east Asia, Orang-utangs outside a few islands in Indonesia; by contrast, humans have been able to live across a vast swathe of Africa, Europe and Asia for at least half a million years. Our genetic 'speciality' is precisely that we are not specialised, not constrained by any limited range of instinctive behaviour.

What is more, 'naked ape' views rest on very simplistic models of ape behaviour. Until the 1960s nearly all studies of apes were carried out in zoos, like Solly Zuckerman's famous 1930s account of life in the chimpanzee enclosure at London Zoo. They fitted the apes into a wider model of behaviour based on baboon studies (although baboons are monkeys and have quite substantial genetic differences with all the apes). They were seen as almost completely vegetarian, with little learning capacity and nothing that could, by any stretch of the imagination, be called culture. Above all they were seen as innately aggressive, with the males involved in continual, vicious sexual competition for females and kept in order only by a hierarchy of 'dominance' imposed by the most successfully aggressive 'alpha male'.

In the last 30 years studies of chimps, pygmy chimps and gorillas in the wild have challenged any such model,[20] suggesting that drawing conclusions about ape behaviour from life in zoo cages is about as valid as drawing conclusions about human behaviour from case studies of long term inmates in Dartmoor.[21] The main conclusions that can be drawn are:

i) Chimps and pygmy chimps are much more sociable than used to be thought. Aggressive confrontations are much less frequent than friendly interactions. Most aggressive confrontations are settled without violence.[22]

ii) Males are not involved in continual, bitter competition to dominate females. 'In the chimpanzee troop, unlike the Savannah Baboon, the dominant male is relatively tolerant of other males' attention to females: sexual promiscuity is the natural order of things...'[23] 'Generally there is little sign of jealousy or aggression'. Females initiate many sexual contacts and their co-operation is essential if males are to have special relationships with them.[24]

iii) The role of 'dominance' among chimps and gorillas has been overstated in past. There is no single hierarchy for all activities among chimps, and among gorillas 'dominance' often seems closer to what we would call leadership than to domination.[25]

iv) There is much more learned and socially transmitted behaviour than used to be thought, and much more use of primitive tools. Chimps use· stones to break nuts, sticks to collect termites from holes, and leaves as sponges to pick up liquids for drinking.

v) Chimps are not completely vegetarian. They hunt small animals (for instance, small monkeys) when the opportunity arises and so get about 10 percent of their diet from non-vegetarian sources. And hunting is a *social* activity: some chimps will chase the monkeys, others will lie in wait, ambush and kill them.

vi) Apes do not behave as competing individuals when it comes to consuming food. If one chimp finds a source of good food—a bush well endowed with edible shoots, for instance—it lets others know. And although common chimpanzees consume vegetarian foodstuff individually (except for the mother who provides food for her young offspring), they share meat with each other,[26] while pygmy chimps share some vegetarian food as well.

vii) Elementary forms of communication play a significant role among apes. Gestures are used not merely to attract attention but also to indicate certain intentions—as when a female pygmy chimp tells a male how she wants sex.[27] And a range of sounds are used for different purposes, for signalling danger or a plentiful source of food.

viii) The social behaviour of apes varies from band to band within each species, showing that it depends not merely on instinctive, genetically programmed, factors but also on the natural terrain they live off and the learned techniques they have for coping with this.

Most of these developments are more marked in pygmy chimps than among common chimps and gorillas. There is more sharing of food, more female initiation of sexual activity, and more of a break with the 'baboon' dominance model of social interaction since a group of females tends to play a central role in holding the troop together.[28]

This has led to suggestions that 'pygmy chimps offer may clues to the nature of the 'missing link' between apes and humans'.[29] Be that as it may, the evidence from apes in the wild, and from pygmy chimps in particular, challenges the usual image of innately aggressive and competitive behaviour. It also shows how in certain conditions elements of what we usually think of as uniquely human forms of behaviour arise among humanity's nearest relatives—and so could also have begun to arise among our common ancestors of more than 4 million years ago.

Our ancestors

We know very little for certain about our ape and early human (or hominid) ancestors. But what we do know tends to point to the adoption of two-legged walking by creatures, Australopithecines (meaning 'southern apes').[30] These were, in most other respects, closer to apes than to human beings, with brains still little more than chimp size, averaging 385 to 500 cubic centimetres and with no definitive evidence of tool making among them.[31] Hence their classification as apes, not humans.

The first *human*[32] remains are from 2-2.5 million years ago. The brain is substantially bigger (by up to 50 percent) than that of the Australopithecines and chimps,[33] and the species has been called *homo habilis* (or 'handy man') because it was first found, in the Olduvai gorge in east Africa, alongside stone tools. The shape of its teeth suggests a mixed diet of meat and vegetation, as against the overwhelmingly vegetarian diet of the modern great apes.

By about 1.6 million years ago, humans with considerably larger brains—usually designated as a new species, *homo erectus* ('upright man'), were to be found in Africa and were soon spreading out from Africa to the Eurasian landmass. Over the next million years brain size continued to grow until it reached about 1,000 cubic centimetres—as big as that of some modern humans, even if smaller than our average. By now teeth were clearly adapted to meat eating, showing that hunting went along with the gathering of vegetarian foodstuffs. Stone tools were shaped into standard patterns (usually referred to as the *acheulean*) for different jobs—hand axes, cleavers, scrapers, and so on. And, significantly, the males were on average only about 20 percent larger than the females (as opposed to twice as large among the Australopithecines and the great apes). This indicates that defence against predators must have depended much more on co-operation within each group and the use of tools as weapons than on the physical prowess of any individual male.

From about 500,000 years ago a variety of human types were to be found through Africa, Europe and Asia which resembled modern humans in having large brains (in some cases bigger than ours), and thin skulls. These are designated 'archaic *homo sapiens*', as the earliest version of our own species. The best known of them are the Neanderthals, who lived in Europe and parts of the Middle East from about 150,000 to about 35,000 years ago.

Finally, anatomically modern humans (often known as *homo sapiens sapiens*) seem to have evolved in Africa and possibly the Middle East 200,000 to 100,000 years ago.[34] By 40,000 years ago they were spread throughout Africa, Asia and Europe and were making the first landings in Australia. By 12,000 years ago at the latest they had crossed from north east Asia to the Americas.[35]

There have long been arguments about the relation of modern humans to the Neanderthals. When the first Neanderthal skeleton was found 140 years ago, it was seen as representative of a species much more primitive than ourselves, with many 'beastial' ape-like characteristics (hence the colloquial use of 'Neanderthal' to mean animal-like or barbaric). Forty years ago it was still assumed to be an evolutionary blind alley—'a human type which evolved in the colder climes of ice age Europe before dying out'.[36] Then the intellectual pendulum swung in the opposite direction: the emphasis was on the large Neanderthal brain and its similarities to ourselves.

Today the pendulum has swung at least part of the way back again, with the most popular view being that the modern humans evolved along a completely separate line from the 'archaics', originating from a group of *homo erectus*, normally identified as living in Africa. But there is still substantial resistance to this 'out of Africa' view from those who see some continuity between at least some of the archaics and ourselves.[37] Such is the paucity of evidence the arguments may never be finally resolved.[38] And, however important the debate is from a purely scientific perspective, it is not, in itself, particularly significant when it comes to understanding the nature of modern humans.[39]

A species born from blood?

Much 'naked ape' theorising is based on the assumption that our ancestors were engaged in continual bloody combat both with other species and with each other. Thus Ardrey argues, 'man emerged from the anthropoid background for one reason only: because he was a killer'.[40] From this the conclusion is drawn that murder is in our genes, held in check with difficulty by the mechanisms of civilisation. Such views were encouraged by the ideas on early human evolution developed by Raymond Dart after discovering the first Australopithecine remains. He claimed his bone finds showed that hunting was the major factor in the evolution of our earliest non-ape ancestors, that there had been 'the predatory transition from ape to man'.[41] Such views are still peddled in some quarters. But much of the evidence deployed to justify them has been discredited. Dart's piles of bones were probably not the result of human hunting. Our nearest cousins, especially the bonobos, are not particularly aggressive. And, as we shall see, war is non-existent and vegetation has supplied more nourishment than meat in those surviving societies that are similar to those our ancestors lived in until about 10,000 years ago.

One interpretation of the 'out of Africa' position would, however, back up the 'born from blood' thesis. It rests on the claim that geneticists have proven that certain of our genes originated with a single woman in Africa between 100,000 and 200,000 years ago. Humanity began with her, it is said, with her descendants spreading out from Africa, 'replacing ancient,indigenous humans all around the world...in an abrupt and violent manner'.[42] The implication is that modern humans engaged in primeval genocide against peoples who were very similar to themselves and that this points to ingrained, warlike characteristics built into our very nature.

But the whole argument rests on an elementary confusion between what happens with genes and what happens to the bearers of those genes. Every individual has at least one pair of genes for each genetically transmitted characteristic, one from its mother and one from its father.[43] But both genes do not necessarily have equal impact on the individual's physical make-up and sometimes one will be 'dominant', completely masking the existence of the other, although each has an equal chance of being passed on to the individual's offspring. Thus, a child with one parent with blue eyes and one with brown can itself have brown eyes, but still be able to transmit blue eyes to its own children.

Evolution takes place when a new form of a gene appears which can change the physical characteristics of an individual, so increasing the chances of that individual surviving to breed. Eventually, the new form of the gene will completely replace the old. But in the interim (which may be a very long time) successive generations of individuals can carry both forms of the gene, with some individuals displaying the new characteristics but still passing on to some of their offspring genes for the old characteristic. Likewise those displaying the new characteristic can transmit the gene for the old characteristic to some of their offspring. When the new gene comes to predominate, it usually does so among people who share a common ancestor (the first possessor of the gene) but who have many other ancestors as well.[44] So an African origin for modern humans does not entail us all having one, and only one, distant female ancestor, whose descendants wiped everyone else's; rather it means we had at least one shared ancestor as well as many others.

Allan Wilson, who did the first genetic research suggesting the shared African ancestor, certainly did not believe she was the single source from which we came. As two of his colleagues wrote shortly after he died about such interpretations: 'they have confused the migration and extinction of genes with those of populations. There is no suggestion that Eve was the first, and, at one time, the only, woman'.[45]

Chris Stringer, one of the most eminent members of the 'single origin' school, recognises that 'during the few thousand years of possible coexistence of Neanderthals and modern *homo sapiens*, extensive gene flow could have occurred between groups...'[46] At a 1987 conference on human origins there was 'a consensus that although there are considerable morphological differences between archaic and modern *homo sapiens*, hybridisation or local continuity between the two groups cannot be ruled out'.[47] This possibility is reinforced by the fact that the two groups coexisted for some thousand years in certain areas, living in the same sites (although not necessarily together) and using similar tools.

Even if humans did not interbreed with the Neanderthals and other archaic members of our species, it does not at all follow that they displaced them by violence. It does not require violence for one animal population to replace another within a few thousand years. It only requires that one is more successful than the other at getting a livelihood from the environment. This leads to its numbers growing, depleting the resources available to the other until its birth rate is no longer sufficient to make up for its death rate. Models have been suggested for how this could have happened in the case of modern humans and Neanderthals within a mere 1,000 years, without one butchering the other.[48]

Brain, culture, language and consciousness

Much more important than the argument over the exact line of ancestry of modern humans are other questions with which it is often interlinked. These concern the origins of culture and language.

The debate arises because skeletal and stone tools do not, in themselves, tell us how our ancestors lived, the degree to which they communicated with each other, how successful they were at gathering vegetarian foodstuffs and hunting, still less whether they told each other stories, engaged in rituals or had inner thoughts. The structure of the cranial skeleton does not even let us know in detail how the brain was constructed, let alone what it did. And the remaining stone tools of our ancestors cannot tell us anything about their wooden and bone tools (which were probably much more prevalent, since these substances are easier to shape than stone), whether they used animal skins and vegetarian matter for decoration (which would imply imagination) as well as simply to eat and keep warm.

So, just as there are elaborate, opposed conjectures about the genealogies of the physical bodies from which skeletons come, there are completely contradictory interpretations of the development of their minds and cultures.

There are two main sets of theories. First are those which see culture and language arising very early in hominid history, at least by the time of *homo habilis* (2 million years ago) as human beings co-operated to use tools to get a livelihood. The development of culture, language, the brain and human intelligence is seen as a long, cumulative process, beginning 2 million years ago and continuing until the arrival of the first fully modern humans, some 100,000 or more years ago. The requirement of coping with the environment and the upright posture adopted by the ancestral hominids led, in each generation, to the natural selection of those genes which encouraged intelligence and sociability. As Nancy Makepiece Tanner has put it:

> *Selection would intensely favour the more intelligent young who could effectively execute the new behaviour... Reorganisation (of the brain) could have happened quite rapidly: young who did not make it and died before reproductive age did not pass on their genes. Selection would have favoured young who were curious, playful and cued in to the behaviour of other group members, imitating tool making skills and environmental know-how, learning to recognise and to interact with a wide and diverse social network.*[49]

Most such interpretations have built on the work of Glyn Isaacs, who argued that collections of animal bones alongside tools at Olduvai pointed to the existence among *homo habilis* of 'home bases' to which they carried the carcasses of hunted animals to be shared out among themselves.[50] The tools themselves, it is claimed, could not have been made without a level of manual dexterity and intelligence way beyond that of the apes. As John Gowlett argues:

We know certainly that tool making goes back for at least 2 million years... Through the process of detaching hundreds of flakes...in sequence...each individual step is subordinate to the ultimate goals...The striking of individual flakes requires manual dexterity and hand-eye co-ordination, as well as an appreciation of the fracture properties of stone. More than this, it requires the ability to 'see' where the flake will come off.[51]

Along with this stress on tool making and intellectual development goes a claim that the skull of *homo habilis* points to a specifically human-like organisation of the brain, complete with the first development of areas adapted to speech (Broca's and Wernicke's areas), which is 'strongly suggestive that even 2 or 3 million years ago natural selection was operating on eco-niche adaptation and that cognitive and social behaviour was surely the main focus'.[52]

According to this view, the successive enlargements of the brain over 2 or 3 million years correspond to the increased dependence on communicative and cognitive skills, which in turn were necessary for the transmission of knowledge about increased tool making, for co-operative gathering and hunting and for coping with the much denser networks of social interactions which grew out of both these activities.

Some proponents of this account claim there is archaeological evidence which backs it up: the finding of 'base camps' among *homo habilis*, the remains of fire use among *homo erectus*, 'ritual burial sites', the remnants of ochre skin painting and of hut building among archaic human beings. All these are said to point to a growing complexity of social life, to growing transmission of culture, to increased symbolic communication, and to expressions of intelligence and artistic imagination similar to, even if less developed than, those among modern humans.

If this model of human evolution is correct, it vindicates Engels' account. As Charles Woolfson has said, it means that 'the broad outlines of Engels' theory are, by and large, confirmed by contemporary research, and that, in this respect, Engels' essay is a brilliant scientific anticipation of what is now thought to be the likely pattern of human evolution'.[53]

The new idealist challenge

But this model has faced some sharp challenges in the last few years. These have rested on a number of claims.

Firstly, that much of the archaeological evidence is unreliable. Isaacs' *homo habilis* 'base camps' could have been little more than early human versions of the chimpanzees' nests and the animal bones the result of individual scavenging of animal remains left by other carnivores, not of socially organised hunting.[54] Skull remains do not tell enough about the shape of the brains they once enclosed for us to deduce the existence of specialised areas (Broca's and Weinecke's areas) devoted to speech.[55] Remains which allegedly show hut construction among *homo erectus* and the use of decoration among archaic *homo sapiens* can, in fact, be explained in very different ways that do not involve any high level of culture. Alleged ritual burials could just as well have been the result of natural events—the collapsing of cave roofs on their occupants, for example.[56]

Secondly, the most convincing evidence we have, the stone tools that remain, change very little through the million year long duration of *homo erectus* and the hundred thousand long history of the Neanderthals. What is remarkable, it is claimed, is not that there is change, but that there has not been much greater, much more rapid, much more systematic advance. This does not occur until the 'upper palaeolithic' cultures of the modern humans some 35,000 years ago. Until then, it is claimed, the tool production did not differ qualitatively from what happens among non-human mammal species.[57] And it is only then that we find unchallengeable evidence of artistic production (cave paintings) and ritual behaviour (ceremonial burial, etc).

Thirdly, it is claimed that neither *homo erectus* nor the Neanderthals had a larynx capable of making more than a fraction of the range of sounds made by modern man, and that, they were, therefore, incapable of language as we know it.[58]

Finally, it is said, the model rests on an outdated, gradualist version of evolutionary theory, in which species change a little at a time as individual genetic mutations arise and are selected. More recent evolutionary theory accepts the possibility of what Gould and Eldridge call 'punctuated evolution' according to which genetic change can take place in bursts.[59]

The overall impact of these different arguments has been to encourage a fashion in recent years which sees 'a distinctively human way of life' as arising very late in history, as a result of a 'human revolution' which first produced culture and langauge. A recent exposition of the argument puts it like this:

__Homo erectus__ had very nearly a modern brain capacity, but apparently very little in the way of human culture to show for it. If human origins are taken to mean the beginnings of a recognisably human culture, then the first 3.5 million of the 4 million years of hominid history must be countered still as a period of pre-history...[60]

It seems likely that the most momentous changes occurred only after the evolution of __homo sapiens__. They may even have begun later still, after anatomically modern humans replaced the early varieties of __homo sapiens__.[61]

If this is true, then Engels' account was fundamentally misconceived. Something other than co-operative labour must have been behind the evolution of humanity. But the argument has huge holes in it which cannot be plugged by materialist explanations.

The evidence on stone tools does not prove that no advance in culture occurred. Stone would never have been the only substance used by our *homo habilis* and *homo erectus* predecessors to make tools, even if it was the one most able to survive the rigours of time. They certainly used wood, bone, animals skins and fire to cope with their environment, and would probably have found ways to make twine of various sorts for trapping animals and for carrying.[62] All of these could have been as important to them, if not more important, than stone, and could have been used in innumerable, changing, ways which left next to no evidence. What is more, a slow change in stone tools is not the same as no change at all. And it certainly does not prove they were made by creatures without cumulative intellectual and cultural development.

As McGrew points out, there is an enormous gap between the tools used by chimps and those used by *homo habilis*, let alone *homo erectus*:

Chimps are skilful makers and users of tools...there are certain things chimps have not been seen to do... They do not make flaked stone tools... They do not use digging sticks to get at roots... They do not use missiles or ladders to get at out-of-the way fruit.[63]

S T Parker and K R Gibson, using Piaget's conceptual framework for language development in humans, claim that evidence suggests that early hominids would have had 'intelligence and language comparable to that of young children'.[64] Thomas Wynn argues by the end of the Acheulian period, 300,000 years ago, early humans had already reached the second highest stage in human intellectual development, that of 'concrete operations', with the 'almost perfect symmetry of hand axes' pointing to an aptitude for 'reversibility, conservation, correction of errors, and so on'.[65]

Stone tools could have changed very slowly simply because they were adequate to the tasks set them—in the same way that some basic tools of carpentry show little change from Ancient Egyptian times through to the early 20th century. And even if the stone tools changed slowly, this does not mean they were easily made or could be the result of people simply copying others without giving any thought to what they were doing.

Certainly, stone tools cannot be used to justify claims of an enormous gap between the first modern humans and the later 'archaic' humans. Not only did both groups coexist for many tens of thousands of years, but also that they shared cultures. Until 40,000 years ago the modern humans of Europe and the Middle East used the same sort of 'Mousterian' tools as the Neanderthals (as is acknowledged by Adam Kuper, who accepts the fashionable view that a 'distinctively human culture' only goes back 25,000 to 35,000 years.)[66] Yet the last surviving Neanderthals of 35,000 years ago had learnt to use some of the same more advanced technologies as their modern human neighbours.[67]

Even after modern humans had moved on to these new technologies, change was often very slow, with 'no major technological developments, no significant increase in man's ability to generate energy' for a long period.[68] In what is now France, for example, there was a gap of up to 20,000 years between the arrival of 'upper palaeolithic' culture 35,000 years ago and the Magdalenian cave paintings at La Marche. And it was another 10,000 years before agricultural techniques replaced hunting and gathering in the area.

The picture, then, is one of a slow development of techniques over 2 or 3 million years, with some acceleration 200,000 to 150,000 years ago just as the Neanderthals and the first modern humans were appearing. Further acceleration took place 30,000 to 35,000 years ago, among both the growing modern human population and the declining Neanderthal population; further rapid change at the time the cave paintings some 15,000 years ago; very rapid development with the rise of agriculture 10,000 to 5,000 years ago; and massive acceleration over the last thousand years. This suggests that, although there could have been important biological differences between archaic and modern humans, the speed of innovation did not, necessarily, depend on this. Something else had to be involved.

Even if *homo erectus* and the archaic humans had a much more limited vocal range than modern humans—and some paleontologists challenge this conclusion[69]—this does not mean that Neanderthals and other archaic humans lacked language completely. It simply means they were not as good at communicating with each other as ourselves. As Lieberman, the arch-exponent of the view stressing the linguistic limitations of the Neanderthals, himself writes: 'The computer modelling does not show the Neanderthal hominids totally lacked speech or language; they had the anatomical prerequisites for producing nasalised versions of all the sounds of human speech save [i], [u] and [a] and velar consonants, and probably had fairly well developed language and culture'.[70]

Finally, the argument that punctuated evolution can take place does not, in itself, prove that it did take place in such a way as to produce culture and language suddenly. And there is one powerful argument against this—that of brain size. If the evolution of humanity was the result of very rapid changes towards the end of a period of millions of years, then that is when you would expect the most characteristic feature of *homo sapiens*—the massive size of our brain compared to our bodies—to arise. The original formulation of the punctuated evolution hypothesis by Gould and Eldridge in fact held to this view, contending that the brain hardly increased in size for the million years *homo erectus* existed. But, as Stringer points out, there is 'little evidence' to back up this view.[71]

That leaves a problem for any theory which sees the 'human revolution' as occurring all at once half a million years ago with the replacement of *homo erectus* by *homo sapien*, let alone 35,000 years ago after the evolution of anatomically modern humans: why did late *homo erectus* have a brain twice the size of the Australopithecines, and the Neanderthals a modern sized brain? It could not have been simply to undertake the mental operations which could be done by their ancestors millions of years before.

At the same time, it is inconceivable that our forebears of a million years ago could have survived unless they had already developed ways of co-operating together to cope with their environment and of transmitting knowledge to each other on a qualitatively greater scale than is to be found among our ape cousins. For by that time they were already moving out of the African valleys where their species originated to colonise much of Eurasia, showing they were capable not just of living in a certain restricted ecological niches, but of adapting a variety of environments to their needs—learning to discriminate between those newly encountered varieties of plants that were edible and those that were poisonous, learning to hunt new sorts of animals, learning to protect themselves against new predators, learning to cope with new climates.

The dialectic of labour and intellect

The direct archaeological evidence for social labour—or for any other form of behaviour—among our forbears is necessarily weak. But the circumstantial evidence is overwhelming.

Look at the features that distinguished *homo erectus* from the apes. It walked on two legs and lost the easy escape route from predators of fleeing into the trees; its young took considerably longer to mature (and so needed a longer period of protection by their elders); the males of the species were now only on average 20 percent larger than the females, not 100 percent, and so were not built mainly for defence; it experienced considerable reduction in the size of the canines (the long pointed side teeth with which monkeys and apes can threaten would-be predators and to kill small animals for food); its back teeth (molars) were adapted to a diet which included much meat, while excluding any vegetable matter that required much grinding down during chewing; the hand was reshaped, with the development of a thumb that could hold and manipulate small objects; female sexual interest was no longer concentrated mainly around the time of ovulation; and, as we have seen, there was an enormous increase in brain size.

A creature with this combination of features could only survive if it had developed some means of replacing some of the physical characteristics it had lost. It had to be able to defend its young for longer periods of time than its ape cousins despite losing apes' enormous canines, tree climbing abilities and large male build. It had to be able to cope with a greater variety of vegetation than them despite having molars that were not as good at grinding. It had to find some way to cut up the flesh of animals, whether it hunted them itself or merely relied on finding carcasses left by other predators. All of these things point to an enormous dependence on the use of artifacts of various sorts to defend, to cut up, to dig, to gather and to grind. They also point to a much greater level of social organisation than is found among even the most sociable of apes: it is this which probably explains the change in the pattern of female sexuality, encouraging permanent ties between the sexes rather than the frenetic coupling concentrated around a couple of days a month to be found in common chimps. But to transmit the knowledge of the necessary techniques and to cope with the enormous level of social co-operation involved in social living on this scale required a much higher level of brain power than previously. Over many millennia those creatures whose genes changed in such a way as to best enable them to learn from, to communicate with and to care for each other would have an advantage when it came to surviving and reproducing. Natural selection would bring about the evolution in the direction of ever larger, denser and more complex neural networks, capable of directing and learning from intricate motor functions of the hand and of using minute changes in gesture or voice to communicate.

Only if you see things in this way can you explain why our species was already endowed with the capacities 35,000 years ago to develop a whole new range of technologies. The explanation lies in 2 million years of cumulative evolution, with labour at each stage encouraging the adept hand, greater sociability and the larger brain. And, at each stage, the adept hand, greater sociability and the larger brain made possible more advanced forms of labour. But all this makes *labour* the real missing link in the story of human evolution, as Engels rightly insisted.

Such labour had enormous implications for the brain. Those best at the co-operating with others in tool production and use would have been those whose brains underwent changes in structure and size that made them better at co-ordinating the motor functions controlling the hands with vision and hearing, while also becoming more responsive to the signals of others of their kind.[72] A cumulative process would soon have been underway in which survival depended on culture, and the ability to partake in culture upon a genetic endowment that encouraged the combination of sociability, communication, dexterity and reasoning power.

It is this which explains why our forebears were able, a million or so years ago, to move out of their African ancestral home into the very different climatic conditions of Eurasia, and why the Neanderthals were able to survive the harsh conditions of the European ice age for 100,000 years or more. However great or little their differences from us, they could not have survived unless they had at least substantial rudiments of culture, language and intelligence. After all, they were like us in one very important respect: they had nothing else to protect them—no body fur, no great speed in flight, no tusks or claws, no ready ability to disappear into the trees.

It is this which also explains the development of those most peculiarly human attributes, language and consciousness. The distinctive feature about human language, as opposed to the sounds and gestures made by other animals, is that we use words to refer to things and situations that are not actually present in front of us. We use them to abstract from the reality that confronts us and to describe other realities. And once we can do this to others, we can also do it to ourselves, using the 'inner speech' that goes on inside our heads to envisage new situations and new goals. The ability to do these things cannot have arisen at one go. It must have grown up over many generations as our remote ancestors learnt in practice, through labour, to abstract from and to change immediate reality—as they began to use sounds and gestures not merely to indicate what was immediately in front of them or what they immediately desired (which is what some animals do) but to indicate how they wanted to change something and how they wanted others to help them. In tool use we know there was a significant change from the ape to the early humans: the ape picks up a stick or stone to use as a tool; the early humans of 2 million years ago were already not only shaping the stick or stone, but using other stones to do the shaping, and, undoubtedly, learning from each other how to do this. This implies not merely conceptions about immediate things (food stuffs), but about things once removed from immediacy (the tool that can get the food stuff) and twice removed from immediate reality (the tool that can shape the tool that gets the food stuff). And it also implies communication, whether by gesture or sound, about things two stages removed from immediate conditions—in effect, the first use of abstract nouns, adjectives and verbs. The development of labour and the development of communication thus, necessarily, go hand in hand. And as they both develop, they both encourage the selection of those new genes which made people more adept at both: the more agile hand, the larger brain, the larynx that made a wider range of sounds.

Such developments do not involve just quantitative changes. As the growth of labour, the growth of sociability and the growth of language reinforced each other, encouraging the selection of a whole range of new genes, new networks of nerve cells would emerge in the brain, making possible whole new ranges of interaction between people and the world around them. This may well explain why suddenly new species of humans developed that lived alongside and then superseded those that went before, as with the successive emergence of *homo habilis*, of *homo erectus*, of the various sorts of archaic human. Thus, it may well be the case that modern humans eventually replaced the Neanderthals because they were able to communicate more quickly and clearly with each other (although we will probably never know for certain if this was so).

So there has to be a recognition of how quantity turns into quality, of how through successive changes animal life gave birth to that new form of life we call 'human', which had a dynamic of its own, shaped by its labour and its culture not by its genes. But this should not lead to a collapse into a new idealism which sees culture and langauge as emerging from nowhere in the fairly recent past. If such an approach is fashionable in some circles, it is not because it can provide a scientific, materialist account of our origins, but because its fits in with the much wider mood of the intelligentsia since the late 1970s. In virtually every discipline there has been the attempt to separate off the development of language and ideas from the development of material reality. As in the days of Marx and Engels, the struggle for science is a struggle against both idealism and mechanical materialism—with idealism today taking the form of 'post modernist' fashions, and mechanical materialism of sociobiology.[73]

Loose ends

There are many details in the story of human evolution that are not yet resolved and which, because of the paucity of the evidence, may never be resolved. This accounts for a whole series of ongoing debates which produce heat at academic conferences and give rise to nice titbits for science journalists.

There is, for example, a fascinating debate about why a group of apes adopted two-legged walking in the first place. Most authorities say it was because climactic change broke up the forests in which the ancestral apes lived, presenting the ancestral apes with a choice between retreating into the remaining forest or adapting to a more open environment. Natural selection would then have picked out genetic traits among the groups which retreated into the forest adapted to that sort of life, the traits we find in today's gorillas. And in the same way it would have picked out among the grassland dwellers the 'co-operative' and culturally transmitted tool using traits we find among humans: 'The hominids obtained less succulent and probably much harder to find plant foods in the new environment, the east African savannah. They specialised by becoming more intelligent and bipedal, and by using tools'.[74] As against this, others claim archaeological evidence points to the first two-legged apes living in forests, not bush and grassland.[75]

There is another debate about the role of hunting in the first steps along the hominid line. The revival of discussion on the social aspects of human evolution was given an enormous boost by the 1966 Man the Hunter conference convened by Richard Lee and Irven DeVore which drew together archaeologists and anthropologists studying present day hunter-gatherer societies. As the title of the conference suggests, the stress was on hunting as the formative social activity.[76] But this was soon challenged by those[77] who said the archaeological evidence for *homo habilis* pointed to individual scavenging (the eating of animals already killed by other carnivores) not collective hunting. This in turn led to the rejoinder that our ancestors would have had every incentive to scavenge collectively (numbers would have frightened off the carnivore that killed the prey in the first place, while there was little point in the individual hominid hogging for him or herself a carcass far too big to be eaten by one person before it went mouldy).[78]

At the same time, from another direction, it was stressed the early bipeds would necessarily have been unsuccessful hunters, but that to rear their young and to be successful gatherers of vegetarian food they would have had to become social tool users: 'To all indications the ancestral chimp-like population of 5 million years ago possessed behavioral and anatomical elements basic to the development of a gathering adaptation in which a whole range of savannah plant foods could have been exploited with tools...'[79] The young had to be undergo extensive socialisation if they were to learn to perform such tasks, which put a premium on the 'mother-offspring tie', with females 'as the necessary centre of the social group: Appropriate motor patterns for making and using gathering tools for digging, knocking down, scraping, opening or dividing foods, for carrying implements, food and babies, and for defence from predators, had to be learnt'.[80]

Finally, there is the debate already referred to, in passing, on the relations between the different hominid specimens that have been found—the various sorts of Australopithecus, *homo habilis*, *homo erectus*, the various sorts of 'archaic humans', the Neanderthals and modern humans.

But none of these disagreements among the professionals should obscure one of the most fascinating developments in intellectual history over the last 30 years—the vindication of the line of analysis laid out in the unfinished, unpublished pamphlet which Frederick Engels wrote after reading Darwin. Trigger tells how:

> *Engels' work demonstrates that it was possible to conceptualise the modern materialist theory of human evolution already in the 1870s. Yet Darwin's essentially idealist concepts about human evolution were clearly more compatible with the beliefs of most middle class scientists in Western Europe than were those of the arch-revolutionary Engels. Hence it was not surprising that Engels' work was ignored...*

The result was that the search for origins spent three quarters of a century going up blind allies until, in the 1960s, 'Kenneth Oakley, Sherwood Washburn and F Clark Howell laid the groundwork for the construction of a new theory of evolution that, while arrived at largely inductively, closely reassembled Engels' long forgotten work'.[81]

II The origins of classes and the state

The Part Played by Labour ended with a few paragraphs suggesting how, once the human species was established biologically, its labour on the world then led to successive changes in its social institutions. *The Origin of the Family, Private Property and the State*, written eight years later, built on these insights, developing an overall account of the evolution of class society.

It held that originally humans had lived in societies without private property in sense in which we use the term today (ie no private wealth, as opposed, say, to tooth brushes), without any division into classes, and without any domination of women by men. But changes in the way humans co-operated to produce their livelihoods led to the replacement of these 'primitive communist' societies by a succession of forms of class society, of which modern capitalism is the most recent. And with class society came the state and different forms of family in which women were oppressed.

If *The Part Played by Labour* was ignored by established social science, *The Origin of the Family* was systematically denounced. The whole idea of 'primitive communism' was dismissed as a fairy story. The experience of the American anthropologist Eleanor Leacock was typical. She tells how it was 'generally accepted when I was a student that "the communism in living" referred to by Lewis Henry Morgan and Frederick Engels had in fact never existed'.[82]

In part, the attack on Engels was political, linked with the general attack on socialist ideas. But the attack also corresponded to a general ahistorical, anti-evolutionary trend in sociology and social anthropology. Whereas in the 19th century these disciplines had originated as speculative attempts to show how all of human history had grown organically into the marvel of modern capitalism, in the 20th century the trend was in the opposite direction—to reject any notion of social evolution whatsoever. There were many accounts of life within individual cultures. There were attempts to show how the different aspects of particular 'primitive' societies had the 'function' of keeping society going. There were even attempts to provide a 'theory' for the functioning of each and every society, of which the most grandiose and the most fruitless were the writings of Talcott Parsons. But there was a repudiation of any attempt to account for social evolution.

Yet throughout this period, the actual researches of social anthropologists proved the existence of vast number of societies in which classes, the state or women's oppression as we know it did not exist—for instance Margaret Mead's *Coming of Age in Samoa*, Ruth Benedict's *Patterns of Culture*, even Bronislaw Malinowski's *Argonauts of the Western Pacific* and *Sex and Repression in Savage Societies*, and Meyer Fortes' and Evans Pritchard's *African Political Systems*.

Only in one discipline, that of archaeology, did notions of evolution persist. This may have been partly because archaeologists found human bones and artifacts embedded in geological layers laid down at different points in the past and were therefore prone to see some as succeeding others. But it was also because the most eminent figure in British archaeology was a left wing socialist, V Gordon Childe, who was attracted to a Stalinised version of Marxism in the 1930s and used some of Engels' insights to come to terms with inadequacies in his own previous accounts of cultural change (which had depended on elaborate schemes by which culture 'diffused' from one society to another).[83]

Then in the late 1960s the intellectual climate changed—a change which could not be divorced from wider upheavals of the decade. On the edges of the academic world some anthropologists (among them Marxists like Eleanor Leacock and anti-imperialists like Richard Lee) began to work with archaeologists (who were often influenced by Gordon Childe) to elaborate evolutionist interpretations of human society. They effectively re-established the validity of ideas that had been anathematised for

two generations, especially the contention that for hundreds of thousands
of years humanity lived in societies without classes, private property and
the state.

Today, an influential non-Marxist like Ernest Gellner can accept that
for a vast period humans lived in as 'hunter/gatherers... defined by the
fact that they possess little or no means of producing, accumulating or
storing wealth', in societies 'characterised by a low degree of division of
labour'.[84] And Richard Lee can argue quite respectably: 'Before the rise
of the state and the entrenchment of social inequality, people lived in for
millennia in small scale kin based social groups, in which the core institutions of economic life included collective or common ownership of
land and resources, generalised reciprocity in the distribution of food,
and relatively egalitarian political relations.'

This does not mean we can simply take all of Engels arguments and
treat them as sacrosanct. He himself noted in 1891 that what he had
written in 1884 needed to be revised to take account of 'important
progress' in knowledge. And we live not seven, but more than 100 years
on from that. As Gailey has noted, in a study very much in the tradition
laid down by Engels, much of the 'ethnographic' (ie anthropological) data
in *The Origin of the Family* has been overtaken by further researches.[85]
There is a core to Engels' argument in *The Origin* which remains
extremely valuable. But it is necessary to disinter it from a range of factu-
ally incorrect data and speculative arguments which have been treated as
gospel since by some would-be Marxists and used by opponents to dis-
credit all of Engels' insights.[86]

Primitive communism

Engels' starting point was a reformulation of the point he and Marx had
made back in 1845-6, that the ways human beings secure a living from
nature determine how they co-operate with each other and so lay the
basis for societies in which they live:

> The determining factor in history is, in the last resort, the production and
> reproduction of immediate life... On the one hand the production of the means
> of subsistence, of food, clothing and shelter and the tools required therefore;
> on the other the production of human beings themselves, the propagation of
> the species. The social institutions under which men of a definite epoch and
> definite country live are conditioned by both kinds of production...[87]

Morgan, quite independently of Marx and Engels, had come to a
somewhat similar conclusion:[88]

> *Mankind are the only beings who may be said to have gained an absolute control over the production of food... Without laying the basis of subsistence mankind could not have propagated themselves into other areas...and ultimately over the whole surface of the earth...*
>
> *It is accordingly probable that the great epochs of human progress have been identified more or less directly with the enlargement of the sources of subsistence.*[89]

Engels followed Morgan in dividing human history into three great stages—savagery, barbarism and civilisation. Each had 'a distinct culture and mode of life more or less special and peculiar to itself' and rested on a particular way of achieving a livelihood:[90]

> *Savagery—the period in which the appropriation of natural products, ready for use, predominated; the things produced by man were, in the main, instruments that facilitated this appropriation.*
>
> *Barbarism—the period in which knowledge of cattle breeding and land cultivation was acquired, in which methods of increasing the productivity of nature through human activity were learnt.*
>
> *Civilisation—the period in which knowledge of the further working-up of natural products, of industry proper, and of art, was acquired.*[91]

The terms themselves reflected the prejudices of the late 19th century, of the idea of so-called 'primitive' societies as 'savage' and 'barbaric'. But Morgan and Engels, who both by and large rejected those prejudices, were able to use these distinctions to grasp what is central to any scientific study of human social development: the distinction between societies where human beings get a livelihood through gathering berries, nuts and roots and hunting wild creatures (so called 'hunter-gatherer' or 'foraging' societies); societies where human beings cultivate the land and herd mammals ('agricultural societies'); and societies which are to a greater or lesser extent urbanised ('civilisation' in the literal sense of being based on towns).[92] This in turn enabled Engels to challenge many orthodox prejudices about society.

Most reactionary thinkers claim 'primitive societies' are markedly hierarchical, under the sway of brutal, aggressive and murderous males.[93] Since these societies have existed much longer than 'civilisation', it is said to follow that human nature is likewise brutal, aggressive and murderous.

Engels' view was very different. He argued that early societies were organised along completely different lines to class societies, using as his model Morgan's account of the North American Iroquois. There was no private property in them and no division into classes. And they were not held together by a state in the sense of 'a special public authority separated from the totality of those concerned in each case'. Instead, they were organised through extended, interlinked 'consanguine' groupings (that is, of people who were related to each other, or at least thought they were)—groupings which Engels called 'gentes', 'clans' or 'phatries' and which modern anthropologists usually call 'lineages':

> *This gentile constitution is wonderful in all its childlike simplicity. Everything runs smoothly without soldiers, gendarmes or police; without nobles, kings, governors, prefects or judges; without prisons, without trials. All quarrels and disputes are settled by the whole body of those concerned...Although there are many more affairs in common than at present—the household is run in common and communistically by a number of families, the land is tribal property, only the small gardens being temporarily assigned to the house-hold—still, not a bit of our extensive and complicated machinery of adminstration is required.*
>
> *There can be no poor and needy—the communistic household and the gens know their responsibility towards the aged, the sick and those disabled in war. All are free and equal, including the women. There is as yet no room for slaves nor, as a rule, for the subjugation of alien tribes...*
>
> *This is what mankind and human society were like before class divisions arose...*[94]

Modern studies of surviving hunter-gatherer and early agricultural societies have upheld the essential core of Engels' account. Hunting-gathering peoples live in what are usually called 'band societies'—based on loose knit groups of 30 or 40 people which may, periodically, get together with other groups into bigger gatherings up to a couple of a hundred strong. There is no formal leadership, let alone class division within these societies.

> *Individual decision makings are possible for both men and women with respect to their daily routines... Men and women alike are free to decide how they will spend each day: whether to go hunting or gathering, and with whom...*[95]
>
> *There was no differential access to resources through private land owner-ship and no specialisation of labour beyond that of sex... The basic principle of egalitarian band societies was that people made decisions about the activ-ities for which they were responsible.*[96]

Individual band members enjoy a level of autonomy infinitely greater than the mass of people in class societies. But it is not accompanied by selfishness in their relations with each other. On the contrary, the stress is on generosity, on individuals helping each other:

Food is never consumed alone by a family: it is always shared out among members of a living group or band... Each member of the camp receives an equitable share... This principle of generalised reciprocity has been reported of hunter-gatherers in every continent and in every kind of environment.[97]

There is a very strong disdain for the competitive notions which are taken for granted in our society. As Richard Lee tells of the !Kung[98] people of the Kalahari (the so-called 'Bushmen'):

The !Kung are a fiercely egalitarian people, and they have evolved a series of important cultural practices to maintain this equality, first by cutting down to size the arrogant and boastful, and second by helping those down on their luck to get back in the game... Men are encouraged to hunt as well as they can, but the correct demeanour for the successful hunter is modesty and understatement.[99]

One of the !Kung reports:

Say a man has been hunting. He must not come home and announce like a braggart. 'I have killed a big one in the bush!' He must first sit down in silence until I or someone else comes up to his fire and asks, 'What did you do today?' He replies quietly, 'Ah, I'm no good at hunting. I saw nothing at all...maybe just a tiny one'. Then I smile, because I know he has killed something big.[100]

An early Jesuit noted of another hunter-gathering people, the Montagnais of Canada: 'The two tyrants who provide hell and torture for many of our Europeans do not reign in their great forests,—I mean ambition and avarice...as they are contented with a mere living, not one of them has given himself to the devil to acquire wealth'.[101] There are no chiefs or bosses in such bands. Thus the Mbuti Pygmies of the Congo:

never have chiefs... In each aspect of Pygmy life there might be one or two men or women who were more prominent than others, but usually for good practical reasons... The maintenance of law was a co-operative affair... The more serious of crimes, such a theft, were dealt with by sound thrashing which was administered co-operatively by all who felt inclined to participate, but only after the entire camp had been involved in discussion of the case... Pygmies dislike and avoid personal authority.[102]

Among the !Kung 'patterns of leadership do exist', but they are very different to power as we know it. In discussions the opinions of some individuals tend to have more impact than others. 'These individuals are usually older people who have lived here the longest...and have some personal qualification worthy of note as a speaker, an arguer, a ritual specialist, or a hunter.' But,

> *Whatever their skills !Kung leaders have no formal authority. They can only persuade, but never enforce their will on others... None is arrogant, overbearing, boastful or aloof. In !Kung terms, these traits absolutely disqualify a person as a leader... Another trait emphatically not found among traditional camp leaders is a desire for wealth or acquisitiveness.*[103]

What is more—and on this Engels was wrong—there was very little in the way of warfare among hunter-gatherers. There might occasionally be clashes between different bands, but these were of marginal importance.[104] Among the !Kung, for instance, there is a sense in which a water hole and the area of land around it is 'owned' by group and passed from generation to generation. But other groups may use the land, provided they ask permission. 'Disputes between groups over food are not unknown among the !Kung, but they are rare...'[105]

Such evidence refutes completely the claims that the whole prehistory of humanity, from the time of the Australopithecines right through the emergence of literacy, was based on a 'killing imperative', that 'hunter-gatherer bands fought over water holes that tended all too often to vanish under the baking African sun', that we are all 'Cain's children',that 'human history has turned on the development of superior weapons...for genetic necessity', and that, therefor, only a thin veneer of 'civilisation' conceals an instinctive 'delight in massacre, slavery, castration and cannibalism.'[106]

The 'primitive communist' attributes of band societies can only be understood by looking at the way they subsist. The normal size of bands is restricted by the need to find enough food each day in the area of their camp. Within that area, the individual members will continually be moving, from one source of plant food to another or in pursuit of animals. And the band as a whole will have to move on every so often, as the food supplies in a locality get used up. The continual movement precludes any accumulation of wealth by any band member, since everything has to be easily carried. At most an individual may have a spear or bow and arrow, a carrying bag or a few trinkets. 'The ultimate value is freedom of movement...the desire to be free from the burden and responsibilities which would interfere with the society's itinerant existence'.[107]

The stress on the value of generosity follows from the way the hunters and gatherers are intensely dependent on each other. The gatherers usually supply the most reliable source of food, the hunters that which is most valued. So those who specialise in hunting depend for their daily survival on the generosity of those who gather, while those who specialise in gathering—and those who are temporarily unsuccessful in the hunt—rely on valued additions to their diet from those who manage to kill animals. And the hunt itself does not usually consist of the individual male hero going off to make a kill, but rather a group of men (sometimes with the auxiliary assistance of women and children) working together to chase and trap a prey.

There is nearly always a division of labour in these societies between the men and the women, with the men doing most of the hunting and the women most of the gathering. This is because a woman who is pregnant or breast feeding a child could only take part in the hunt by exposing it to dangers—and thus threatening the reproduction of the band. But this division does not amount to male dominance as we know it in present day society. Both females and males take part in key decisions, such as when to move camp or whether to leave one band and join another. And the conjugal unit itself is loosely structured. The spouses in any of these societies can separate without suddenly jeopardising their own livelihood or that of their children.[108]

Thus Engels was right in insisting that there was no systematic domination of women in these societies. However, he was probably wrong in one important detail—he overestimated the role played by lineages in most hunting gathering societies. The bands of surviving hunter-gatherers are *loose and flexible*. People are free to enter and leave them. They are not tightly controlled by lineage groups, even though the members of a band will often be related to each other and, through intermarriage, have loose ties to other bands.[109]

Engels' belief in the power of the gens or clan among *all existing* 'primitive societies' was a result of the anthropological knowledge of his time. He relied mainly on Morgan's first hand account of the Iroquois and his second hand account of Polynesian society—both early agricultural (or 'horticultural') societies—rather than hunter-gatherers, about which neither Engels nor Morgan knew very much.

Existing hunter-gatherer societies are not necessarily the same as those all of humanity once lived in. Peoples like the !Kung, the Mbuti, the Eskimos and the Australian aborigines have a history as long as a our own—and their history will have been influenced first by the impact of neighbouring agricultural societies and then, traumatically, by Western colonialism.[110] So their patterns of social life could be different in many respects to those of our common forebears. These may possibly have had strong lineage structures, as Engels thought, but we have no evidence to prove it.

On the question of egalitarianism, however, we are on much firmer ground. The stress on sharing, the strong co-operative values and the flexible make-up of the bands must have characterised the life of our forebears for tens of thousands of years, just as it characterises modern hunter-gatherers. These values fit perfectly with the needs of the nomadic, hunter-gatherer life. They are not the sorts of values found in class societies, and so their existence among surviving hunter-gatherers cannot be a result of external pressures. Lee quite rightly stresses, 'for all its economic and military power and its near monopoly of the ideological apparatus, the capitalist state has not succeeded in eradicating innumerable pockets of communalism [primitive communism]'.[111] This in itself points to primitive communism as a stage prior to the rise of class society, as the condition of all of humanity at one stage in our history.

This is immense of importance for any arguments of 'human nature'. For if such a nature exists it was moulded, by natural selection, during the 2.5 million year long epoch of hunting and gathering between the first appearance of *homo habilis* and the first planting of crops by 8th millennium BC *homo sapiens*. Lee is quite right to insist:

> *It is the long experience of egalitarian sharing that has moulded our past. Despite our seeming adaptation to life in hierarchical societies, and despite the rather dismal track record of human rights in many parts of the world, there are signs that humankind retains a deep-rooted sense of egalitarianism, a deep rooted commitment to the norm of reciprocity, a deep rooted...sense of community...*[112]

The first agriculturalists

More than 99.9 percent of humanity today live in societies that have been moulded by a change that began about 10,000 years ago. It involved the establishment of settled villages, the use of new, more varied and more intricate kits of stone, wooden and bone tools (hence the term 'neolithic', meaning 'new stone age'), the use of clay pots for storage and cooking, and, perhaps most importantly, the first cultivation of the soil.

Today this change is usually referred today by Gordon Childe's term 'neolithic revolution'. Engels equated it with the transition from 'savagery' to 'barbarism'. He argued it began with the introduction of pottery and then continued in the Eastern hemisphere (Eurasia and Africa) 'with the domestication of animals', and in the Americas 'with the cultivation of edible plants by means of irrigation and with the use of adobe (bricks dried in the sun) and stone for building'.[113] In the Eastern hemisphere, but not in the Americas, there followed an 'upper stage of barbarism' which 'begins with the smelting of iron.' 'Here for the first time we encounter the iron ploughshare drawn by cattle, making possible land cultivation on wide scale and, in the conditions of the time, virtually unlimited increase in the means of subsistence. And 'in connection with this we find also the clearing of the forests and their transformation into arable and pasture land—which again would have been impossible without the iron axe and spade. But with this there also came a rapid increase in population and dense population in small areas...'[114] These changes in production during 'barbarism', Engels went on to argue, laid the basis for the first development of class society:

> *To whom did this new wealth belong? Originally, doubtless to the gens. But private ownership of herds must have developed at an early stage... On the threshold of authenticated history we find everywhere the herds are already the separate property of the family chiefs, in exactly the same way as were the artistic products of barbarism, metal utensils, article of luxury and, finally, human cattle—the slaves.*
>
> *For now slavery too had been invented. The slave was of no value* [while] *human labour power at this stage yielded no noticeable surplus as yet over the cost of its maintenance. With introduction of cattle breeding, of metal working, of weaving and, finally, of field cultivation, this changed...*[115]

Engels' account is wrong on a number of significant points. Class society and civilisation did develop in central and south America as well as in Eurasia and Africa. Cultivation of the land (although not using the plough), began at about the same time as the domestication of animals, not after it. The first form of class society was not slavery, which seems to have been a marginal form of exploitation of the oppressed classes until Graeco-Roman times. Yet his overall picture of the rise of class society is basically correct.

The whole organisation of society did undergo radical change as human groups developed new ways of getting a livelihood. At different times they turned from hunting-gathering to cultivation, independently of each other (in several regions of the Americas, at least three distinct parts of Africa, the uplands of Iraq, the Indus valley, Indochina, the valleys of central Papua-New Guinea, and China[116]). And where cumulative change went furthest it did lead to the first division into classes, the first states and the first systematic oppression of women. But the full change took place over a very long period of time—4,000 or 5,000 years in the most studied case, that of Mesopotamia (present day Iraq). And in most societies it never got this far, so that even a century and a half ago millions of people were still living in non-class agricultural societies.

The first form of agriculture (often called 'horticulture') involved clearing the land (by cutting away at woodland and brush with axes and then burning off the rest), and then planting and harvesting seeds or tubers, using a hoe and or a digging stick. Usually, after a couple of years the fertility of the land would be exhausted. It would be allowed to return to the wild and a new area was cleared for cultivation. The crop yield from a given area of land was not nearly as great from this 'slash and burn' shifting agriculture as from later forms based on irrigation or the plough, but it was considerably greater than to be obtained by most forms of hunting and gathering.

This in itself had immediate social consequences. People no longer needed to be on the move all the time, as with hunting and gathering; indeed, it would have been disastrous to move between sowing and harvesting. For the first time, it made sense to construct heavy clay pots and to store things in them. And the local food supply was often enough to sustain five or ten times as many people as before, so permitting village life for the first time.

Changes also, necessarily, took place in the internal structure of each social group. On the one hand, the individual household became less reliant on co-operation with the rest of the group for obtaining its subsistence: group-wide co-operation was often needed in clearing the land, but the each household could sow and harvest its own patch of cleared land by itself. On the other hand, there had to be ways of ensuring that households with lots of labour but few mouths provided assistance to those which have lots mouth but little labour—especially those with lots of young children.[117] For children represented the future labour supply of the village as a whole, and if they were not adequately cared for, the group itself would eventually die out.

The move to agriculture produced, in fact, a very important change in the group's needs when it came to *reproduction*. Under hunting and gathering, the need to carry children, both on the daily round of gathering and on the periodic moves of the whole camp, led to a tight restriction on the birth rate. Women could not afford to have more than one child who required carrying at a time, and so births were spaced every three or four years (if necessary through sexual abstention, abortion or infanticide). With fixed village life based on agriculture, by contrast, not only did the child not have to be carried after it was a few months old, but the greater the number of children, the greater the area of land that could be cleared and cultivated in future. Provision for reproduction became central to the dynamics of the society.

Something else had to be provided for if the group was to flourish— some new mechanism of social control. A big dispute in a band of hunter-gatherers can be solved simply by the band splitting or by individuals leaving it. This option is hardly open to a group of agriculturalists once they have cleared and planted their land. They can only survive argument, conflicts and infractions of social norms if there is a much more developed superstructure of control than among hunter-gatherers.

This can explain the much enhanced role of lineages. They bind people much more tightly in early agricultural than in most hunter-gatherer societies. People now have clearly spelt out sets of rights and obligations vis-a-vis members of other households with whom they are related, either directly through kinship or indirectly through intermarriage or age group associations. Individuals who haven't got enough food can expect to get it from those designated as 'uncles' or 'cousins' in their lineage (not just immediate relatives, also second, third, even fourth cousins and so on). And the way to attain social prestige is to have enough surplus food at one's disposal to enable one to be a big giver.

The lineages, by preventing any individual household going hungry, ensure the reproduction of the group as a whole. But that is not all. As they become responsible for exercising social control over their members, they become much more formalised in their mode of operation. Decision making begins to be concentrated in the hands of some members of the lineage—usually those who are among the eldest. And in many societies things go a stage further so that some lineages come to have more prestige than others. The point can even be reached, as in Tonga even before contact with Europeans, in which the leading people ('chiefs') in prestigious lineages are able to escape from the burden of productive work and begin to try to turn themselves into an exploiting class.[118]

The first hierarchies

Why does this differentiation happen? The most plausible explanation goes along the following lines: Once human groups settle down in one place they can begin to store considerable quantities of food and other valuable. Those lineages which are most successful at this—even if purely for accidental reasons, like being lucky enough to cultivate land which is more fertile than the average—will be able to make bigger gifts than other lineages, and so gain greater prestige. And, similarly, within each lineage, certain households will be able to become wealthier than others and again earn great prestige. The very values of generosity built into such a society encourage a differentiation of status.

This leads to the emergence of what anthropologists call 'big men', individuals who gain prestige because of the wealth at their disposal. Yet, and this is very important, these individuals do not use this wealth for their own well being. They gain prestige precisely because they give it to others.

In its most developed form, a whole system of collecting and giving way wealth arises. 'Big men' use their prestige to gather in their hands any surplus left in the hands of other members of their lineage. But they then reinforce their prestige by giving the surplus back, through great ceremonial feasts for those who are directly and indirectly related to them. And a particular lineage can raise its prestige above that of other lineages, to whom it is connected by intermarriage, by giving feasts for those lineages.

The system is one in which some individuals and some lineages have higher prestige than others, in some cases culminating in establishment of hereditary chiefs and chiefly lineages. But it is not a class system, in which one section of society consumes the surplus which another section produces. Despite the establishment of hereditary or semi-hereditary hierarchies in terms of prestige, the mode of production remains communal, with consumption patterns marked by egalitarianism and sharing.

Richard Lee notes that 'a large number of pastoral and horticultural societies in the third world share the same traits' of 'communal property concepts' as hunter-gatherer societies. 'In numerous chiefdoms described by anthropologists in Africa, Oceania and lowland South America one notes, for example, much of what tribute the chiefs receive is redistributed to subjects, and the chiefs' power is subject to checks and balances by the forces of popular opinion and institutions'.[119] Thus among the Nambikwara of South America:

> *The chief must not just do well. He must try, and his group will expect him to try, to do better than the others… Although the chief does not seem to be in a privileged position from the material point of view, he must have under his control sufficient surplus quantities of food, tools, weapons and ornaments… When an individual, a family or a band as a whole, wishes or needs something, it is to the chief that an appeal is made. Generosity is, therefore, the first attribute to be expected of a new chief.[120]*

This can even lead to the leader having a harder time materially than those under him. Thus among the New Guinea Busama, the clubhouse leader 'has to work harder than anyone else to keep up his stocks of food…he must toil early and late—"his hands are never free from earth, and his forehead continually drips with sweat".'[121] In such societies many core values remain much closer to those of hunter-gatherer societies than to those we take for granted in class societies. Thus, an early 18th century observer of the Iroquois horticulturalists noted, 'If a cabin of hungry Iroquois meets another whose provisions are not entirely exhausted, the latter share with the newcomers…without waiting to be asked, although they expose themselves thereby to the same dangers of perishing as those whom they help…'[122] And a similar story emerges in a classic study of the Nuer pastoralists.[123]

Yet, these communal, egalitarian values often face the beginnings of a challenge, with household trying to evade their wider obligations in a way that does not happen among hunter-gatherers. Hidden beneath the egalitarian, communal ideology are often found incipient tendencies to place the needs of the household above the needs of the community. The Bemba in East Africa, for instance, will hide beer when a visit from an elderly relative takes place, telling him, 'Alas, we are poor wretches, we have nothing to eat'.[124] Among the Maoris there is a saying, 'Broil your rat (a favourite dish) with its fur on, lest you be disturbed by someone'.[125] After a hurricane caused acute shortages among the Tikopia—a people noted for their generosity—households began to avoid eating when people with whom they were meant to share were present.[126]

This contradictory behaviour is not the result of some inherently selfish 'human nature', but of a contradiction built into the productive system. Production itself does not rely on co-operation from the whole group, as in hunter-gatherer societies, but is based, by and large,on the care of crops and animals by the individual household.[127] The lineage and group are concerned with redistribution and reproduction, rather than production. As Karen Sachs puts it, there is a 'contradiction' in this 'mode of production' between lineage-based 'relations of production' and 'forces of production' that mainly depend on households.[128]

The survival of society depends on *both* the individual concerns of households which sustain production and the co-operative, altruistic, sharing within the group which ensures reproduction. And this means that the household can put up resistance to its obligations to the wider society if conditions arise in which its own survival is at stake. It is not a question of individual benefit versus social welfare, but of the needs of one element in the mode of production clashing with other elements.

Usually the household succeeds in reconciling the contradictory pressures, and the system does not break down. But it not difficult to see how internal changes (new productive techniques) or external pressures (natural catastrophes, exhaustion of the land, the impact of other societies) could create conditions of acute crisis in which the old order would no longer be able to continue, leading some wealthy household or lineages to break completely with their old obligations. What had been wealth to be given away to others in return for prestige then becomes wealth to consume while others suffer. 'In advanced forms of chieftainship…what begins with the would-be headman putting his production to others' benefit ends, to some degree, with others putting their production to the chief's benefit'.[129]

There is another very important change in the transition from hunter-gathering to agriculture. For the first time systematic warfare makes sense. Wealth that is stored is wealth that can be stolen from other groups of agriculturalists. Whereas clashes between rival bands are very rare among hunter-gatherers, 'Organised warfare for the purpose of defending or expanding territory is endemic…among horticulturalists'.[130]

But warfare allows some individuals and lineages to gain great prestige as they concentrate loot and the tribute from rival societies into their hands. Hierarchy becomes more pronounced, even if it remains hierarchy associated with the ability to give things to others. And to this extent, warfare is a factor opening up the possibility of class relations emerging in the face of some great social crisis.

Thus, Christine Ward Gailey suggests the attempts between 1100 and 1400AD by the highest ranking groups of chiefs in Tonga to cut themselves off from their obligations to lower ranking people—to attempt to form themselves into a ruling class—were a result of their victory in battle over the inhabitants of other islands.

The origins of agriculture

One problem has long perplexed those who have studied the transition from hunting-gathering to agriculture. Why did people make the change?

It used to be thought the change must have led to such improvements in people's lives as to make them readily accept it. But today there is a lot of evidence refuting any such simple notion. In many hunter-gatherer and horticultural societies people have actually worked less and been at least as well fed as in societies based on intensive agriculture. Thus the !Kung of the Kalihari desert may seem to have lived in a region devoid on any great resources to sustain human life. But they enjoyed a balanced diet and a calorific input rather higher than the average in modern India—and did not need to work more than three or four hours a day. They seem to have lived in what Marshall Sahlins has called, 'the original affluent society'.[131]

This explains why many hunter-gatherer societies have refused to make the transition to agriculture, even when they have been fully aware of certain agricultural techniques. They identify agriculture with an unnecessarily heavy workload.

More recent accounts of the transition from hunter-gatherer to agricultural societies focus, instead, on how certain changes could have produced tensions in hunter-gatherer societies *before* the transition to agriculture. In particular they stress that not all hunger-gatherer societies are continually on the move. Some have found a more or less static source of food to sustain them in fixed camps, which sometimes develop into villages several hundred strong. This, for instance, is true of the original inhabitants of the north west pacific coast of America, who sustain themselves from plentiful supplies of fish. Significantly, in such societies there is already some incipient social stratification: because a surplus can be stored and because a relatively large social group has to be held together, some people gain prestige (although not power or higher living standards) by fulfilling these tasks.[132] At the same time, however, life for the majority of people has advantages over that with nomadic hunter-gathering. Young children do not repeatedly have to be carried long distances, and so there is no longer any need to space births, whether by abortion and infanticide or by abstention from sex. And the larger permanent social groupings provide more opportunities for socialising, opportunities that are usually restricted among nomadic hunter-gatherers to the few weeks in the year in which several different bands camp together.

If life is easier for nomadic hunter-gatherers than for agriculturalists, it is easier still for *non*-nomadic hunter-gatherers, providing they have a large, static food supply. It is not surprising that some nomadic hunter-gatherers should opt for the new way of life and that under such conditions, there should be rapid population growth.

However, the new way of life depended on the ready availability of copious local supplies of wild foodstuffs. If these supplies disappeared for some reason, people faced immense problems. Their communities were too large for them to return to a way of life based on small, wandering bands. That would involve a complete break with an established way of life, massive social disruption, the learning (or relearning) of survival techniques—and probably starvation on a wide scale at first. And so they had an incentive to look to new ways of getting food, even if this involved an intensification of work.

This is what seems to have happened in the fertile crescent of the Middle East. About 11,000 BC climatic conditions in the region changed in such a way as to provide local 'Natufian' peoples with copious source of both meat (from herds of antelopes) and wild grain, so that they could begin to live in large, sedentary groups (villages) without having to abandon the hunter-gatherer mode of subsistence. But after about three millennia, ecological conditions changed again, and they could no longer rely on the wild herds and wild grains to feed them. 'The imbalance between population and resources is reflected in dietary stress, female infanticide and declining meat consumption'.[133]

At this point human survival for the inhabitants of the society depended upon changing their way of life. There were two directions in which change could go: towards putting effort into cultivating the crops and herding the animals they had previously collected and hunted, or, alternatively, to an abandonment of village life by splitting into small bands which would wander the land seeking naturally occurring food supplies which were not to be had close at hand. In fact, Natufians seem to have gone in both directions. Some used their knowledge of plant and animal life to undertake the planting of seeds and the domestication of herds, others reverted to the life style of their nomadic ancestors. We do not know on what basis individual groups made their choice. But it seems likely that those that adopted farming did so by accepting a reorganisation of the local economy under the direction of those prestigious individuals previously responsible for the collecting and redistribution of surpluses.[134]

Such an account an explains of why the transition to agriculture took place, independently, in so many different parts of the world.[135] It was the result of the emergence of hunter-gatherer societies which became so successful at exploiting local food resources that they grew too big to adapt when, after hundreds or thousands of years, those resources dried up. At that point they had either to change or die.

Once the transition to agriculture had taken place among any group in a region, something irreversible had happened. The populations of those societies practicing agriculture began to grow much more rapidly than those of societies that still depended on hunting and gathering. The surpluses which their sedentary life style enabled them to store provided the basis for increased specialisation in the making of artifacts, initially of stone, later of copper and brass. And among the new artifacts were the weapons they made and stockpiled for fighting each other—weapons that could also be used to drive neighbouring hunter-gatherers from the most productive soil. The new farming societies began to spread out from their place of origin, budding out into new areas as they grew, conquering or converting the hunter-gatherers around them. So, for instance, farming spread from the fertile crescent uplands some 8,000 to 9,000 years ago across the plains of the region and through south east Europe 7,000 to 8,000 years ago and then into north Europe by 4,500 to 4,000 years ago.[136]

Hunting and gathering did not disappear everywhere. Ecological niches with abundant wild animal life remained in the middle of agricultural areas, allowing the survival for millennia of societies that opted to stay with hunting and gathering. And groups of agriculturalists sometimes found it expedient to return to hunting and gathering as they moved into new areas. Nevertheless, there is no mistaking the overall trend towards the dominance of whole regions by agriculture, with the remaining hunter-gatherers being driven into the areas not suitable for agriculture—the forests, the deserts, the arctic wastes.

The first class societies

Very few agricultural societies developed into full class societies as a result of their own internal development. This began to happen in Mesopotamia about 6,000 years ago, in Egypt, Iran, the Indus Valley and China several hundred years later, on the middle Nile (in what is now

Sudan) and the eastern Mediterranean a thousand years after this, and in Meso-America, the Andean region, the Ethiopian highlands, and west and south east Africa between 2,500 and 1,000 years ago.[137] In all these cases the main pressures for the development of a new social order were internally generated. But in most other parts of the world external pressures were necessary. The old purely horticultural or agricultural societies continued to persist until foreign trade, military defeat or colonisation led to change. This was true, for instance, of northern Europe until between 2,500 and 1,000 years ago, and of highland New Guinea right through until the early 1930s.

Engels associated the rise of class society with intensive agriculture and the first use of metals. Gordon Childe accepted a similar view, calling the process of change, 'the urban revolution' (although, unlike Engels, he recognised that it followed thousands of years after the first settled agriculture of the 'neolithic revolution').

On the one hand, the population growth associated with early agriculture eventually ran, in every locality, into limits in the amount of land that could be cultivated using existing techniques. 'The growth of the neolithic populations was eventually limited by contradiction in the new economy.' This encouraged an increasing resort to warfare, with 'stone battle axes and flint daggers' becoming increasingly common in 'the later stages of the neolithic revolution in Europe'. On the other, the self sufficient neolithic village could never escape from the threat of natural catastrophe:

> All its labours and plans might be frustrated by events still beyond its control: droughts or floods, tempests or frosts, blights or hailstorms, might annihilate crops and herds... Its reserves were too small to tide it over any prolonged succession of disasters.

The urban revolution eventually offered a way out of both problems:

> The worse contradictions of the neolithic economy were transcended when farmers were persuaded or compelled to wring from the soil a surplus over and above their domestic requirements and when this surplus was made available to support new economic classes not directly engaged in producing their own food.

But this, in turn, required technical advance—'additions to the stock of science':

> The thousand or so years immediately preceding 3,000 BC were perhaps more fertile in fruitful inventions and discoveries than any period in human

*history prior to the 16th century AD. Its achievements made possible that
economic reorganisation of society I term the urban revolution'.*[138]

The advances in technology included the discovery of how to smelt
copper and then of how to alloy it with tin to produce bronze, the use of
the plough instead of the hoe and of animal power (at first oxen) to drag
it through the soil, the employment of the first wheeled carts (and war
chariots), the building of regular channels and dams for irrigation, new
ways of building and sailing of boats.

All of these changes involved what Childe calls 'modifications in
social and economic relations'—changes in the relations of people with
each other, as well as in their relations with nature. Metal smelting was a
much more skilled occupation than pot making, and came to depend on
groups of highly skilled specialists, passing the secrets of their trade on
from generation to generation. The use of the plough tended to increase
the division of labour between the sexes, since it was a form of heavy
labour not easily done by women bearing or nursing children. The
building and maintenance of regular irrigation channels tended to mean
the co-operation of dozens or even hundreds of households, and encouraged a division between those who supervised work and those who
undertook it.

The use of wheeled carts and sailing craft encouraged growing trade
between widely separated groups of agriculturalists—giving people
access to a range of useful things they could not produce themselves.
The increased productivity of labour as a result of these changes enabled
the average size of settlement to rise enormously, until in some regions
the villages of the neolithic period gave way to cities. And the enlarged
surplus resulting from the increased productivity provided an added
motive for war preparations.

Gordon Childe describes the transformation that occurred in
Mesopotamia, as people settled in the river valley of the Tigris and
Euphrates. They found land which was extremely fertile, but which
could only be cultivated by 'drainage and irrigation works', dependent
upon 'co-operative effort'.[139] A much more recent study of Mesopotamia
by Maisels suggests that people who had already learned agriculture on
naturally irrigated land found, in fourth millennium BC, 'the river channels flowed between levees [mud banks] which had only to be locally
breached to extend the productivity of nearby areas. High and sustained
levels of output could thus be attained given the right agricultural conditions.' But not all this increased output was consumed immediately.
Some was put into reserve:

*Surpluses were required for exchange against pastoral and other subsistence
products, while further stores had to be held against years of drought, pests,*

or growing season damage, for instance by storms... Such reserves...mean
permanent means of organising production and consumption so there is
always a safety margin.[140]

Over thousands of years the agricultural settlements based on the new
methods of irrigation grew into towns, and the towns into cities. The
storage of grain came to require sizeable buildings which, standing out
from the surrounding land, symbolised for people the continuity and
preservation of social life. Those who supervised the granaries became
the most prestigious group in society. In short, temples emerged which
were watched over by priests.[141]

With the foundation of a permanent grouping of priestly administrators something else, of enormous historical importance, arose: a system
of signs for keeping account of society's wealth, the first alphabet. As
Gordon Childe put it:

> *To keep account of the receipts and expenditure of the deity the priestly cor-*
> *porations administering the temple estate devised and sanctioned a system of*
> *conventional signs—ie writing; the only written documents* [until 2,800BC]
> *are account tables. Thus the accumulation of a substantial social surplus in*
> *the temple treasuries—or rather granaries—was actually the occasion of the*
> *cultural advance that we have taken as the criterion of civilisation.*
>
> *The deity may be regarded as a representative or projection of the com-*
> *munity, and the priests who served him would therefore be servants of the*
> *community, though doubtless better paid than the rest of god's people.*[142]

Over the generations, the priestly layer became increasingly separate
from the rest of society, until it formed a class with quite distinct interests. Gordon Childe describes how, 'Favoured priests practised various
forms of extortion (overcharging for burials, for instance) and treated the
god's (ie the community's) land, cattle and servants as their own private
property and personal slaves, quoting an edict of the city of Lagash from
around 2,500 BC:

> *The high priest came into the garden of the poor and took wood therefrom. If*
> *a great man's house adjoined that of an ordinary citisen', the former might*
> *annexe the humble dwelling without paying any proper compensation to its*
> *owner.*

'This archaic text', he concludes, 'gives us unmistakeable glimpses of
a real conflict of class... The surplus produced by the new economy was,
in fact, concentrated in the hands of a relatively small class'.[143]

In Mesopotamia, the first exploited class were not slaves conquered
in war, as originally suggested by Engels (and accepted to some extent

by Gordon Childe), but '*erin*' people, formerly independent peasant households who had been forced into dependency on more powerful groupings, especially the temple, and who worked for rations and wages at digging canals, cultivation or in military service.[144]

The scale of exploitation grew until it was massive. T B Jones tells how in Lagash about 2,100 BC:

> *A dozen or more temple establishments were responsible for cultivating most of the arable land. About half (the crop) was consumed by the cost of production (wages for workers, feed for draft animals and the like) and a quarter went to the king as royal tax. The remaining 25 percent accrued to the priests.*[145]

The ordinary labourer's normal subsistence was three *silla* (about 2.4 litres) of grain a day, plus supplements of beer and oil. This diet was probably deficient in protein, minerals and vitamins, but still amounted to 3,000 calories a day, 1,000 calories a day more than most people in India or Sub-Saharan Africa get today.[146] So much for the wonders of capitalism compared with other class societies!

Mesopotamia was probably the first—and has certainly been the most studied—example of the transition to 'civilisation'. But as we have seen it was not the only one. The conditions that led to the first elements of urban life and of class division occurred, as we have seen, in several parts of the world. Engels was misled by the evidence available at his time to see them arising from the use of iron by the 'pastoral' semitic and Indo-European speaking peoples of Eurasia. What is more, there were many more instances of agricultural societies developing, on their own accord, to a level where hundreds or even thousands of people could be mobilised to construct imposing stone edifices—as with the stone temples of third and fourth millennium BC Malta, the third millennium BC stone circles of which Stonehenge is the best known example, 18th century AD statues of Easter island and stepped platforms of Tahiti.[147]

Sometimes the development towards 'civilisation' would be influenced by one that had occurred elsewhere.[148] But this does not alter the fact that the processes leading to the formation of towns and cities, and often to the invention of writing, began independently in several different locations, because of the internal dynamic of society once agriculture advanced beyond a certain point. This makes nonsense of any attempt to claim that one group of the world's people are somehow 'superior' to others because they arrive at 'civilisation' first.

In place after place, different peoples arrived at a similar end point, summed up by Gordon Childe as 'the aggregation of large populations into cities; the differentiation within these of primary producers (fishers, farmers, etc), full time specialist artisans, merchants, officials, priests and rulers; the use of conventional symbols for recording and transmitting information (writing), and equally conventional standards of weights and measures of time and space leading to some mathematical and calendrical science'.[149]

But the exact route from hunter-gathering through horticulture and agriculture to civilisation did vary considerably from one society to another.[150]

Studies of the beginnings of stratification within contemporary 'communal' agricultural societies do suggest this can take different paths—sometimes with lineage elders emerging as tribal chiefs, sometimes with 'big men' turning into village headmen, sometimes with whole lineages developing into priestly castes, sometimes with some household coming to control others. Some fully established class societies do seem to have developed in the way Engels talked about, through the immediate growth of private property in land, crops and animals. But in others the evidence points to a ruling class which initially exploited the rest of society without private property—along lines which Marx and Engels referred to (somewhat misleadingly) as 'The Asiatic mode of production'.[151] In these cases class exploitation remained hidden within old communal forms of social organisation, rather than being openly revealed through private property. It was, however, just as surely class exploitation, with the old 'communal' organisation of production in reality completely transformed by the enforced payment of tribute to the exploiting priests or bureaucrats. The heads of communal organisations (whether villages, lineage groups or extended households) no longer served their needs alone, but increasingly became also the means by which the demands of the ruling class were imposed on their fellows.[152]

The divergent forms under which class society emerged must not make us forget the enormous similarities from society to society. Everywhere there was, in the beginning, primitive communism. Everywhere, once settled agricultural societies were formed, some lineages, lineage elders or 'big men' could begin to gain prestige through their role in undertaking the redistribution of the little surplus that existed in the interests of the group as a whole. Everywhere, as the surplus grew, this small section of society came to control a greater share of the social wealth, putting it in a position where it could begin the crystallise out into a social class.

What is more, even where it crystallised into a collective social class, it could, over hundreds of years, give birth to classes of private property owners. This certainly happened in Mesopotamia[153] and ancient India, 'where not only is there evidence to prove the existence of private property, but also...the role of private property changes significantly over the centuries',[154] and may have happened in Titohuacan in Central

America.[155] Even in Egypt, where the power of the monarchy was enormous, there was a tendency for both temples and the governors of local provinces ('nomes') to develop economic power of their own by the end of the old kingdom (about 2,000 BC), and by Ptolemaic times a new warrior caste owned about half of the land.[156] The German-American ex-Marxist Wittfogel attempted to develop an overall theory of 'Oriental despotism', applicable to all these societies, in which economic power was completely in the hands of an all-powerful collective ruling class; but his own early studies of China suggest a different picture, in which a state bureaucracy, local gentry and merchants were all involved in bitter battles for control in 5th century BC China.

How class began

So far we have seen that there was, indeed, a transition from hunter-gatherer societies to urbanised societies, and that parallel to that went a transition from primitive communist to the class societies. About the fact of this transition there can today be no doubt. This, in itself, is an enormous vindication of Engels. It also undercuts some of the most basic anti-socialist arguments about humans being so intrinsically selfish as to make a co-operative commonwealth impossible.

But still unresolved are a couple of important points about the origins of class rule and the state: why did people move from hunter-gathering to agriculture and then cities? Why did they accept the rise of ruling classes? Why did those rulers come to exploit rather than serve the rest of society?

These are questions Engels did not fully answer. As Gailey points out, his explanation in *The Origin* seems at points to amount to just blaming greed—some people found they had a surplus in their hands and used it to the detriment of others.[157] In *Anti-Dühring* he puts forward a fuller account, with the stress being on the initial advantages to society as a whole of having the surplus set aside in such a way that it could not be immediately consumed by the producers. But he still does not explain why people should then be motivated to consume much of this themselves, or why others should accept this.[158]

There is an argument among academic evolutionists over precisely this question. E R Service has put forward what may be termed a 'functionalist' theory of the rise of the state (and by implication, of classes). Rulers, it says, arose because it was in everyone's interests that they should do so. 'This development fulfilled the tremendous potentialities that lay in centralised leadership...' and arose from 'the simple attempts of primitive leaders to perpetuate their social domination by organising such benefits for their followers'.[159] As against this, Morton Fried argues that the formation of the state was not 'functional' for *all* of society, but was part of a the process by which one section of society exploited and coerced the rest.[160]

But this does not explain why a group which had not previously exploited and oppressed should suddenly start doing so, nor why the rest of society put up with this new exploitation and oppression.

The only way to answer such questions lies in Marx's stress on the interaction between the development of relations of production and forces of production.[161] Classes arise out of the divisions which occur in society as a new way of advancing production emerges. A group discovers it can increase the total social wealth if it concentrates resources in is own hands, organising others to work under its direction. It comes to see the interests of society as a whole as lying in its own control over resources. It defends that control even when that means making others suffer. It comes to see social advance as embodied in itself and in the protection of its own livelihood against sudden outbreaks of scarcity (due to harvest failure, pests, wars etc) that cause enormous hardship to everybody else.

It is not difficult to see how the spread of farming led to pressures for changes in production that required direction from above. The first farming communities probably established themselves in localities with exceptionally fertile soil. But as they expanded, survival came to depend on coping with much more difficult conditions. That required a further reorganisation of social relations. Renfrew has argued:

> *The relatively small neolithic population could in fact select soils such as fertile alluvial areas whose potential yield was many times greater than the areas later taken into cultivation... The spread of settlement to areas where yields were more vulnerable to fluctuations in rainfall, for instance, would have increased the need for redistributive mechanisms which would allow the local surpluses to be fully used.*[162]

D R Harris has made a similar point in relation to tropical agriculture in Africa and south east Asia. At first it was,

> *small scale and depended on ecosystem manipulation rather than the creation of artificial ecosystems by large scale transformations... The techniques... normally being limited to human labour using simple tools such as axes, knives, planting sticks and hoes'. 'The unit of labour' was 'the family', and there was no need for a 'level of social organisation more complex than that of the simple segmentary tribe.*[163]

But agriculture that produces more also demands 'units of labour greater than the family' and 'a more complex' level of 'social organisation' which is achieved through 'the medium of ranked chiefdoms and socially stratified states with a dependent peasantry'.[164]

Groups with high prestige in preceding, non-class societies would set about organising the labour needed to expand agricultural production by building irrigation works or clearing vast areas of new land. They would come to see their own control of the surplus—and the use of some of it to protect themselves against natural vicissitudes—as in everyone's interest. So would the first groups to use large scale trade to increase the overall variety available for consumption. So too with those groups who were most proficient at wresting surpluses from other societies through warfare. In this way, the advance of the forces of production in each locality would turn groups and individuals who previously gained prestige by fulfilling redistributive or ceremonial functions into classes which imposed the demand of surplus extraction upon the rest of society.

In many parts of the world societies were able to prosper right through to modern times without resorting to labour intensive methods such as the use of heavy ploughs or extensive hydraulic works. This was true of much of North America, the islands of the Pacific ocean, inland Papua-New Guinea, and parts of Africa and south east Asia. But in other conditions survival came to depend on adopting new techniques. Ruling classes arose out of the organisation of such activities, and so did towns, states and what we usually call civilisation. From this point onwards, the history of society certainly was the history of class struggle.

Such groups could not keep the surplus in their own hands at times when the whole of society was suffering great hardship unless they found ways of imposing their will on the rest of society, unless they established coercive structures, states, and legal codes and ideologies to back them up. But once such structures and such ideologies were in existence, they would perpetuate the control of the surplus by a certain group even when it no longer served the purpose of advancing production. A class which emerged as a spur to production would persist even when it was no longer such a spur. And it would be protected by a military-juridicial-ideological superstructure which could constitute a growing burden on the production of society as whole.

This was shown dramatically with all the first great civilisations when, after longer or shorter period, they collapsed amid enormous internal discontent: the great crises of Sumerian society around the beginning of the second millennium BC, the temporary disintegration of the Egyptian state at the end of the old kingdom around 1,800 BC, the collapse of the Mycenean and Cretan civilisations after the middle of the second millennium BC, the collapse of the Teotihuacan civilisation in Central America around 700 AD. It has been shown repeatedly since, from the fall of the Roman Empire to the present day crisis of world capitalism.

Class was then, as Marx and Engels always insisted, a necessary development once scarcity faced society. But, as they also insisted, once a class is established in power, further advance depends on the fight against it. Engels wrote of the downfall of primitive communism:

> This organisation was doomed to extinction. It...presupposed an extremely undeveloped form of production, that is, an extremely sparse population spread over a wide territory, and therefore the almost complete domination of man by external nature, alien, opposed, incomprehensible to him...
>
> The power of these primordial communities...was broken by influences which from the outset appear to us as a degradation, a fall from the simple moral grandeur of the ancient...society. The lowest interests—base greed, brutal sensuality, sordid avarice, selfish plunder of common possessions— usher in the new civilised society, class society... And the new society...has never been anything but the development of the minority at the expense of the exploited and oppressed great majority; and it is so today more than ever.[165]

We could not go back to primitive communism even if that were what we wanted. It would mean wiping out 99.9 percent of humanity (the population of Southern France under foraging 30,000 years ago was about 400 and of the whole world 10,000 years ago about 10 million). But Marx and Engels insisted that this is not necessary. Capitalism has created so much wealth that, for the first time in human history, it is possible to conceive, not of a primitive communism, but of an 'advanced communism'. What is more, if we do not move to this, we will not see a simple continuation of existing society but a regression through 'the mutual destruction of the contending classes'. As Engels put it at the end of *The Origin of the Family*, we reach 'a stage in the development of production at which the existence of classes not only will have ceased to be necessary, but will become a positive hindrance to production'.[166]

III The origins of women's oppression

The Origin of the Family was not, of course, just about the rise of classes and the state. It was also about the origins of women's oppression. A central argument is that women were not subordinate to men until the rise of classes, that 'the first class antagonism which appears in history coincides with the development of the antagonism between man and woman in monogamous marriage, and the first class oppression with that of the female sex by the male'.[167]

On this Engels was undoubtedly right. The evidence, meticulously

put together by Eleanor Leacock and others, is that there was no domination of men over women among the nomadic hunter-gatherers European
settlers encountered in the 17th to 19th centuries.[168] There was a division
of labour between men and women, with men doing most of the hunting
and women most of the gathering. But since gathering usually produced
more of the average diet than hunting, this did not necessarily lead to any
higher evaluation of men and their work than of women and theirs. The
anthropologist Ernestine Friedl does accept that in the few societies, for
instance among Australian aborigines, in which meat was the central
component of the diet, men were more highly ranked than women.[169] But
she insists:

> *Individual decisions are possible for both men and women with respect to*
> *their daily routines... Men and women alike are free to decide how they will*
> *spend each day: whether to go hunting or gathering and with whom...*

She notes that when it comes, for instance, to discussion on whether
to move camp to a new area, women and men both take part.[170] And
women still exercise enormous powers in their own right. So, for
instance, among Australian aborigines, 'older women exercise influence
over their own marital careers, and on those of their sons and daughters',
and married women often have affairs with young unmarried men—a
state of affairs anathema to the sexual codes of conduct of almost all
class societies.[171]

Anthropologists of the Eleanor Leacock school go even further. They
discount the evidence accepted by Friedl for men ever having higher
status than women, arguing that this simply reflects prejudices of the
Western observers who gathered it.[172]

Class society's notions of 'the place of women' are also absent in societies based on horticulture. There is sometimes the beginning of a
hierarchy which gives men a higher standing than women, just as there can
be the beginning of a hierarchy between lineages and households. Men (or
at least, *some* men) may have greater decision making power than women.
But there is still no systematic oppression of women. Women retain their
own spheres of decision making, and can counter decisions made by their
spouses.

Structures usually exist which restrict who people can marry, and this
is interpreted by the influential structuralist school of anthropology,
inspired by Claude Levi Strauss, as meaning that women are treated
simply as objects of negotiation between men. But, as Karen Sachs,
Christine Gailey, Ernestine Friedl and others have emphasized, it is not
men as such who lay down who people are permitted to marry, but the
'kin corporate' lineages. And older women as well as older men usually

have a say in these decisions.

This is most obviously the case in societies which are described by anthropologists as 'matrilineal' and 'matrilocal'. In matrilineal societies descent is reckoned down the female line: someone's most important ties are not be to their father (who belongs to a different lineage), but with their mother and their mother's brother; in the same way, a man's main responsibility is not to his biological children but to his sister's children. In matrilocal societies a man does not run a household himself, but moves into one run by his wife, her sisters and her mother.

Where society is both matrilocal and matrilineal, men exercise very little authority in the households in which they actually live. A man's formal rights and responsibilities are always with another household, which is part of another lineage—that of his mother, his sister and her children. There they may exercise some authority—which is why these societies are not 'matriarchies', societies ruled by mothers. But their absence from that household necessarily means this is a limited authority, no greater than that of the women.

Significantly, the structuralist school, with its insistence that women are everywhere the object of arrangements between males, hardly refers to such instances.[173]

Not all matrilineal societies are matrilocal. Among, for instance, the Ohaffia, an Ibo people in Eastern Nigeria, descent is reckoned along the female line but residence is in with the husband's kin. But even here wives are not subordinate to husbands.[174] In this society, 'divorce is usually granted merely at the wish of either spouse', 'daughters are highly prized', and 'the relationship…of husband and wife…seems to be one of mutual respect and accommodation to each other'.[175]

Finally there are horticultural societies where descent is through the male line and residence after marriage is with the husband's family. But even here women still have much greater influence than is usual in class societies. This is exercised through the lineages. A woman is not just a wife, a subordinate in a strange household and lineage. She is also a sister, someone with influence in the decision making of her own lineage. And her husband's kin will want to maintain good relations with that lineage. Her position as a wife gives her husband's kin (including his mother and sisters) some control over her productivity. But her position as a sister in turn gives her some claim over the produce of her brothers and their wives. In the course her lifetime, she will move from being mainly regarded as a subordinate, as a 'wife', to being mainly seen as a 'sister' and 'mother'. And as such she is a 'controller' of 'labour and productive means'.[176]

This is not a world of isolated nuclear families in which the individual woman is subject to the whims of her partner. Nor is it a world of patriarchal households in which fathers lay down the law for wives, children and servants. It is a world in which everyone, male or females, is tied into a network of mutual rights and responsibilities which vary from one stage in life to another, delimiting people's freedom in various ways, but still leaving them with more autonomy than is general in class societies.[177]

The movement of a woman from one household (that of her father), to another (that of her husband) is seen by structuralist anthropologists as an 'exchange' of women between men. But the woman does not move between men, but between lineages, each of which involves other women. Her standing is such that she is seen as a loss to one household and a gain to another. The husband's father often had to hand over goods to her parental household (what is called by Europeans the 'bride-price') to compensate for its loss, a situation markedly different to that in societies which devalue women, where the women's family have to pay a dowry to get rid of her. And in marrying, the woman herself can gain 'an increase in individual status and autonomy', as Gailey tells of Tonga.[178]

The structuralists confuse reciprocal obligations that tie different lineages together in pre-class societies with the commodity exchange of capitalism, and so confuses a situation in which 'women move back and forth as valued people, actively operating within and manipulating the networks of relations their moves creates' with their reduction to virtual commodities.[179]

The confusion is made easier by the integration of the economies of almost all surviving horticulturalists into the world economy with the use of money.[180] People's need for money to spend on market goods leads them to see old relations of reciprocal obligation in a new way, as a means of realising cash. It is usually males who relate directly to the market outside the village and this tends to give them a power and a standing they never used to have. Contact with the capitalist world causes the horticultural societies to mimic its social relations—and Western anthropologists then claim this proves those social relations typical of capitalism are universal to all societies.

Any scientific analysis of early agricultural societies has to cut away such distortions.

We may never know whether matrilineal descent was once universal, as Eleanor Leacock suggests, since we have no way of studying in detail preliterate societies before the impact of the world economy. What we can say, however, is that there was no universal experience of female oppression and that it only became a systematic aspect of society with the division into classes and the rise of the state. On this Engels was 100 percent right.

Minor mistakes

Engels was, however, badly wrong on a couple of subordinate questions which he himself took so seriously as to make *The Origin of the Family* a misleading work if not read critically.

He took over from Morgan the view that the classifications of relatives that exist in lineage societies (where, for instance, every woman in the lineage who is of your own generation is called 'sister', every male of your parents' generation is called 'uncle', as so on) harked back to a previous, quite different form of social organisation.[181] The system of classifying relatives was, he held, a 'social fossil' that enabled one to decifer the history the family. He also took over from Morgan the conclusion that these 'fossils' proved that there had existed a stage of 'group marriage', when a group of brothers married a group of sisters.[182] This, he argued, was 'characteristic of savagery', while 'the pairing family' was characteristic of barbarism.[183]

In fact, as we have seen, nomadic hunting and gathering ('savagery') is not characterised by strong lineages let alone group marriage but by the flexible organisation of couples and their children into bands.[184] Engels saw lineage organisations as relics of a time when sexual relations had a 'naive, primitive, jungle character'.[185] In fact, they were complex mechanisms which co-ordinated society once early agriculture had allowed the formation of villages of hundreds of inhabitants—they were in fact, an expression of the development of the forces of production, not some hangover from old 'relations of reproduction'. Engels was wrong, not because his basic Marxist methodology was wrong, but because he did not apply it consistently enough.

He was also mistaken to try to decipher an even earlier form of the family, that which he refers to as 'primitive promiscuity'. He claimed such a stage must have existed as ancestral apes evolved into humans, because it alone could have prevented 'jealous males' disrupting all attempts at the co-operation needed to cope with nature. Yet, his logic breaks down only a page or so later, when he notes, 'jealousy is an emotion of comparatively late development'—a conclusion which, as we have seen, research into gorillas and chimps suggests to be correct.[186] And his own conception of what 'primitive promiscuity' amounted to is by no means clear, since at one point he suggests it was little more than what we would today call 'serial monogamy', based on 'separate pairings for a limited time'.[187]

In fact, Engels here makes the mistake of falling into blind speculation about a very long period (more than 3 million years) about which neither he nor we know anything with certainty. We do not know whether the ancestral apes were organised in male centred groups like the common chimpanzees or female centred groups like the pygmy chimps, and we certainly do not know how the form of organisation characteristic of modern nomadic hunter gatherers arose. It is preferable to stick with what we do know—that the relations between women and men among surviving hunter-gatherers, have been very different to those taken for granted in class societies and embodied into most notions of human nature.[188]

There is one other mistake that Engels himself did not actually fall into, but which is often ascribed to him by both supporters and opponents. That is the use of the term 'matriarchy' implying a period of female rule prior to that of male domination. Those who employ it presuppose there has always been something akin to class domination and the state, but that at one time it was under aegis of women not men. Engels explicitly rejected any such notion. He took over the term 'mother right' from the German writer Bachofen to describe the reckoning of decent along the female line which, he believed, was universal at one stage. But he added, 'I retain the term for the sake of brevity. It is however an unhappy choice, for at this social stage there is no such thing as right in the legal sense'.[189] Certainly, the characteristic of both hunter-gatherer and early agricultural societies is that both women and men take part in decision making, not that either excludes the other.

Engels' argument revisited

Engels is at his best when he describes the rise of women's oppression, 'the world historic defeat of the female sex', as he put it, and relates it to the rise of class society. Yet his argument sometimes falters when he tries to spell out mechanisms behind this defeat. He does not show why it is necessarily *men* who dominate in the new class society. He says men came to produce both the food and the tools of production, that this necessarily gave them ownership rights and control over the surplus,[190] and that they wanted to pass on ownership to their sons, not to their wife's relatives. But he does not show *why* they should suddenly get this desire after thousands of years in which their closest relationships were with their sisters' children.[191] Two sorts of attempts have been made to fill the gap in his argument.

First there is the account of those like Eleanor Leacock and Christine Gailey who have emphasized the impact of the rise of the state in smashing the old lineages in which women exercised their influence. The state subordinates the rest of the society to the newly emerging ruling class. But that means destroying 'the relative authority and autonomy' of the old kin communities. Insofar as they survive, it is as transmission belts for imposing the demands of the state and the ruling class on the mass of people. And this involves taking not just productive, but also reproductive decisions away from the members of these communities. Women, as the biological reproducers, lose out.[192]

But this account, by itself, does not explain any better than Engels' why women should not have an equal share of power and influence with men in the new ruling class and state—nor why women should usually also be reduced to a subordinate role among the exploited class. It explains the collapse of the old order, but not the gender hierarchy that exists in the new.

An alternative account, put forward in different ways by Gordon Childe and Ernestine Friedl, stresses the productive role of women and the role played by biology at different points in historical development.

Childe points out that in the early neolithic period women played a major role in production. There was a division of labour, in which men looked after the flocks and herds. But the key to the neolithic revolution, he argued, was:

> to discover suitable plants and appropriate methods for their cultivation, devise special implements for tilling the soil, reaping and storing the crops and converting it into food... All these inventions and discoveries were, judged by ethnographic evidence, the work of the women. To that sex too may be credited the chemistry of pot making, the physics of spinning, the mechanics of the loom and the botany of flax and cotton.[193]

And, 'owing to the role of women's contributions in the collective economy, kinship is naturally reckoned in the female line and the system of "mother right" prevails'.[194]

All this changed, however, once the plough replaced the hoe and the digging stick as the major agricultural implement. Stock keeping was already a male sphere, and the plough turned arable farming into one as well, sharply reducing women's place in production:

> The plough...relieved women of the most exacting drudgery but deprived them of their monopoly over the cereal crops and the social status that it conferred. Among the barbarians whereas women normally hoe plots, it is men who plough. And even in the oldest Sumerian and Egyptian documents the ploughmen really are males.[195]

Ernestine Friedl argues that the relative standing of men and women in horticultural societies depends on their contribution to production. There are, for example, some horticultural societies in which women produce the basic crops and men the ones that are exchanged, and others in which men produce the basic crop and women the one that is exchanged.[196] It is in the first sort that men have the higher standing. 'The prevalence of male dominance is a consequence of the frequency with which men have greater rights that women to distribute goods outside the domestic group'.[197]

She points out that certain activities tend in most societies to be done by men rather than women. In some hunter-gatherer societies women do hunt, but 'are barred from hunting in the later stages of pregnancy... [and] after childbirth by the burden of transporting the child'.[198] In early agricultural societies, crafts can be done by either sex, but 'metal working is almost entirely a man's skill'.[199] And in most societies— although not all—men are the only warriors.

An interaction between biological imperatives and social needs underlies such changes in the division of labour. The human species has to reproduce itself if any society is going to survive. But the scale of its reproduction—how many children are needed from each adult woman— varies enormously. In a nomadic hunter-gatherer society, as we have seen, there is a premium on spacing children so that no woman is responsible for more than one infant at a time. By contrast, for agricultural societies, each child is, potentially, an extra cultivator, and there is the need to compensate for a higher death rate, the result of a greater vulnerability to infectious diseases, and the ravages of interminable wars.[200] So the higher the birth rate the more successful that society is likely to be. It is in the interests of the whole society (including its women) for women not to take part in activities (such as warfare, long distance travel and heavy agricultural tasks) which expose them to the greatest risks of death, infertility or abortion—or which expose to danger infants dependent on their mother's milk for food.

This would explain why women often do most of the food producing in societies which rely on the hoe and the digging stick, but not in those which rely on the plough or on cattle herding. The first set of activities may involve hard and tiring physical labour, but is not likely to affect the reproduction rate unduly in the way that the second set would. The women of such a society are of more value to the village, the lineage or the household when it comes to physical reproduction than the men— and so are kept clear of activities which might endanger them, or at least their reproductive potential.

The result is that women are central to production, as well as reproduction, in hunter-gatherer and early agricultural societies. But they are excluded from the sorts of production that produce the biggest surplus with the rise of heavy agriculture, the urban revolution, and the shift from 'communal' or 'kin corporate' society to class society.

An account just in terms of the plough and cattle farming is not sufficient, since classes emerged in the New World a millennium and half before the European conquest led to introduction of the plough.[201] However, there was a turn to a different sort of heavy agriculture with the first use of local irrigation works. And there was a growth of other activities from which women were usually excluded by their reproductive role—long distance trade and warfare. All these activities increased the surplus available to a particular society. All of them tended to be performed by men rather and women. And all of them encouraged the transformation of highly esteemed groups of people into dominating classes.

Most of the men who carried through the burden of these new productive activities did not become part of the dominant class. Most ploughmen did not become princes and most soldiers did not become warlords, and neither of them made up the priesthood which often came to constitute the first ruling class and which *never* got involved in heavy work of any sort. But the new forms of production encouraged the breakdown of the old lineage based communal forms of organisation, the key element in the account of Gailey and Leacock.

So long as much of food production was carried out by women it made sense to everyone for land and other means of production to be under the control of lineages running through the female line. This guaranteed a continuity of cultivation across generations. A woman, her sisters and their spouse would be able to look forward to their daughters cultivating the lineage's land and so providing for them in their old age. The fact that land did not pass to the son did not matter to either the mother or the father, since he would not be responsible for the main burden of food production.

Once, however, the main food producers became the men, the situation changed. A couple became dependent on the production of the next generation of males to keep them once they were no longer physically able to provide fully for themselves. The survival of any particular household came to depend much more on the relationship between the males in one generation and the next than between the females. Relying on the father's sisters sons, who would themselves work on land controlled by other lineages (that of their wives) was much less dependable than trying to keep the couple's sons attached to the parental household. Patrilineality and patrilocality began to fit in with the logic of production much more than matrilineality and matrilocality.

The replacement of shifting (or slash and burn) agriculture by continual cultivation of the same land encouraged this development. It necessitated measures to improve the land over more than one generation, measures which would be carried through mainly by the men and would therefore be encouraged by a new stress on relations between successive generations of male cultivators, tied to the same piece of land.

Finally, the rise of classes and the state at the expense of the lineages encouraged male dominance among the lower classes once men were the main producers of the surplus. It was on them that the newly emerging authorities would place responsibility for handing over part of the crop. And they would then have to impose these demands on the household unit as a whole, beginning to direct its work and control its consumption.

Class, the state and women's oppression

Whether or not matrilineal-matrilocal relations were originally universal hardly matters in this scheme. For, even if they had only existed in a minority of cases, they would almost everywhere by replaced by patrilineal relations once agriculture developed beyond a certain point. And the development of classes and the state would, in turn, begin to transform patrilineality—descent through the male line, checked by a complex network of kinship relations—into patriarchy, the domination of the household by the senior man.

But the development of classes and the state did not take place over night. It was a process taking hundreds, even thousands of years. Those who made up the first ruling classes were those whose ancestors had acquired high standing in the pre-existing non-class societies by concentrating in their hands resources, albeit resources to be redistributed back to the rest of society. And since these societies had already begun to make the transition to patrilineality, they tended to be male.

What was involved was not one single moment of transition, but a long, dialectically developing process. The move to patrilineality would encourage the emergence of men as the key figures controlling society's resources. This, in turn, would encourage the emergence of patriarchy in the households. And patriarchy in the household would then encourage the domination of males within the ruling class and the state. They would begin to turn the old control of lineages over marriage arrangement to their own advantage, so that the intermarriage between lineages that had once bound whole societies together through ties of reciprocity was transformed into a conscious 'exchange of women' aimed at enhancing the flow of resources into the hands of the dominant male line.

Women, who had been key producers as well as reproducers, now became subservient to males at all levels of society. Among the exploited classes they still worked. But even in the frequent cases where they actually produced more than the men in total terms, they did not produce and control the key surpluses which determined the household's relationship the rest of society, and so were still subordinate to the men (or, more accurately, to the one man who ruled over both the women and the younger men in the patriarchal farming or artisan household). The only exceptions were in the occasional cases where the absence of the male from the household (for instance in some fishing communities or among some groups of artisans when there was the early death of the husband) or the participation of the women in certain forms of trade (for instance, in parts of West Africa) gave them control over the surplus. The woman, in these cases, became a sort of female patriarch. But these cases were necessarily the exception, never the rule. And, of course, in cases where production was based on gang labour by slaves, there was no household and no male dominance at all at the base of society.

Among the ruling classes women became oppressed in a different way. They became playthings in the manoeuvring between different rulers, used to enhance the standing of one at the expense of another. So although they participated in the exploitation of the rest of society, they were rarely full equals to the ruling class men, initiating events on their own behalf. And in extreme instances, they were confined to a world of their own, a world of purdah or of the harem, in which the only sort of participation they could hope for in the wider world was at one remove, through manipulation of the affections of a husband or a son. Again, there were occasional exceptions, of the queen or the dowager who took total power into her own hands. But again, the exception never became the rule.

Engels, then, may have been wrong in his explanation of some of the processes involved in the rise of the patriarchal family. But he was right to insist on its historical novelty and to see it as a 'world historic defeat' for women, as not simply a 'revolution', but 'one of the most decisive ever experienced' in the history of humanity, He was also right to add that it happened in a way which 'need not have disturbed one living member' of the society.

The transformation in the reality at the top and bottom of society was necessarily reflected in transformations in ideology. Among the remains of prehistoric societies of the early neolithic period female statuettes abound, suggesting the worship of goddesses, while phallic statues are lacking.[202] Once class societies develop, the stress is increasingly on the role of gods, with the great religions which dominated from the 5th century BC onwards across most of Eurasia characterised by the omnipotence of a single male god. The ideology of both rulers and ruled became one of male dominance, even if female figures were sometimes allowed a subordinate role.

Engels also insisted on something else. The further development of the means of production brought about further changes in the form of the family and the character of women's oppression. This, he claimed, happened with the replacement of the ancient slave mode of production by feudalism, which, according to him, was accompanied by the replacement of the 'patriarchal household' by the 'monogamous family'. 'The new monogamy...clothed the domination of men in milder forms and permitted women to occupy, at least with regard to externals, a far freer and more respected position than in ancient antiquity'.[203]

The details of the change do not concern us here. What is important is Engels' insight that there have been variations, even within class society, in the nature of the family and the character of women's oppression. The whole process cannot be subsumed under one single category of 'patriarchy' in the way that many modern feminist theorists have tried to do. There have always been enormous differences between the families of the exploiting class and the exploited classes: you cannot simply equate the family of the Roman slave owner and the family of the Roman slave, nor the family of the feudal lord and the family of the feudal peasant. And there have been considerable differences in the family as you move from one ruling class to another. A society in which ruling class women play a public but subordinate role—as in feudal Europe as viewed by Chaucer or Boccacio—is different in significant respects to one in which they live in purdah. A society in which bride-price exists is different than one in which dowry payments exist. To say this is not to ignore women's oppression in each case, but to insist on the changes it undergoes—a precondition for recognising it is not some expression of human nature, but a product of concrete historical developments, something that can be done away with by further developments.

Some of the most important passages in *The Origin of the Family* begin to outline these further developments. Engels emphasises that even under capitalism the women of the working class enter the workforce, and so get incomes of their own—on a scale unknown in previous class societies:

> *Since large scale industry has transferred the woman from the house to the labour market and the factory, and makes her, often enough, the bread winner of the family, the last remnants of male domination in the proletarian home have lost all foundation—except, perhaps, for some of that brutality towards women which became firmly rooted with the establishment of monogamy. Thus the proletarian family is no longer monagamian in the strict sense, even in cases of the most passionate love and strictest faithfulness of the two parties… The woman has regained, in fact, the right of separation, and when the man and woman cannot get along, they part.*[204]

But if the entry of women into the paid workforce offers the potential for liberation, the continued organisation of reproduction within the individual family prevents the realisation of this potential:

> *When she* [the proletarian woman] *fulfils her duty in the private service of her family, she remains excluded from public production and cannot earn any-*

thing; and when she wishes to take part in public industry and earn her living
independently, she is not in a position to fulfil her duties.[205]

Thus women in existing society are in a contradictory situation. They
can see the possibility of full equality and therefore challenge male dominance with a confidence unparalleled since the destruction of communal
production. But there are still hindered from achieving this equality
unless they forego having children. No amount of legislation could overcome this painful contradiction, although, Engels insisted, legislation
was to be welcomed, since it would bring into the open the need for a
further, revolutionary, change:

> *It will then become evident that the first premise for the emancipation of*
> *women is the reintroduction of the entire female sex into public industry; and*
> *that this again demands the quality possessed by the individual family of*
> *being the economic unit of society be abolished...*
> *With the passage of the means of production into common property the*
> *individual family ceases to be the economic unit of society. Private house-*
> *keeping is transformed into a social industry. The care and education of*
> *children becomes a public matter.*[206]

This will transform completely relations between the sexes. Once the
obsession with reproduction and property rights is gone, Engels argues,
people will be free to relate to each other in, new, genuinely liberated
ways. We can only 'conjecture' about what the new relations will be
like:

> *That will be settled after a new generation has grown up...Once such people*
> *appear, they will care not a rap about what we today think they should do.*
> *They will establish their own practice and their own public opinion..on the*
> *practice of each individual—and that's the end of it.*[207]

If other sections of *The Origin of the Family* suffer from using outdated material and, occasionally, for the use of circular arguments, these
passages shine because of their modernity. Engels was, in fact, far ahead
of his time when he wrote them. As Lindsey German and others have
written, after virtually abolishing the family among the working class in
the early stages of the industrial revolution, capitalism sought to impose
a form of the bourgeois family in the second half of the 19th century as
the only way of ensuring the socialisation of the next generation of
workers.[208] Hence attempts to use the law and religious preaching to limit
women's involvement in the workforce. Since the Second World War,
however, the relentless drive of capital accumulation has everywhere
broken through these restraints, so that even in countries dominated by

Catholic moralising or by Islamic codes, the proportion of women in the workforce has climbed relentlessly, while in parts of Britain women are now the majority of the employed working class.

Yet, reproduction remains privatised, even if the state is compelled to play a much larger role than in Engels' time in the provision of social services and education. Most women are wage earners and expect, as never before, to live a life of independence, yet still find themselves forced back into bearing the burden of childcare within the confines of the nuclear family. Out of this has grown a resistance among both women and men to many things which were taken for granted in the past—unequal pay, sexual stereotyping of jobs, the treatment of women's bodies as commodities, domestic violence, frustrating and soul destroying marriages. It is a resistance that raises everywhere the vision of a better life for all, yet within a society which prevents that vision becoming a reality.

Conclusion

Very few scientific writings from 100 years ago still inspire current research. This is not surprising, given the explosion of research, knowledge and theorising that has accompanied the frenetic accumulation of capital. *The Part Played by Labour* and *The Origin of the Family, Private Property and the State* were attempts both to develop and popularise the insights of the science of their time. It is an enormous credit to Engels and to the method that he and Marx developed in the mid-1840s that they still provide us with insights which are lacking in so many present day writings on the evolution of our species and of society. They contain much which has to be discarded or rejigged on the basis of what had been discovered since Engels died. But what remains is still of immense value. It forms an invaluable starting point for anyone who wants to make sense of the mass of empirical material produced on an almost daily basis by archaeologists and anthropologists. And so it helps us today to refute the nonsense of 'sociobiologists' and 'naked ape' theorists when they claim that capitalism is inevitable because it rests on the foundations of an unchanging 'human nature'.

Engels and natural science

PAUL McGARR

Engels and Marx had a lifelong interest in natural science. Both saw their politics growing from a materialist world view of which science was an integral part. Science, argued Marx, 'underlies all knowledge'.[1]

Of the two founders of the Marxist tradition, Engels followed science more closely. He planned a major work setting out his approach to science, its history, place in society and the philosophical arguments surrounding it—but never completed it. Notes survive—some complete chapters, others in very rough form—which have been collected together and published as *The Dialectics of Nature*.[2] Engels never managed to fully develop his ideas. He was forced to break off work on *The Dialectics of Nature* to deal with arguments inside the then growing socialist movement. In Germany a now long forgotten professor, Dühring, had become fashionable among sections of the German workers' movement. Engels was pressed by Marx, who was working on *Capital*, to write a polemic against Dühring.

This division of labour between the two men was typical, with Engels usually taking on the job of defending their joint views in public debate. Engels did not approach his task with enthusiasm. He wrote to Marx, 'It is all very well for you to talk. You can lie warm in bed and study Russian agrarian conditions in particular and rent in general with nothing to disturb you. But I am to sit on the hard bench, swill the cold wine, suddenly interrupt everything again and tackle the boring Dühring'.[3]

Dühring's arguments are of little substance and Engels was scornful of what he called Dühring's 'bumptious pseudo-science' in which he 'speaks of all possible things and some others as well'.[4] Nevertheless, Engels took the opportunity in his polemic, known as *Anti-Dühring*, to lay out the basic world view that he shared with Marx. As Dühring had drawn on science to justify some of his arguments, Engels replied by spelling out some of his own ideas on science. Engels intended to resume work on *The Dialectics of Nature*, but was prevented from doing so by Marx's death. Engels found most of his energies then tied up in preparing Marx's unfinished *Capital* for publication, and also in meeting the growing demands placed on him to defend Marxism within the socialist movement.

Nevertheless, despite the unfinished nature of Engels' project, it is possible to gather a fairly clear idea of his arguments about science. Ever since, those views have been the subject of fierce controversy, both among Marxists and between Marxists and those hostile to socialism. In the process Engels' views have been distorted by both enemies and many would be friends.

The usual charges against Engels are twofold. On the one hand, he is accused of a crude and mechanistic form of materialism. On the other hand, he is charged with using notions drawn from the idealist philosopher Hegel which have no place in a materialist world view. Engels' critics often manage to attack him for both these faults in the same breath, not noticing the contradiction. In fact the whole thrust of Engels' writings on science is a polemic against both the views with which his critics tax him.[5] John Rees deals in detail elsewhere in this book with many of these attacks on Engels.[6] The aim of this chapter is to lay out what Engels said in his writings on natural science. In doing so I quote Engels' words extensively and occasionally at length since they have too often been attacked on the basis of crude distortions. Engels' arguments are then examined to see how they stand up against the enormous developments in natural science in the century since his death.

Natural history and the history of science

Engels enthusiastically welcomed every advance in a scientific understanding of the world. He located this attitude in the context of the battle between the two basic ways of understanding the world which have run through human history—materialism and idealism. The basic premise of materialism is that there is an objective world which exists independently of and predates human beings, human ideas and consciousness—or those of any supposed god. Most materialists would also hold that the world has definite ways of behaving, laws, which can be discovered and understood. Materialism, in its various forms, has long been opposed by another approach, idealism. This is the notion that the world is dependent on, has no existence apart from, some idea or consciousness. Most often this has meant some form of religion in which a god or non-physical being was a necessary precondition of all existence.

For most of human history idealism, usually in the form of religion, was the dominant approach in seeking to understand and explain the world. The balance, however, was decisively shifted in favour of materialism by the scientific revolution of the 16th and 17th centuries, associated with figures like Copernicus, Galileo, Kepler and Newton. Engels saw this revolution as intimately connected with the development of modern bourgeois society and the defeat of the old feudal society. It was a turning point in human history, a time when 'the dictatorship of the Church over men's minds was shattered', the 'greatest progressive revolution that mankind had so far experienced'.[7]

'Natural science', Engels wrote, 'developed in the midst of the general revolution and was itself thoroughly revolutionary'.[8] The first step in the scientific revolution was the theory put forward in 1543 by Copernicus that the Earth went round the sun and not the other way round. In throwing the Earth and man out of their place at the centre of the universe this marked a fundamental challenge to the old religion dominated view. Kepler went further and showed that the planets all moved not on perfect circular orbits, as established authority decreed, but rather on ellipses. Moreover, Kepler put forward the then revolutionary notion that the motions of the planets and motions of bodies on Earth could both be explained on the basis of the same physical principles.[9]

Galileo, using the telescope, recently developed for military purposes, shattered many other old established notions by showing that the Earth was not unique in having a moon. Jupiter had several. He found that the sun, in the established view a perfect, unblemished body, had dark spots. He also conducted systematic experiments and was the first to formulate an understanding of acceleration—change of velocity—which was a crucial step in explaining the dynamics of moving bodies. Newton went further still. He showed how all motion, from apples falling from trees to the trajectory of cannonballs and tides on Earth, to the motion of the Moon and all the planets, could be explained on the basis of his famous three laws of motion and the law of gravity. He also invented, along with the philosopher Leibniz, the mathematical calculus. This for the first time enabled processes involving continuous change to be precisely handled by scientists—for example velocity and acceleration.

Galileo and Newton were 'giants', but they were also products of the society they lived in. The problems they thought about and worked on were those thrown up by a society in which the bourgeoisie was expanding its wealth and power, and so transforming the way human beings interacted with nature.

The bourgeoisie's drive to expand trade and production meant it had a vital interest in understanding and exploiting the natural world. It was this that lay behind the great scientific breakthroughs. Engels, in several of the sections of *The Dialectics of Nature* which remain as rough notes and sketches, links the development of science to the development of production. 'From the very beginning the origin and development of the sciences has been determined by production'.[10] Engels never had time to spell out his argument, but a flavour of his approach can be gleaned from a few paragraphs:

> *If, after the dark night of the Middle Ages was over, the sciences suddenly arose anew with undreamt-of force, developing at a miraculous rate, once again we owe this miracle to production. In the first place, following the crusades, industry developed enormously and brought to light a quantity of new mechanical (weaving, clockmaking, milling), chemical (dyeing, metallurgy, alcohol) and physical (spectacles) facts.*

This 'not only gave enormous material for observation, but also itself provided quite other means for experimenting than previously existed, and allowed the construction of new instruments.' In addition, 'geographical discoveries—made purely for the sake of gain and, therefore in the last resort, of production—opened up an infinite and hitherto inaccessible amount of material of a meteorological, zoological, botanical and physiological (human) bearing'.[11]

Engels saw that scientific developments themselves changed society and production. Equally he understood that science also developed through its own internal dynamic—through attempts to make theories internally and mutually consistent. His point was to emphasise what was often forgotten: 'hitherto, what has been boasted of is what production owes to science, but science owes infinitely more to production'.[12] As so often in his notes on science, Engels is forced to end with a hope he was never able to fulfil, 'this to be studied further and in detail and to be developed'.[13]

Though the scientific revolution was a huge leap forward, it had a peculiar and one sided nature. 'What especially characterises this period is the elaboration of a peculiar general outlook, the central point of which is the view of the absolute immutability of nature.'[14] At the core of this 'Newtonian' world view was the notion that 'in whatever way nature itself might have come into being, once present it remained as it was as long as it continued to exist.'

The planets and their satellites, once set in motion by the mysterious first impulse, circled on and on in their predestined ellipses for all eternity. [The Earth] *has remained the same without alteration from all eternity, or, alternatively, from the first day of creation. The 'five continents' of the present day had always existed, and they had always had the same mountains, valleys and rivers, the same climate, and the same flora and fauna, except in so far as change or transplantation had taken place at the hand of man. The species of plants or animals had been established once and for all when they came into existence.*[15]

In contrast to the history of mankind, 'which develops in time, there was ascribed to the history of nature only an unfolding in space'.[16] All change, all development in nature, was denied. And as a result 'natural science, so revolutionary at the outset, suddenly found itself confronted by an out and out conservative nature, in which even today everything was as it had been from the beginning and in which—to the end of the world or for all eternity—everything would remain as it had been since the beginning'.[17]

Though science had challenged religion it was 'still deeply enmeshed in theology'.[18] This static world view meant it often could give no answer to important questions. 'How did the innumerable species of plants and animals arise? And how, above all, did man arise, since after all it was certain that he was not present from all eternity?' To such questions 'natural science only too frequently answered by making the creator of all things responsible. Copernicus, at the beginning of the period shows theology the door; Newton closes the period with the postulate of a divine first impulse'.[19]

Scientific developments in the 19th century challenged this static view of nature. These developments were spectacular, almost on a par with those of the years of Galileo and Newton. Too often the impression is given that the basic picture established by Newton underwent little change until the scientific revolution of the early 20th century associated with people like Albert Einstein. Nothing could be further from the truth. Nineteenth century science, growing in the midst of the industrial revolution, transformed our understanding of nature. Above all these developments proved that 'nature also has its history in time',[20] that everything in nature 'does not just exist, but comes into being and passes away'.[21] This insight is the cornerstone of the whole of Engels' approach to natural science.

The first breach in the static view of nature 'was made not by a natural scientist but by a philosopher'.[22] The great 18th century German philosopher Immanuel Kant put forward the hypothesis that the Earth and solar system had evolved from a spinning gaseous cloud. Later the French scientist Pierre Laplace developed the scientific details of Kant's notion. The details of the theory are thought not to be correct today, but it is right in many essential points. What mattered at the time was that, 'if the Earth was something that had come into being, then its present geological, geographical and climatic state, and its plants and animals likewise, must be something that had come into being; it must have had a history'.[23]

This argument soon derived support from another quarter. 'Geology arose and pointed out that not only the terrestrial strata formed one after another and deposited one upon another, but also the shells and skeletons of extinct animals and the trunks, leaves and fruits of no longer existing plants contained in these strata'.[24] The new geology, developed first by Charles Lyell, indicated that 'not only the Earth as a whole but also its present surface and the plants and animals living on it possessed a history in time'.[25]

There remained, however, a contradiction between the new geology, with its view of the changing Earth, and the then assumed constant nature of plants and animals on the Earth. In this context Engels makes the perceptive comment:

> *Tradition is a power not only in the Catholic Church but also in natural science. For years Lyell himself did not see the contradiction, and his pupils still less. This can only be explained by the division of labour that had meanwhile become dominant in natural science, which more or less restricted each person to his special sphere, there being only a few whom it did not rob of a comprehensive view.*[26]

Meanwhile physics too had undergone enormous developments in the 19th century. New sciences, of heat, electricity and magnetism had grown up alongside the already established understanding of the mechanics and dynamics of material bodies. These advances were intimately connected with the industrial revolution then transforming capitalist society. For instance, thermodynamics, the science of processes involving heat, was developed directly out of attempts to understand the principles behind, and improve the efficiency of, steam engines.[27]

At first these advances gave rise to a whole series of separate theories with each phenomenon being explained on the basis of a distinct physical, natural force. But in the mid-19th century a series of scientists forged a revolutionary breakthrough. Meyer in Germany and Joule in England first showed that mechanical motion could be transformed into heat and vice versa. Others then showed that both could be transformed into electricity, magnetism and chemical forces. They 'proved that all so-called physical forces, mechanical forces, heat, light, electricity, magnetism, indeed even so called chemical force, become transformed into one another under definite conditions without any loss of force occurring'.[28]

The point was not just that science had demonstrated the transformations, but also that these transformations were law governed. Underlying them all was the principle dubbed the 'conservation of energy', which remains among the most fundamental principles of science. The total amount of energy remained the same but it could be transferred from one form to another. It was another mighty blow against the static world view. 'With that,' Engels wrote, 'the special physical forces, the as it were immutable "species" of physics, were resolved into variously differentiated forms of the motions of matter, passing into one another according to definite laws.'[29] Later in the 19th century things were taken further when scientists showed that not only could heat and mechanical motion be transformed into one another, but that heat was in fact nothing more than the greater or lesser mechanical motion of the atoms or molecules of which a body was composed.

Chemistry too had undergone 'wonderfully rapid development' and 'attacked the old ideas about nature'. Until the 19th century there seemed to be an unbridgeable gulf between 'organic' chemistry, that of living organisms, and 'inorganic'. Now 'the preparation by inorganic means of compounds that hitherto had been produced only in the living organism proved that the laws of chemistry have the same validity for organic as for inorganic bodies, and to a large extent bridged the gulf between inorganic and organic nature'.[30]

The old world view had come under attack 'in the sphere of biological research also'. Biology had undergone a revolutionary transformation which had shattered for ever many of the old notions. 'The more deeply and exactly this research was carried on, the more did the rigid system of an immutably fixed organic nature crumble away at its touch'.[31] These developments culminated in Darwin's *Origin of Species* in 1859, and its theory of evolution by natural selection which put an end to the idea of fixed unchanging species. It showed that all species, including humans, had evolved from common ancestors. Engels enthusiastically wrote to Marx, 'Darwin, whom I am just reading, is magnificent—there has never been until now so splendid an attempt to prove historical development in nature'.[32]

In every field Engels pointed out how the old ahistorical, unchanging view of nature had been challenged if not shattered by the results of science in the 19th century. In the new outlook 'all rigidity was dissolved, all fixity dissipated, all particularity that had been regarded as eternal became transient'.[33] At the social level Marx and Engels had argued, in *The Communist Manifesto*, that in capitalist society 'all fixed fast-frozen relations...are swept away, all new-formed ones become antiquated before they can ossify. All that is solid melts into air'.[34] In society this was based on capitalism's 'constant revolutionising of production, uninterrupted disturbance of all social conditions'.[35] Now the same process had pushed science to the point where it had undermined the old static view of nature and shown that change, constant transformation, was built into nature.

This view was not entirely new. In fact many of the great philosophers of classical Greece had such a view. After the one sided static world view born of the scientific revolution, modern science had 'once again returned to the mode of outlook of the great founders of Greek philosophy, the view that the whole of nature, from the smallest element to the greatest, from grains of sand to suns, from Protista [very simple organisms] to man, has its existence in eternal coming into being and passing away, in ceaseless flux, in unresting motion and change'.[36] But there was an essential difference. 'What in the case of the Greeks was a brilliant intuition, is in our case the result of strictly scientific research'.[37]

The dialectics of nature

The recognition that nature has a history, that everything in nature is subject to change, comes into being and passes out of existence, is the starting point of Engels' approach. But then it is necessary to understand how such change unfolds.

The first step in all real science is to examine separate phenomena, the 'details' of which 'the picture of appearances' is made up. 'So long as we do not understand these [details], we have not a clear idea of the whole picture'.[38]

A necessary starting point was that 'in order to understand these details we must detach them from their natural or historical connection and examine each one separately, its nature, special causes, effects etc.'[39] Engels emphasises over and again the importance of this breaking up of nature—gathering, examining and seeking to understand facts about separate aspects of nature—as the first step in building up a real understanding:

> The analysis of nature into its individual parts, the grouping of the different natural processes and objects in definite classes...these were the fundamental conditions of the gigantic strides in our knowledge of nature that have been made during the last four hundred years.[40]

The same approach remains the basic method by which most science proceeds, and must proceed, today. Both in Engels' day and today many scientists would argue that this approach is what science is about, and that they have no need of 'philosophy' beyond this. But such an approach, often called empiricism, is not enough to understand the whole picture. It has severe inbuilt limitations.

Engels points to how many scientific 'empiricists' of his day had fallen prey to all sorts of claims by mystics, spiritualists and mediums. 'The shallowest empiricism that spurns all theory and distrusts all thought', Engels insists, 'is the most certain path from natural science to mysticism'.[41]

> *Natural scientists believe that they free themselves from philosophy by ignoring it or abusing it...[but] they cannot make any headway without thought...[and] hence they are no less in bondage to philosophy, but unfortunately in most cases to the worst philosophy.*[42]

The great danger is of 'observing natural objects and processes in isolation, apart from their connection with the vast whole; of observing them in repose not in motion; as constants, not as essentially variables; in their death, not in their life'.[43]

> *Things and their mental reflexes, ideas, are isolated, are to be considered one after the other and apart from each other, are objects of investigation fixed, rigid, given once and for all...a thing either exists or does not exist; a thing cannot at the same time be itself and something else. Positive and negative absolutely exclude one another; cause and effect stand in a rigid antithesis one to the other.*[44]

'At first sight', says Engels, 'this mode of thinking seems to us very luminous because it is that of so called common sense. Only sound common sense, respectable fellow that he is in the homely realm of his own four walls, has very wonderful adventures directly he ventures out into the wide world.'[45] He warns that breaking apart, considering separately aspects of nature, 'justifiable and necessary as it is in a number of domains whose extent varies according to the nature of the particular object of investigation, sooner or later reaches a limit, beyond which it becomes one-sided, restricted, abstract, lost in insoluble contradictions.[46]

Engels gives a series of examples to illustrate the point: 'For everyday purposes we know and can say, eg whether an animal is alive or not. But upon closer inquiry, we find that this is in many cases, a very complex question...it is just as impossible to determine absolutely the moment of death, for physiology proves that death is not an instantaneous momentary phenomenon, but a very protracted process'.[47]

Again even the notion of identity—to talk of this plant, that animal or this person—is frequently misleading.

The plant, the animal, every cell is at every moment of its life identical with itself and yet becoming distinct from itself, by absorption and excretion of substances, by respiration, by cell formation and death of cells, by the process of circulation taking place, in short by a sum of incessant molecular changes which make up life and the sum total of whose results is evident to our eyes in the phases of life—embryonic life, youth, sexual maturity, process of reproduction, old age, death.

The young boy, the mature man and the aged man are the same person, yet they are continually changing and different. 'Abstract identity', Engels says, 'suffices for everyday use where small dimensions or brief periods of time are in question; the limits within which it is usable differ in almost every case and are determined by the nature of the object'.[48]

The point is of more general validity. It is necessary in beginning to detach aspects of nature from the rest, to isolate them from their connections, to focus on their existence, not their coming into being, passing away or transformation. But this can only partially grasp the reality of nature. We construct an understanding based on abstracting from some *facets* of the *totality* of nature. This process of abstraction helps us to look beneath surface appearances and see the essence of what is happening. These insights are then reintegrated into the totality from which they have been extracted, the better to explain the original appearance.

One simple example is Newton's law of gravity. The core notion of this is that all bodies fall at the same rate—they are all accelerated at the same rate by the force of gravity. A consequence of this law is that a feather and a cannonball dropped from a tower will hit the ground at the same time. But we know that in reality a cannonball will hit the ground before a feather. To begin to explain what is really going on is quite difficult. We, like Newton, must abstract from appearances. Put aside the size and shape of the various objects. Put aside the air through which they fall. Imagine—or try to approximately construct—a situation in which we can ignore these factors. Only then can we grasp and formulate the underlying reality of a uniform acceleration due to gravity. And only then can we use that understanding to move back towards and explain the appearances. We can explain the various times at which objects acutally hit the ground by showing how air resistance, the shape of an object and so on produce deviations from what would be expected simply on the basis of the underlying natural law.

Engels argues that a similar process underlies all science. The very notions of 'matter' and 'motion', for instance, are of precisely this character. He attacks those who fail to see these concepts are abstractions from real experience, and ask about what is 'matter as such' or 'motion as such'.[49]

Matter as such and motion as such have not yet been seen or experienced by anyone, but only the various, actually existing material things and forms of motion. Matter is nothing but the totality of material things from which this concept is abstracted, and motion as such nothing but the totality of all sensuously perceptible forms of motion; words like matter and motion are nothing but abbreviations in which we comprehend many different sensuously perceptible things according to their common properties. Hence matter and motion can be known in no other way than by investigation of the separate material things and forms of motion.

Engels gives as an analogy, 'We can eat cherries and plums, but not fruit, because no one has so far eaten fruit as such'.[50]

Abstraction from appearance to understand the underlying essence is always based on focusing on some facets of nature and ignoring others. As a result, any such understanding *always* breaks down, is shown to be only partially correct, beyond certain limits. It fails to fit reality where what has previously been ignored can no longer be left out of the picture. We will see later how, for example, the 250 year old Newtonian law of gravity broke down in exactly this fashion in the early 20th century. Again, the centuries old notion of matter as billiard-ball-like lumps or particles broke down at the same time and in a similar manner.

Engels insists therefore that a fully rounded understanding which seeks to overcome these problems must be based on seeing 'things and their representations, ideas, in their essential connection, concatenation, motion, origin and ending'.[51] He calls for a 'comprehensive view of the interconnections in nature by means of the facts provided by empirical natural science itself'.[52]

Engels called the approach he was arguing for 'dialectical'. (The word derives from the philosophers of ancient Greece and means seeking truth through critical inquiry, disputation and argument.) It is a critique of static, fixed categories usually used in science—categories valid within certain limits, which differ according to the case, but which prove to be inadequate to fully grasp the nature of reality. There was no question for Engels of fitting facts about nature into some preconceived schema. 'In every field of science, in natural as in historical science, one must proceed from the given facts...the interconnections are not to be built into the facts but to be discovered in them, and when discovered to be verified as far as possible by experiment'.[53]

Engels goes on to argue that having understood the details of how particular processes develop in nature a number of key general features can often be seen. He calls these 'laws of the dialectic'. They are not laws in the sense of, say, Newton's law of gravity, but operate at a quite different level of abstraction. They are ways of seeing the underlying pattern of a process of change after having worked out and understood the concrete details of the process concerned.

The first and most important of these is 'the transformation of quantity into quality', which Engels says is 'rather obvious'.[54] Indeed it is, but it is nonetheless important for that. Modern science has shown, Engels argued, 'that in nature, in a manner exactly fixed for each individual case qualitative changes can only occur by the quantitative addition or quantitative substraction of matter and motion (so called energy)'.[55]

He gives a series of examples to illustrate the point. For instance, he takes the example of water (which has often been derided, but is a precise and excellent example). On heating water quantitative change, more or less heat, produces no qualitative change between certain limits. However, at certain critical points—the boiling and freezing points—a similar quantitative change then produces a dramatic qualitative transformation. The water freezes and becomes ice, or boils into steam. This is not just a question of human thought. Water does freeze and boil, did so long before human beings existed and, no doubt, will continue to do so long after we cease to exist.

Engels argues that this pattern—of the transformation of quantitative change into qualitative change at critical points—is a fairly general phenomenon in nature. 'Every metal has its temperature of incandescence and fusion, every liquid its definite freezing and boiling point...every gas has its critical point at which it can be liquified by pressure and cooling'.[56] He gives a whole string of other examples from science—which demonstrate that he was remarkably well informed of many of the very latest advances in natural science. Chemistry, he argued, 'can be termed the science of the qualitative changes of bodies as a result of changed quantitative composition'.[57]

For instance, 'the case of oxygen. If three atoms unite into a molecule instead of the usual two we get ozone, a body which is very considerably different from ordinary oxygen in its odour and reactions'.[58] And Engels points to the discovery of the periodic table of elements by Mendeleyev, in which he showed that certain qualitative properties of elements are periodic functions of their atomic weights, as further demonstration of how in nature quantitative change is at certain points transformed into qualitative leaps.

Engels noted that 'probably the same gentlemen who up to now have decried the transformation of quantity into quality as mysticism and incomprehensible transcendentalism will now declare that it is indeed something quite self-evident, trivial and commonplace, which they have long employed, and so they have been taught nothing new.' Well, Engels replied, 'if these gentlemen have for years caused quantity and quality to be transformed into each other, without knowing what they did, then they will have to console themselves with Molière's Monsieur Jourdain who has spoken prose all his life without having the slightest inkling of it'.[59]

Engels goes on to argue that change in nature is also often characterised by 'the interpenetration of opposites'[60] or the 'motion through opposites which asserts itself everywhere in nature'[61] or development through 'contradictions'. And he argues that a further characteristic typical of processes of change is 'the negation of the negation'—development through a new synthesis emerging which surpasses and transforms the elements of the 'contradiction'. To see changes in the way Engels describes is for him not a substitute for understanding the 'particular process' itself.[62]

Engels gives a series of examples to illustrate the kind of processes he means. In *Anti-Dühring*, a polemical work, some of these examples are fairly trite and some are circular processes which do not really demonstrate the qualitative development that Engels claims to be illustrating. But scattered among the notes in *The Dialectics of Nature* a picture of what he is grappling with can be found. For instance, Engels discusses the question of living organisms, what following the best scientific understanding of his day he calls 'albuminous bodies' (today we would talk of bodies based on DNA, RNA and protein molecules). A condition of existence of any living organism is that it 'absorbs other appropriate substances from its environment and assimilates them':

> Non-living bodies also change, disintegrate and enter into combinations in the natural course of events, but in doing this they cease to be what they were. A weather worn rock is no longer a rock, a metal which oxidises turns into rust. But what with non-living bodies is the cause of destruction, with albumen is the fundamental condition of existence...this uninterrupted metamorphosis [which] essentially consists in the constant self-renewal of the chemical constituents of these bodies.
>
> Life therefore consists primarily in the fact that every moment it is itself and at the same time something else; and this does not take place as the result of a process to which it is subjected from without...on the contrary...[it] is a self-implementing process which is inherent in, native to, its bearer.[63]

The first point is about how things maintain their unity, their identity, in the face of external impulses, effects and pressures to change. These pressures 'negate' the object (quite literally in the example of rust Engels mentions). But some material objects have the capacity to react quite differently to such pressures—in so far as such an object absorbs these pressures, and in the process may change itself while preserving itself, it 'negates the negation'. Indeed, in the second paragraph quoted above, Engels hints at the possibility of self, or internally generated, change— that is, a self contained totality which evolves under the impact of its own internal 'contradictions' (though the particular example he uses does not quite fit). Engels himself never fully developed these ideas, but he is trying to grasp the essence of a pattern, or possibility, of a process of change exhibited by some aspects of the natural world. It is not a formula nor is it a substitute for an investigation and explanation of 'the particular nature of each individual case'.[64]

Engels has sometimes been attacked because some of the science he quotes has since been shown to be wrong. For instance, Engels did believe in the ether, a supposed medium filling all space through which light waves propagated. He was also inclined to accept, for example, the doctrine in evolution known as Lamarckism, the notion that, in addition to natural selection, evolution may also be based on the inheritance of acquired characteristics. We should remember, however, that in the first case *all* scientists of Engels' day supported the notion of the ether, and in the second case most biologists of Engels' day, including Darwin, agreed with him on the possible inheritance of acquired characteristics. Both these views have since been shown to be wrong. But it is unfair to attack Engels for sharing views supported by the best scientists of his day. We should also remember that Engels' writings on science are preliminary thoughts, often rough notes, rather than a fully worked out view. He ends *The Dialectics of Nature* with, 'All this has to be thoroughly revised'.[65]

Engels insisted, however, that his general approach was backed up by the findings of modern science. 'Nature is the proof of dialectics, and it must be said for modern science that it has furnished the proof with very rich materials, increasing daily'.[66] How does this claim stand up against the developments in science in the 100 years since Engels' death?

Science after Engels

In the century since Engels' death almost every area of science has been radically transformed by new breakthroughs in our understanding of nature.

Geology, for instance, has been revolutionised by the theory of plate tectonics, or 'continental drift'. Instead of seeing the land masses on the Earth's surface as permanent features we have a scientific understanding of the way they have developed, changed and moved during the Earth's history. Nor is this a finished process: the continents continue to move today. New land is continually being created and existing continental material destroyed. The new understanding means we can begin to explain the development and change of natural phenomena from mountain ranges to oceans and earthquakes in a way that was impossible before. The understanding of plate tectonics also casts new light on biological evolution.

For a long time many geologists resisted the theory of plate tectonics, despite the growing evidence in its favour. It has only been fully accepted in the last 30 years or so. These scientists would perhaps have been less resistant to the new understanding if they had been accustomed to think in the spirit of Engels' argument that all of nature changes, that what appears to be static and fixed usually turns out to be otherwise. Of course Engels knew nothing of plate tectonics, but his general attitude did lead him to warn against the idea that 'the five continents of the present day had always existed'.[67]

Biology has undergone an even more revolutionary transformation since Engels' death. First Mendelian genetics, then in more recent decades molecular biology—and a host of other advances—have transformed our understanding of living organisms. But, as so often with powerful new breakthroughs, the very success has bred a distorted one sided view among many biologists. In biology this is often linked to political and ideological questions—as arguments about human biology easily lead to arguments about human nature and society.

The fashionable approach, at least among molecular biologists, is best termed a 'reductionist determinism'. In this view everything about, say, human biology and behaviour is a mechanically and directly determined consequence of our genes—strings of DNA molecules inside every cell in our bodies. At its most extreme this leads to claims that there are genes for aggression, homosexuality, criminality, homelessness and the like. It leads to sociobiology, in which human behaviour and social development are viewed as a direct consequence of our genes—so war, sexism, racism and so on are seen as a product of our biological evolution. And it leads to a view of human beings as robot like receptacles manipulated by 'the selfish gene'. Without going this far many biologists argue as though genes are all that really matter, all we need to know to understand our biology and even our behaviour.

Most of this is a mixture of poor science, ideology, and fanciful 'just-so' stories about evolution. Some of those pushing such arguments are motivated by reactionary politics. Others are influenced, often unconsciously, by the money available for research in these areas—molecular biology and genetics are big business today. Some are simply carried away with the real success of molecular biology and genetics in advancing our understanding into generalising from this to a mistaken overall view, in much the same way as Engels argued happened to many scientists after the 16th and 17th century scientific revolution.

Fortunately, there are a growing number of eminent biologists who forcefully challenge this approach. Two of the most well known who have written popular works expounding their view are Richard Lewontin in the US and Steven Rose in Britain. They argue that a proper understanding of biology, and of the huge advances of recent decades, demands a totally different approach, what they themselves call a 'dialectical biology'. Moreover, these scientists frankly acknowledge that their general approach is inspired by Engels, as can be seen from the work contained in such books as *Not in Our Genes*, *The Making of Memory*, *The Doctrine of DNA* and *The Dialectical Biologist*[68]—none of which demand a formal or technical training in biology.

There are two reasons for dealing in greater detail with the advances in physics since Engels' death. Firstly, the revolution in physics of the last 100 years has been the most spectacular in any science. It has radically transformed the most basic notions which underpinned all previous science. Secondly, while in biology there are at least some eminent working scientists, even if they are a minority, who argue for a dialectical approach, this is not the case in physics.

The difference can be illustrated from a glance at the 1993 shortlist for the prestigious annual Rhone-Poulenc science book prize. The eventual winner was *The Making of Memory* by Steven Rose. This is a beautifully written account of how science works by someone who has made major contributions to it. It is also a sharp critique of reductionist and determinist biology and an unashamed defence of what the author has called 'a dialectical biology'.

Steven Rose's book was in fact a surprise winner of the award. The pre-award favourite was instead *The Mind of God*, a book on modern physics by the eminent theoretical physicist Paul Davies. In it he claims the lesson of physics today is that, 'We have to embrace a different concept of understanding from that of rational explanation. Possibly the mystical path is a way to such an understanding'.[69]

Davies's previous work was also a popular best seller on modern physics written with John Gribbin, a respected scientist, an astrophysicist by training and physics consultant for the reputable *New Scientist* magazine. The title of their book indicates their key argument. It is called *The Matter Myth*. Their central thesis is that 'materialism is dead... During this century physics has blown apart the central tenets of materialist doctrine in a sequence of stunning developments'.[70] They go on to indicate what these developments are: 'first came the theory of relativity...then came the quantum theory...another development goes further, the theory of chaos'.[71]

If these authors, and they are fairly typical of much that passes for serious thinking about modern physics, are right it is a serious matter. It is therefore worth looking at the argument in some detail. In fact, far from undermining materialism the very advances cited by these and similar authors are in fact huge advances in a materialist understanding of nature. Moreover, they are also a marvellous confirmation of the general arguments put forward by Engels, weighty evidence for the necessity of a dialectical approach to understanding the natural world.

The first two of the scientific advances cited, relativity and quantum theory, were part of the revolution which transformed science in the first few decades of this century, most famously associated with the work of Albert Einstein.

This revolution arose from a profound crisis in science. By the time of Engels' death there were a series of glaring contradictions between different branches of physics. Theories which successfully explained different physical phenomena contradicted each other in fundamental ways. It was out of the attempt to resolve these contradictions that the new scientific revolution was born. A new, deeper understanding was built which went beyond the previous contradictory elements, and at the same time showed why these had worked within certain limits. This process is a fairly typical one in the history of science. In the historical development of scientific ideas Engels' arguments about how change takes place are well grounded.

Relativity theory was developed by Einstein between 1905 and 1915. The first step, known as 'special relativity', was born of a contradiction between theories of motion, dynamics, on the one hand, and theories of electromagnetism—phenomena such as radio and light waves as well as electric and magnetic forces—on the other. In dynamics, Newton's laws of motion had stood the test of over two centuries. Then in the 1860s James Clerk Maxwell had put the understanding of electromagnetism on a similar footing by describing all electromagnetic phenomena in terms of a series of simple and beautiful laws. Maxwell's equations were a huge breakthrough, they enabled the prediction of radio waves and led to a host of other developments, and they remain today a key element of modern science.

The problem, though, was that there was a contradiction between Newton's laws and Maxwell's. The crux of the matter is that Newton's laws appeared to remain the same for any two observers moving at constant velocity relative to each other while Maxwell's didn't. This led to all sorts of contradictions. For example, it meant two different physical explanations of the electrical dynamo and motor—one converting electricity to motion, the other the reverse—processes which appeared in fact to be connected. Einstein solved the problems by going beyond both existing theories.

The cornerstones of relativity are two principles about nature first put forward by Einstein in 1905. The first—in view of the contradiction between Newton and Maxwell—was to insist that the laws of physics must be the same for any observer no matter what their velocity. The second principle is that the velocity of light is constant, the maximum velocity possible in nature, *and* that its velocity is independent of the motion of the source of that light.

It is the last part of this that seems outrageous. Imagine measuring the speed of a ball thrown to you and finding it to be the same whether the ball is thrown by a motionless friend standing nearby or from another friend speeding by in a supersonic aircraft. Since the speed of such balls would not be the same why should it be for light? But when looking at nature we should always bear in mind Engels' warning about the dangers of 'sound common sense'. For in fact it does turn out that if you measure the speed of light it is always the same, no matter how fast you yourself or the source of the light may be moving. This is now a well established fact of nature.

A series of consequences follow from Einstein's arguments which seem to challenge commonsense notions of time and space. These new notions have since been tested and confirmed in countless experiments. The old notions are themselves abstractions, generalisations, from how the world behaves when things are moving at low speeds relative to ourselves. Einstein showed that those notions break down and do not fit the way real material objects behave at speeds which begin to approach the speed of light. This is why Maxwell's electromagnetic theory, which deals with light waves, did not sit happily with Newton's laws. A crucial element in the new understanding is that what appear to be simultaneous events to one observer may not appear to be so for another observer moving relative to the first. Another consequence is that moving clocks run slow. An accurate clock flown round the world on a jet will show a different time on return to an exactly similar clock left at home. For most phenomena we have direct experience of, the effect is tiny, but it becomes large and important as speeds approach that of light.

Einstein's theory was a key step in the defeat of the notion implicit in Newtonian physics of an absolute space and time, and absolute motion. It was a vindication of the idea that all motion was relative. Also, until Einstein, physics had seen matter, mass, as something dead and inert which had to have energy imparted to it. To be sure, energy could be transformed from one form to another but mass itself was something quite distinct. Now Einstein's relativity, with its famous equation $E = mc^2$, showed that mass could be transformed into energy and vice versa.

Einstein later extended his theory to provide a new explanation of gravity, which had not been incorporated into his earlier theory of 'special relativity'. 'General relativity' starts from a simple fact. In Newton's theory mass appears, but there are two different masses—what are known as the gravitational and inertial masses. One is the mass which is the source of the force of gravity, the other is the measure of a body's resistance to change of motion. In fact the two, though in Newtonian physics quite distinct aspects of matter, are always found to be the same. Weightlessness in a falling lift is one example. Einstein's theory is an attempt to explain facts like this. It attempts to incorporate gravity into the new relativistic dynamics.

General relativity is not, as often presented, simply an exotic tool for speculation about the universe—though it can help in that too. Something as straightforward as the orbit of the planet Mercury around the sun was never fully explained by Newton's laws—despite the best efforts of generations of brilliant physicists, astronomers and mathematicians. General relativity now makes it possible to explain it. Again the theory was spectacularly confirmed in 1919 when its novel prediction that light from stars should bend when it passed close to the sun was shown to be correct.

There certainly are difficult mathematics in general relativity's description of matter and space. For instance, it insists that the geometry of space containing matter is not Euclidean—the kind we are taught at school—but rather what is called 'curved'. A way to try and picture the difference is to compare the kind of geometry possible on the surface of a balloon to that on a flat surface. On the flat surface the three angles of a triangle always add up to 180 degrees. On a balloon this is not true. On a flat surface a line never joins itself no matter how far extended, on a balloon this is again not true. In general relativity, however, the 'curved' geometry is in the three dimensions of space (or, strictly speaking, the four dimensions of space-time) not just on a two dimensional surface, whether flat or balloon like. Despite the difficulties however, the final form of the theory is the most beautiful and elegant in modern physics. And the key notion in the theory is not so difficult. It is simply that the old notion of matter which exists in a passive, unaffected background of space will not do. Rather matter and the space it exists in are connected and influence each other in fundamental ways. The geometry of space and the distribution of matter mutually determine each other.

Neither special nor general relativity are in any way a challenge to materialism. By the turn of the century existing scientific theories simply could not explain a growing number of observed facts of nature and, moreover, the theories that explained different facets of nature contradicted each other. The new theories resolved those contradictions, explained the unexplained, and showed both why the old theories had worked within limits and why they broke down beyond those limits.

Engels certainly had no inkling of relativity theory, or that the 200 year old Newtonian laws of motion and gravity were to be overturned within years of his death. But the development of relativity and its core notions illustrate many of Engels' key arguments. He had insisted that all motion was relative. 'Motion of a single body does not exist, it can be spoken of only in a relative sense'.[72] More importantly, the whole thrust of relativity theory is a precise illustration of Engels' argument that abstractions which fit aspects of nature within certain limits then break down when pushed beyond those limits, and thus require a new understanding. Again the new understanding that matter was not something separate from motion and energy but that each was capable of being transformed into one another in a definite law governed manner is exactly the kind of process Engels pointed to as a unity of opposites, a characteristic revelation of a deeper understanding of nature. Someone who had argued that the science of his day pointed to the fact that motion and transformation were 'the mode of existence, the inherent attribute, of matter' would have been less surprised than many by relativity theory.

Finally, the key notion in general relativity, that space and matter were not mutually opposed aspects of nature, with matter existing against a passive backcloth of space, but that the two were intimately connected and mutually determining, is, again, about as sharp an example as you could find of the interpenetration of opposites, the kind of 'dialectical' understanding Engels argued for and which he insisted scientific advances increasingly demanded.

The second revolution in the early part of the century came with quantum theory. This too came out of glaring contradictions between existing theories and observed facts—especially in the behaviour of small objects like atoms.

Atoms, for instance, simply should not exist on the basis of the old understanding. If Newton and Maxwell were right—even when reconciled by relativity—then every atom should collapse in a burst of radiation in a very short time. This, fairly obviously, is not true. It was out of such problems—and a host of others ranging from the behaviour of metals when ultraviolet light was shone on them to how bodies absorbed and emitted radiation—that quantum mechanics developed.

At first this was done on a fairly ad hoc basis—simply adding in bits to old theories even if these bits flatly contradicted other parts of the theory. But in the 1920s and 1930s a radically new theory was developed. Three aspects of this 'quantum mechanics' are important. Firstly it argues all objects can behave as both waves, like radio waves, and bullet-like particles. So light, usually thought of as a radio-like wave, can behave as a particle, while an electron, a particle, can also behave like a wave. What had previously, and still now to common sense, seemed two mutually exclusive and opposed notions were revealed to be intimately connected, to be two sides of the same coin.

Secondly, quantum mechanics also says there is an intrinsic uncertainty in nature. For instance, an electron can have a well defined and precise position or velocity, but not both at the same time. Thirdly, the theory says some phenomena in nature are inherently probabilistic, governed by chance. So it is impossible to predict in advance, say, which of the various possible energies an electron around an atom will be in or exactly when a radioactive particle will emit radiation.

It suggests this randomness is not the same as that, for example, of rolling a die or tossing a coin, but fundamental. In coin tossing the randomness is a result of our ignorance. If we measured the initial motion of the coin as it left our hands then we could predict which way it would land. The randomness in quantum mechanics is not of this kind, not simply a result of our ignorance. Rather it suggests that, for example, it is not possible even in principle to predict exactly which energy is possessed by an electron around an atom. Instead it suggests that all we can do is predict the probability of it having each of the range of possible energies.

One point should be emphasised. Quantum theory does *not* throw determinism out of the window and leave us with a picture of a world completely governed by chance, random events. It is rather a picture of a world of subtle interplay between chance and necessity. Quantum theory deals with predicting the probability of events, such as an electron around an atom having a particular energy, and how those probabilities evolve in time in a strictly deterministic fashion. Quantum theory deals mostly with very small atomic scales and, as it has to, agrees with older theories on how large, macroscopic, objects behave. Moreover it seeks to explain how uncertainty at the small scale results in the quite predictable and deterministic behaviour characteristic of the larger, macroscopic, scale of which we have direct experience.

Many features of quantum theory seem bizarre and run counter to many common sense assumptions. Yet it makes sense of real facts about nature which on the old understanding could not be explained. It has been spectacularly confirmed in countless experiments. Your TV or pocket calculator wouldn't work if its predictions weren't accurate. It is a step forward in a materialist understanding of the world, not a retreat.

Nevertheless there *are* severe problems in interpreting quantum theory, despite its predictive success. Quantum theory describes matter in terms of something known as a 'wave function'—which sums up the fact that all matter has both wave-like and particle-like attributes. There is deep and unresolved controversy among scientists about what this 'wave function' means. Most scientists think of it as a kind of description of all the possible states open to the matter under consideration at any time and a measure of the relative probability of that matter, say an electron around an atom, being in any of those states. When the matter under consideration interacts with something else, most obviously when it is measured, it is found to be in one definite state. This is called the 'collapse of the wave function'. There is again huge and unresolved controversy among scientists about this process. No one knows the answers.

Many physicists simply get on with using the theory, which has been among the most successful in the history of science. They push the problems to one side. The long time 'orthodox' interpretation of quantum mechanics, usually called the Copenhagen interpretation, is little more than a gentlemen's agreement not to ask awkward questions.

A lot of good things have been written on the problems thrown up by both quantum mechanics and its relation to our understanding of other aspects of nature. As yet, though, they remain unresolved questions. Those who think science is a closed world free of contradiction and with definite answers to all questions are very mistaken.[73]

It is also true that quite a lot of nonsense has been written by quite reputable and otherwise quite sane scientists. Some, for instance, argue that a conscious observer is necessary for the collapse of the wave function. Seeing as the world—and the collapsing wave functions—certainly existed long before human beings, this is simply another way of describing god. Another notion that is quite fashionable is what is sometimes called the 'many worlds' interpretation of quantum mechanics. This argues that every 'measurement' results in the universe splitting into parallel worlds all of which really exist.[74] It avoids the real problems associated with the 'collapse of a wave function' by saying it doesn't really happen, but instead all the possibilities summed up in the wave function really turn out to be true, each in one of a myriad of parallel universes. This may be the stuff of interesting science fiction, but as serious science it leaves a lot to be desired.

Amid all the unresolved problems we should remember that the contradictions and problems with the newer theories are not essentially worse than those with older theories—it is just that we are used to ignoring the earlier problems. For instance, in Newton's theory of gravity, force is supposed to act instantaneously at any distance. A little thought will reveal that this really is a bizarre notion, which didn't stop people using the theory for hundreds of years and continuing to use it within certain limits today. The great 19th century scientist Michael Faraday was one of the few who, long before Einstein, pointed out the difficulty of the 'spooky action at a distance' at the heart of Newton's theory.

Whatever the correct interpretation of quantum mechanics turns out to be, there is no doubting that it is not a challenge to materialism, but a step forward in a materalist understanding. Once again the problems it gives rise to should be set against the fact that the old theories simply could not explain elementary facts about nature while quantum mechanics does, and in addition has led to enormous advances across a whole range of science and technology.

However, given the deep and unresolved problems within it, quantum theory is unlikely to be the last word on how matter behaves at a sub-atomic level. At some point a new understanding will be developed which will resolve some of the problems. No doubt, it will in turn throw up fresh contradictions and problems. John Bell, a leading figure in quantum theory, said:

> *The new way of seeing things will involve an imaginative leap that will astonish us. In any case, it seems that the quantum mechanical description will be superseded. In this it is like all theories.*

And he concluded in a phrase that echoes Engels' whole approach to science: 'To an unusual extent its [quantum mechanics'] fate is apparent in its internal structure. It carries in itself the seeds of its own destruction'.[75]

Engels would have been as shocked and suprised as anyone at the picture of the sub-atomic world thrown up by the development of quantum mechanics. But many of quantum theory's key notions illustrate Engels' arguments about nature. It shows how chance and necessity are not mutually exclusive opposed notions, how in fact chance at one level of nature can give rise to deterministic behaviour at another level. It shows that old notions, of wave-like behaviour and particle-like behaviour, which fit most aspects of nature of which we have direct experience, break down when pushed past certain limits and instead require a new understanding to be developed.

The leading British scientist John Haldane (typically, though, a biologist!) writing in 1940, after discussing Engels and the various points on which he was wrong, commented, 'When all such criticisms have been made, it is astonishing how Engels anticipated the progress of science in the 60 years which have elapsed since he wrote... Had Engels' methods of thinking been more familiar, the transformation of our ideas on physics which have occurred during the last 30 years would have been smoother'.[76] Quantum theory and relativity, though now well established and accepted, were controversial for many years after they were born. Looking back at the controversy after reading Engels, Haldane concluded, 'Had these books been known to my contemporaries, it was clear that we should have found it easier to accept relativity and quantum theory'.[77]

In the decades since the development of quantum theory our understanding of the basic structure of matter has been further revolutionised. Whereas 60 years ago it was thought all matter was made up of protons, neutrons and electrons which were acted upon by eletromagnetic and other forces, now a much richer picture has been uncovered. Protons and neutrons have been shown to be complex systems made up of more 'elementary' objects called quarks. New forces have been discovered and explained, such as the 'colour' force (which, in fact, has nothing do with colour) thought to be responsible for the interaction between quarks. Every few years some scientists think they have found the 'ultimate building blocks' of matter or a 'theory of everything'. But it has always turned out that, once probed beyond certain limits, the ultimate turns out to nothing of the kind, and that matter and its behaviour are an inexhaustible fount of surprises.

Even the notion of the vacuum, empty space, has now been shown to be mistaken on closer investigation. Rather the vacuum seems to be a bubbling sea in which particles, packets of matter and energy, continually froth in and out of existence. This is not just speculation. This process plays a key role, for example, in the spontaneous emission of light by some atoms. The general picture emerging from modern physics is that change, continual process, interaction and transformation are a fundamental property of matter, and of the space which can no longer be seen as separate from it.

The most striking thing about the picture of matter in physics today is how well it sits with Engels' arguments about all of nature having a history, how seemingly separate facets of nature are connected, and how the essence of matter is precisely its continual transformation and change.

For instance, it is now thought that *all* the known forces and particles of nature are connected (all forces are now thought to be carried by particles of matter, or energy—the two are equivalent). The emerging view is that all the fundamental forces of nature are in fact different aspects of a single unified force. Moreover, in this new understanding nature has a history in a sense far more fundamental than even Engels thought possible, though very much in the spirit of his arguments.

It seems that at the very high energies typical early in the history of the universe all the forces were unified. As the universe has expanded and cooled, and so the typical energies of processes have fallen, this symmetry, this unity, has repeatedly been broken until today, at the energies we can now usually have access to, the various forces and their associated particles appear as separate and distinct.

Moreover, all the known 'particles' and 'forces' of matter are simply different and transient manifestations of the same underlying essence (which most scientists would today call energy). They are all capable of being transformed into another. So, for instance, a proton and an antiproton (two particles which are identical except the 'anti' particle has the opposite electrical charge) mutually annihilate each other if they meet. The released energy, or more accurately transformed matter, can then go through further transformations and so give rise to a host of other different 'particles' of matter.

Again the generally accepted explantion for the development of the universe—known as the 'standard cosmological model' or more popularly the 'big bang'—is one in which matter has undergone repeated qualitative transformations when quantitative change has reached critical points. That development has proceeded through a dynamic internal to matter. Differentiated facets of the totality of matter, which has an underlying unity, have been progressively transformed as they mutually interact. We have an evolution from quarks, to protons and neutrons, to neutral atoms, to gas clouds, stars and galaxies, the formation of heavier elements like carbon, the formation of planets and through a series of further transformations to the emergence of organic life and conscious human beings.[78]

At each stage qualitatively novel behaviour of matter emerges. So quarks having existed freely were, when the temperature of the universe fell below a critical point, permanently confined inside particles like protons and a qualitatively new kind of physics emerges (at the energies existing in the universe today free quarks cannot exist). Later, below another critical point, protons and neutrons could capture electrons and the whole possibility of the rich new arena of atomic and molecular processes emerges for the first time. It needed the first such molecules to be further transformed in the very special conditions of stellar interiors, and then those stars themselves to explode in cataclysmic events called supernovae, before the elements crucial to the formation of planets like Earth were even possible. And a further long series of transformations of matter have, billions of years later, resulted in the qualitatively new phenomena of human beings, consciousness and society.

Even a cursory acquaintance with what 20th century physics has uncovered about nature and its various aspects and historical development shows that Engels' general approach is more relevant than ever.

The final development cited as challenging materialism is chaos theory. This has only fully developed in the last 30 years. Many of the problems and issues it deals with were raised by scientists long ago, above all Henri Poincaré at the turn of the century. But the investigation of the problems only became possible with the development of the modern fast computer.

Chaos theory basically says that some physical systems, though governed by laws which predict exactly what something will do, can nevertheless behave unpredictably. The weather is the example most often cited, usually in the picturesque example of the 'butterfly effect'—in which it is said the flapping of a butterfly's wings on one side of the world can ultimately result in changes which accumulate in such a way as to lead to a hurricane on the opposite side of the globe.[79] In fact very simple physical systems also behave in this 'chaotic' way. Three bodies orbiting each other under the influence of gravity, or a simple pendulum swinging over a magnet are two examples. Such physical systems are unpredictable in that their evolution is so sensitive to tiny changes in the initial conditions from which that evolution starts that the only way to see what happens is to wait and see.

This theory has been seized on to argue that any attempt to explain the world, to consciously act to change it in a certain way, is doomed to failure. All we are left with is unpredictability and chaos. Attempts at social or economic planning won't work, the chaos of the market is all that's possible, runs the argument. This is to miss the whole point of the theory. It deals mainly with phenomena which previously were not understood at all. Now where ignorance reigned something can be explained, even if some old notions have to be rethought to do so. In fact chaos theory shows there is a pattern, a structure—albeit often a very complicated one—underlying many phenomena previously not understood at all. The dynamics of heart attacks, or fluid turbulence, to take just two examples, have never been really understood. Now chaos theory has provided the first steps of an explanation.[80]

Chaos is a property of what mathematicians call non-linear systems. Until the last few decades almost all physics for the last 300 years dealt with what mathematicians call linear systems. Linear systems are much easier to deal with mathematically. The basic difference is that in a linear system the whole is equal to the sum of the parts, while in a non-linear system the whole is not simply the sum of the parts—an idea that has been fundamental to a dialectical understanding at least since Hegel.

Great strides forward can be and have been made by studying those parts of nature which can be approximately taken as linear. But all real physical situations are non-linear. Sometimes the non-linear effects can be ignored, but very often they cannot. Because non-linear mathematics is far more difficult to deal with than linear, most science shied away from non-linear problems until the advent of fast computers and chaos theory.

Two key aspects of chaos theory are interesting. Firstly, it shows that at various points small quantitative changes produce large qualitative changes in behaviour. Chaos theory is saying, and explaining why, this—as Engels argued—is a fairly universal feature of the natural world.

Secondly chaos theory shows that in the natural world determinism and unpredictability, seemingly two opposed and mutually exclusive notions, are in fact intimately linked. A process can in a very real and important sense be both at the same time.[81] In quantum theory unpredictability at one level can give rise to deterministic behaviour at another level of nature. Chaos theory shows the opposite is also true. A system can be governed by strictly deterministic laws yet give rise to unpredictable behaviour.

Again this is not a result of ignorance. When specifying the initial conditions of any system there is always a margin of error, summed up in the notion of something being 'correct to within one part in, say, 100 million'. In a 'chaotic' system, no matter how small this margin of error is, it can be shown that a difference still smaller than this will lead to wildly and unpredictably different outcomes in the future evolution of the system. If you say, well, let's make the specification of initial conditions more precise to overcome this divergence the same phenomenon can then be shown for a still smaller difference in initial conditions and so on (this whole notion can be made mathematically precise).

Chaos theory is one of the components which have provided the basis for more recent new developments which are some of the most exciting in science for many years. These have been dubbed 'the science of complexity'.

These developments also draw on new developments in thermodynamics, the science of processes involving heat. Thermodynamics has long sat uneasily alongside other areas of physics. It originated in the work of scientists like Sadi Carnot in the early years of the 19th century and grew directly out of attempts to understand what were the scientific principles underlying the steam engines that were playing a key role in the industrial revolution. Thermodynamics soon began to pose problems as it seemed quite different to the understanding developed in most of the rest of physics. For instance, whereas, say, Newtonian science was deterministic, the laws of thermodynamics were probabilistic.

Secondly, Newtonian science was strictly time reversible. This means that there is nothing in, say, Newton's laws of motion to distinguish changes running forwards or backwards in time. Put crudely a movie of a strictly Newtonian world would not look wrong if it were run backwards. The obvious problem is of course that most real processes in the world are not reversible—try unbreaking an egg or unstirring the milk from your coffee. Thermodynamics deals with such irreversible changes, heat flows from hot to cold, never the other way around. Time, and development in a definite direction in time, plays a key role in thermodynamics, in a way that is not true of most of the rest of the laws of physics.

In short, thermodynamics was not easily reconciled with the laws thought to govern the particles or molecules of which something was composed. This was not helped much even with the scientific revolution of relativity and quantum mechanics—both are still time reversible in the sense described above. In addition most thermodynamic theory was developed around understanding processes involving heat which were near a stable equilibrium—mainly because this was mathematically easier.[82]

In recent years however scientists like the Belgian Nobel Prize winner Ilya Prigogine have started to study thermodynamics when processes are far from equilibrium—which is much more typical of the real world. Other scientists have built on this kind of work and elements of chaos theory to try and look at the connections between different aspects of nature, and in particular to seek to understand the dynamics, the processes of change, which underlie complex physical systems in general, to try and understand the common patterns. It is an attempt, though most of the scientists involved would not use such language, to develop a 'dialectics of nature'.

One of the key notions these scientists have developed is that of emergent properties in complex systems. They point to, and seek to explain, how matter itself at certain levels of complexity develops new behaviour which grows out of the underlying laws, but cannot be simply reduced to these underlying laws. It requires an understanding on that new level.

A picture of nature is beginning to emerge in which at certain points physical systems not only can undergo a transition from regular ordered behaviour to chaotic unpredictable behaviour, but of how matter, once it reaches a certain level of complexity of organisation, can spontaneously generate new higher forms of ordered behaviour. It is a picture of potential development in nature whose essence is exactly that which Engels was grappling with in his discussion of the 'negation of the negation'. Some physical systems can be pushed from a stable ordered state into a chaotic state by some pressure, change or impulse (it is 'negated'). But under certain conditions some of these systems can then develop in such a way as to give rise to new higher forms of ordered behaviour, often with novel properties (the 'negation is negated').

This kind of pattern seems to be typical of many complex systems in nature and scientists are now beginning to seek to understand it. There is some evidence, though it is not established, that complex organisations of matter with genuinely novel and 'creative' properties are those 'on the edge of chaos', systems balanced in a dynamic tension between the tendency towards a dead, stable, repetitive order on the one hand and an unpredictable, disordered, chaotic state on the other.[83]

Where these developments will lead no one yet knows, though one can be certain there will be as much abuse of them as there has been of almost every new scientific development from Darwin to chaos theory. Phil Anderson, who won a Nobel Prize for his work on what is called condensed matter physics, is one of those involved in developing some of this work. He points to the potential of the new science which is beginning to show how 'at each level of complexity entirely new properties appear. And at each stage entirely new laws, concepts and generalisations are necessary. Psychology is not applied biology, nor is biology, chemistry'.[84]

Anderson gives a simple but illustrative example of the point from everyday experience—water. A water molecule is not very complicated: one big oxygen atom with two smaller hydrogen atoms stuck to it. Its behaviour is governed by well understood laws and precise equations of atomic physics. But if a few billion of these molecules are put together they collectively acquire a new property that none of them possesses alone, liquidity. Nothing in the underlying laws governing the behaviour of the individual atoms tells you about this new property. The liquidity is 'emergent'. In turn, argues Anderson, this 'emergent property' produces 'emergent behaviour'. The liquidity can, through cooling, suddenly be transformed into the solid, crystalline structure of ice. Again this behaviour simply has no meaning for an individual water molecule alone.

Further simple examples, by way of illustration, occur with the onset of convection when heating a fluid such as water. At first the heat rises through the fluid by conduction. At a certain critical point, however, and under certain conditions, an abrupt qualitative change in behaviour occurs. Suddenly millions of molecules switch into large scale—by molecular standards—coherent motion in hexagonal convection cells, known as Bénard cells. Again certain chemical reactions exhibit this kind of spontaneous emergence of structure or order. In these 'chemical clocks' millions of molecules undergo rhythmic and structured transformations on a vast scale—again relative to the molecular scale at which the underlying reactions take place. These are examples of what is possible in relatively simple physical systems. The possibilities in more complex systems are correspondingly richer.

The kind of understanding Anderson and similar scientists are beginning to develop is exactly what Engels meant by a dialectical understanding of the change of quantity into quality. It is an understanding which shows how matter itself, through interactions among different facets of the same totality (all have evolved historically from the *seemingly* undifferentiated and homogenous early universe), is qualitatively transformed and develops through history.

It remains true that modern science continues to throw up as many questions as it answers, but just because new questions are posed should not lead us to ignore the many and important answers found over the last century. No doubt some of the various hypotheses put forward today to explain aspects of nature will, as Engels put it 'be weeded out by experience'. Some severe weeding will surely be necessary since, as always in the history of science, theories which explain various parts of nature are riddled with problems and are often mutually incompatible. Quantum mechanics and general relativity, for instance, seem to be incompatible at a fundamental level. Again non-linear processes are increasingly seen as vital in an understanding of nature, but while general relativity and chaos theory are radically non-linear, quantum theory is not. All three are time reversible, in the sense explained earlier, yet the new thermodynamics, not to mention the real world, points to the fundamental importance of irreversible processes in nature.[85]

Which aspects of existing and any new theories are correct, which only of limited value, and which figments of the imagination will become clear when we find a way to tease the answers out of the only ultimate arbiter—matter, in all its many aspects and changes. Lenin, the leader of the 1917 Russian Revolution, in commenting on the scientific revolution of his day put the argument well:

> *Our knowledge is penetrating deeper, properties of matter are disappearing which formerly seemed absolute, and which are now revealed to be relative and characteristic only of certain states of matter. The sole property of matter with whose recognition philosophical materialism is bound up is the property of being an objective reality, of existing outside our mind.*[86]

I have already pointed to the way some leading biologists consciously draw on the tradition founded by Engels. Today some physicists and scientists in other fields are also beginning to recognise the connection between the way they are pushed to think and the approach advocated by Engels. Ilya Prigogine, who has played a key role in the new thermodynamics, for instance says, 'To a certain extent there is an analogy' between the problems he is grappling with and 'dialectical materialism'.

And he says the key understanding emerging from modern scientific developments is that 'nature might be called historical, that is, capable of development and innovation.' And he goes on to comment:

> *The idea of a history of nature as an integral part of materialism was asserted by Marx and in greater detail by Engels. Contemporary developments in physics have thus raised within the natural sciences a question that has long been asked by materialists.*[87]

Richard Levins and Richard Lewontin dedicated their 1985 book *The Dialectical Biologist*, 'To Frederick Engels, who got it wrong a lot of the time but who got it right where it counted'.[88]

Many scientists will say they have no need of philosophy to make sense of nature, that they are simply discovering how nature works. So be it. The science will ultimately stand or fall on its truth, its success in practice, whatever the thoughts in the heads of the scientists or anyone else.

But it is worth noting the dangers many modern physicists, or at least those who think about the meaning of the science they produce, fall into when they reject an attempt to have a consistent materialist, dialectical approach. I quoted earlier physicist Paul Davies's book *The Mind of God* and its talk of possibly needing to embrace 'the mystical path'. He is certainly not alone in such thoughts. Physicist Stephen Hawking concludes his otherwise excellent best seller, *A Brief History of Time*, by talking of 'the ultimate triumph of human reason' as 'to know the Mind of God'.[89] Even Ilya Prigogine ends a generally marvellous book with stuff like 'time is a construction and therefore carries an ethical responsibility' and references to the 'God of Genesis'.[90] It is worth recalling Engels' warning against the illusion that science can do without philosophy and the dangers into which 'sober headed empiricists' can fall. [91]

Conclusion

It should be clear that Engels' general approach to and arguments about science were correct and stand up well against the scientific developments in the 100 years since his death. In fact those developments are a powerful argument for the necessity of a dialectical understanding of nature.

What are the key elements in such an understanding? The first is that nature is historical at every level. No aspect of nature simply exists: it has a history, it comes into being, changes and develops, is transformed, and, finally, ceases to exist. Aspects of nature may appear to be fixed, stable, in a state of equilibrium for a shorter or longer time, but none is permanently so. This is the inescapable conclusion of modern science. Instead of expecting constancy or equilibrium as the normal condition a dialectical approach means expecting change but accepting apparent constancy within certain limits.

The second key element on which Engels was right is the need to see the interconnections of different aspects of nature. Of course it is necessary to break nature up, isolate this or that aspect, in order to understand and explain. But this is only part of the story, and unless complemented by seeing whatever parts have been isolated for study in their interconnections and relationships leads to a one sided, limited understanding. Parts only have full meaning in relation to the whole. This is not any kind of argument for a mystical 'holism'. The real relationships between different aspects of nature must be established and worked out scientifically. It is simply an insistence that such investigation is necessary for a full understanding to be established.

As in most questions there is a connection between the way nature is viewed and the dominant ideology in society. The fact that a way of thinking about nature in which equilibrium is the norm and in which the focus is on isolated parts, 'atoms', is typical is no accident in modern capitalist society. Though originally revolutionary, the capitalist class now has to believe—and tell us to believe—that its way of organising society is best. It has to suggest, whatever the daily accumulating evidence to the contrary, that stability and equilibrium are the normal conditions. It has to suggest that there is no reason why the current way of running society need change radically. Its vision of society is precisly one of atomised individual units. The family, the individual, are paramount. 'There is no such thing as society,' as Margaret Thatcher argued. When this is the dominant ideology in society it is no suprise that it often influences the way scientists think about nature.

What of the general patterns, 'laws', which Engels argued characterise processes of change and development in nature? I would argue that there is no question that Engels' arguments about quantitative change giving rise at certain points to qualitative transformations are generally correct. In every field of science, every aspect of nature, one cannot but be struck by precisely this process. Any attempt to understand the natural world which does not *expect* this to be a typical feature of change and development cannot be reconciled with the developments of modern science. Of course to expect such patterns of change does not tell you anything at all about the specific nature of real processes. The natural world has to be investigated and its behaviour established and explained scientifically.

A consequence of this view, however, is the understanding, more and more supported by modern science, that a radically anti-reductionist view of nature is necessary. As quantitative change gives rise to qualitative transformation, new organisations of matter arise. These have genuinely novel ways of behaving which, while compatible with the laws governing the underlying components, are not simply reducible to them. Biology is not simply applied physics and chemistry. Nor are human behaviour and consciousness simply applied molecular biology. Still less are politics, economics and history applied biology. An understanding is necessary which sees the connections between all these different levels of the organisation of matter, for they are all the result of nothing more than the greater or lesser complexity of organisation of matter—there are no mystical or vital principles at work. But an understanding of nature is also necessary which sees that each level has its own laws, ways of behaving, which cannot be read off from the laws governing a different level.

Throughout nature it seems that things which appear to have any persistence, any stability, for a greater or shorter time, are the result of a temporary dynamic balance between opposing or contradictory tendencies. This is as true of simple physical objects like atoms as of living organisms. When that balance is broken—as it always is at some point—change *can* result which leads to a new development, a transformation to a new situation which is not simply a disintegration or a circular re-creation of what was there before. But this is a potential, a possibility, rather than a general feature. Furthermore the way changes take place, and the kinds of possibilities, tendencies or patterns that can occur are different at different levels of the organisation of matter.

This is especially true of the kinds of processes which Engels talks of as examples of 'negation of the negation'. It seems to have little validity when talking of change in simple physical objects. It becomes important when talking of more complex persistent systems which have the capacity when absorbing impulses to preserve, and possibly transform, themselves. So it fits much better when looking at biological organisms, whose condition of existence is precisely the continual absorption and transformation of external matter. It is even more apparent in the sub-class of living bodies who have reached the further stage of development of consciousness and then self consciousness. These are constantly under the influence of external causation (they are being negated) but by becoming aware of this have the possibility of incorporating it under their own control (above all at the collective, social level) and in the process transforming themselves, and their relations with the external world. Living organisms open up kinds of development, processes of change, which are not there in the same form in the non-living world. Even more so is it the case that with the emergence of human conscious-ness and society new patterns of development and change become possible.

In addition, though, the concept is also important when looking at the evolution of the totality of matter itself. All these various levels of the organisation of matter are different facets of the same material totality, which though differentiated has an underlying unity. This totality has developed to give rise to the different patterns of change exhibited at dif-ferent levels of the organisation, and stages of the history, of the natural world. The levels and the patterns of change open at each are different, but they are connected aspects of the underlying unity.

A genuine dialectical view of nature would require the investigation of all these issues, a study of processes of change and development at every level of nature, their similarities and their differences. To construct such an understanding, based firmly on the real results of a developing scientific understanding of nature, would be the best tribute to Engels' pioneering work which still remains by far the best starting point for the philosophy of science. Engels' arguments on science have for too long been ignored, dismissed or distorted—by socialists sometimes as much as by others. One hundred years after his death it is time that changed. But in learning from Engels and seeking to build on his insights we should do so in the spirit in which he himself worked: 'How young the whole of human history is, and how ridiculous it would be to attempt to ascribe any absolute validity to our present views'.[92]

Notes to Chapter One

1   G Mayer, *Frederick Engels* (London, 1936), p208.
2   Ibid, pp56-57.
3   Ibid, p15.
4   Quoted in F Engels, *The Condition of the Working Class in England* (Moscow, 1973), p313.
5   Quoted in G Mayer, op cit, p49.
6   F Engels, op cit, p60.
7   Ibid, pp111-112.
8   Ibid, p120.
9   Ibid, p167.
10   Ibid, p162.
11   Ibid, p312.
12   Ibid, p261.
13   Ibid, pp333-334.
14   Ibid, p11.
15   F Engels, *On the History of the Communist League* in K Marx and F Engels, *Selected Works* (London, 1968), p436.
16   G Mayer, op cit, pp59-60.
17   F Mehring, *Karl Marx* (Sussex, 1981), p93.
18   Ibid, p95.
19   K Marx and F Engels, *Correspondence 1844-1851* (London, 1982), p4.
20   Ibid, p20.
21   G Mayer, op cit, p69.
22   K Marx and F Engels, *The German Ideology* (London, 1965), pp37-38.
23   Ibid, pp55-56.
24   Ibid, p50.
25   Ibid, p60.
26   Ibid, pp61-62.
27   Ibid, p44.
28   Ibid, pp85-86.
29   Ibid, p503.
30   K Marx and F Engels, *Correspondence*, op cit, p82.
31   O J Hammen, *The Red 48ers* (New York, 1969), p160.
32   F Engels, *Principles of Communism* (Peking, 1977), p3.
33   Ibid, p8.
34   K Marx and F Engels, *Communist Manifesto* (Tirana, 1981), p34.
35   F Engels, *Principles*, op cit, p11.
36   K Marx and F Engels, *Communist Manifesto*, op cit, p25.
37   O J Hammen, op cit, p187.
38   K Marx and F Engels, *Correspondence*, op cit,, p.54.
39   Ibid, pp159-160.
40   Ibid, p165.
41   E Hobsbawm, *The Age of Revolution* (London, 1977), p22.
42   K Marx in *Neue Rheinische Zeitung*, 29 June 1848, reprinted in D Fernbach (ed), *The Revolutions of 1848* (Harmondsworth, 1973), p131.
43   Article in *Deutsch-Brusseler Zeitung*, 23 January 1848, quoted in G Mayer, op cit, p88.
44   Article in *Neue Rheinische Zeitung*, 29 June 1848, reproduced in D Fernbach, op cit.
45   Quoted in O J Hammen, op cit, p234.
46   Ibid, p236.
47   Ibid, p250.

48   F Engels in *Neue Rheinische Zeitung*, 16 February 1849, reprinted in D Fernbach, op cit, p239.
49   F Engels in *Neue Rheinische Zeitung*, 13 January 1849, reprinted in D Fernbach, op cit, pp216-217.
50   F Mehring, op cit, p164.
51   The most detailed criticism from a Marxist point of view comes from R Rosdolsky in Engels and the *Non-historic Peoples: the National Question in the Revolution of 1848*, (Glasgow, 1986).
52   T Carver, *Frederick Engels: His Life and Thought* (Basingstoke, 1989), p201.
53   K Marx and F Engels, *Correspondence*, op cit, p211.
54   K Marx and F Engels, 'Address of the Central Committee to the Communist League (March 1850)', printed in D Fernbach, op cit, p330.
55   L Trotsky, *Permanent Revolution* (New York, 1962).
56   K Marx and F Engels, *Correspondence*, op cit, p241.
57   Y Kapp, *Eleanor Marx, Vol 1*, p112.
58   Quoted in T Carver, op cit, p155.
59   See G Mayer, op cit, pp171-174 and T Carver, op cit, pp153-155, for different interpretations of the correspondence.
60   T Carver, op cit, p159.
61   Y Kapp, op cit, p113.
62   Quoted in ibid, p114.
63   T Carver, op cit, and *The Daughters of Karl Marx* (London, 1984).
64   K Marx and F Engels, *Collected Works Vol 39* (Moscow, 1983), pp434-435.
65   Letter from Marx to Engels in *Selected Correspondence* (Moscow, 1982), p114.
66   Ibid, pp126-127.
67   Ibid, p125.
68   Ibid, p140.
69   Ibid, p163.
70   Ibid, p168.
71   Ibid, p180.
72   Ibid, p209.
73   K Marx and F Engels, *The Civil War in France* in *Selected Works*, op cit, p306.
74   Ibid, p287.
75   Ibid, p285.
76   F Engels introduction, ibid, p259.
77   D Fernbach introduction to K Marx, *The First International and After* (London, 1974), p43.
78   See the article by John Rees in this volume.
79   In K Marx and F Engels, *Selected Works*, op cit.
80   H Draper, *Karl Marx's Theory of Revolution, vol II* (London, 1978), pp308-309.
81   F Mehring, *Karl Marx* (Sussex, 1981), p511.
82   Ibid, p512.
83   F Engels, *Socialism, Utopian and Scientific* in *Selected Works*, op cit, p.398.
84   Ibid, p404.
85   Ibid, p410.
86   Ibid, pp418-419.
87   Ibid, p419.
88   Ibid, p422.
89   Letter from K Marx to Friedrich Adolph Sorge in Hoboken, 19 September 1879, in *Selected Correspondence*, op cit, p309.
90   Ibid, p340.
91   *Speech at the Graveside of Karl Marx* in *Selected Works*, op cit, pp429-430.

92 F Engels, *The Origin of the Family, Private Property and the State* in *Selected works*, op cit, pp449-583. For a fuller view of this and other works by Engels on human origins see the chapter by Chris Harman in this volume.

93 Letter from F Engels to Eduard Bernstein in Zurich, 17 June 1879, in *Selected Works*, op cit, p301.

94 Letter from F Engels to Karl Kautsky in Vienna, 12 September 1882, in *Selected Works*, op cit, p678.

95 A L Morton and G Tate, *The British Labour Movement* (London, 1979), pp162-163.

96 H Draper, op cit, p120.

97 Letter from Engels to J Adolph Sorge in Hoboken in *Selected Correspondence*, op cit, p375.

98 Y Kapp, *Eleanor Marx*, Vol ll (New York, 1976), pp212-213.

99 Quoted in E Hobsbawm, *Labour's Turning Point* (Brighton, 1974), p72.

100 Engels to Sorge in London, 7 December 1889, in *Selected Correspondence*, op cit, p385.

101 Y Kapp, Vol ll, op cit, pp377-380.

102 A L Morton and G Tate, op cit, p204.

103 Y Kapp, Vol ll, op cit, p423.

104 Ibid, p425.

105 Ibid, p549.

106 Engels' introduction to Marx's *The Class Struggles in France* was abridged for publication in *Die Neue Zeit*. For details see chapter by John Rees in this volume. For the introduction see K Marx and F Engels, *Collected Works Vol 27* (London, 1990), pp506-524.

107 Y Kapp, op cit, p446.

108 See F Engels *Socialism, Utopian and Scientific* in *Selected Works*, op cit, pp421-422.

109 C Harman, 'Hidden Treasure', in *Socialist Review* 149 (London, January 1992), p30-31. For a discussion on the argument about socialists and war see G Mayer, op cit, pp285-295.

Notes to chapter two

1 There were voices within the Marxist movement, notably Lukacs and Korsch in the early 1920s, who were critical of this or that aspect of Engels' writings, but these did not extend to a blanket denial of the unity of Marx and Engels' approach as did those which arose after 1960.

2 G Lichtheim, *Marxism: an Historical and Critical Study* (London, 1961).

3 Ibid, p238.

4 Ibid, p245.

5 Ibid, p253.

6 Ibid, p246.

7 Ibid, p237.

8 A Schmidt, *The Concept of Nature in Marx* (London, 1971), p51.

9 Ibid, p55.

10 Ibid, p56.

11 L Colletti, *From Rousseau to Lenin* (London, 1972), p26.

12 Ibid, p62.

13 For Lewis and Avineri, Engels' attempt to give a materialist account of nature was a fundamental mistake and a departure from Marx's method which was exclusively concerned with human society. For Kolakowski: 'Engels' dialectic was formulated under the influence of Darwin's discoveries...the main trend of opinion, shared by Engels...treats human history as a prolongation and a special

case of natural history, and assumes that the general laws of nature apply, in specific forms, to the destiny of mankind.'

This attitude was a mistake, and a break with Marx, since 'the dialectic, which according to Marx is the unity of theory and practice, cannot be formulated so as to relate to nature in itself as it presupposes the activity of consciousness.' Like earlier writers, Kolakowski sees one consequence of this being the adoption by Engels of a copy theory of consciousness. (*Main Currents of Marxism*, Vol 1 pp400-405).

14   P Walton and A Gamble, *From Alienation to Surplus Value* (London, 1976), p64.

15   G S Jones, 'Engels and the End of Classical German Philosophy', in *New Left Review* 79, May/June 1973.

16   E P Thompson, for instance, defended Engels' method against distortions by Louis Althusser (see E P Thompson, 'The Poverty of Theory', in *The Poverty of Theory and Other Essays*, London, 1978), although Thompson's own approach tended to downplay the material and objective factors in any analysis in a way that Engels himself did not. Thompson's hostility to party organisation, also a legacy of his experience in the Communist Party, led him to a much more hostile evaluation of Engels' practical role in the English working class movement (see his *Persons and Polemics* London, 1994, pp10-23). S Timpanaro also mounted a defence of Engels (*On Materialism* London, 1975). Timpanaro has some valuable insights, but he wrongly tends to accept much of the accusation of 'Hegelianism' directed at Engels by his critics.

17   N Levine, *The Tragic Deception, Marx contra Engels* (Clio Press, 1975), p145.

18   Ibid.

19   Ibid, p152.

20   Ibid, p157.

21   Ibid, p175.

22   Ibid, p157.

23   T Carver, *Marx and Engels, the Intellectual Relationship* (Brighton, 1983), p156: 'Engels found his vocation in 1859, rather unfortunately, as a systemising philosopher, setting Marx's work in an academic and philosophical context, drawing out its implications as a universal methodology, and adding...a positivist account of natural science.'

24   Ibid, p157.

25   See the survey of anti-Engels literature in H Sheehan, *Marxism and the Philosophy of Science, a Critical History* (Humanities Press, 1985), pp53-60.

26   T Carver, op cit, p151.

27   N Levine, op cit, p233.

28   Ibid, p232. Even if this were a true picture of Marx's marriage it would be a dubious claim. But, given the enormous pressure of poverty and the family deaths and ill health which accompanied it, Jenny Marx seems to have given her husband a great deal of 'professional and emotional support'. This was certainly Marx's opinion and that of most contemporary witnesses, many of whom stress how close the Marxes' relationship was.

29   T Carver, op cit, pp36-37.

30   Quoted in J D Hunley, *The Life and Thought of Friedrich Engels* (Yale University Press, 1991), p135.

31   Engels, *Selected Correspondence* (Moscow, 1975), p175.

32   Marx, ibid, p176

33   Ibid, p138.

34   Engels, quoted in G Novak, *Polemics in Marxist Philosophy* (New York, 1978), p88.

35 Marx, quoted by Engels, *Anti-Dühring*, in *Marx Engels Collected Works* (*MECW*), Vol 25 (London, 1987), p116. The original is in Marx, *Capital*, *MECW*, Vol 35, part III, ch XI.
36 Ibid, p117.
37 Marx, *Selected Correspondence*, op cit, p177.
38 Ibid, p115.
39 Quoted in D McLellan (ed), *Karl Marx, Interviews and Recollections* (London, 1981), pp77-78.
40 Marx and Engels, *The German Ideology*, *MECW*, Vol 5 (London, 1976), p31.
41 Ibid.
42 Ibid, pp39-40.
43 Engels, *Anti-Dühring*, *MECW*, op cit, p34.
44 Ibid, pp41-42.
45 Ibid, p42.
46 Ibid, pp42-43.
47 Ibid, pp43-44.
48 Marx and Engels, *The German Ideology*, op cit, p40.
49 Ibid.
50 Engels, 'The Part Played by Labour in the Transition from Ape to Man', in *MECW*, Vol 25, op cit, pp453-454. Engels' emphasis.
51 Ibid, pp455-457.
52 Ibid, p459.
53 Ibid, p459.
54 Ibid, p460.
55 Ibid, p461.
56 Ibid, p462.
57 Engels, *Socialism, Utopian and Scientific* (Peking, 1975), p67.
58 Ibid, p68.
59 Ibid, p65.
60 Engels, *Anti-Dühring*, *MECW*, op cit, p111.
61 Ibid, p112.
62 Ibid, p121.
63 Ibid, p124.
64 Ibid, p132. Although it is also true that some of Engels' own examples, often the ones taken over too literally from Hegel, are misleading. The growth of a grain of barley is not, as Engels suggests, a dialectical development. It does not occur as a result of internal contradictions and is perfectly explicable in ordinary scientific terms. Engels' other examples, are often brilliant; see for example his description of the relationship between French and Mameluke cavalry (*Anti-Dühring*, op cit, p119).
65 Engels, *Dialectics of Nature*, *MECW*, Vol 25, op cit, p493.
66 Ibid, pp494-495. Engels' emphasis.
67 Engels, *Ludwig Feuerbach and the End of Classical German Philosophy* (Peking, 1976), p40.
68 Ibid, pp45-46.
69 Engels, *Anti-Dühring*, *MECW*, Vol 25, op cit, pp12-13.
70 Ibid, p35.
71 Even if one accepts the point made by Engels' critics, which I don't, that Engels' critique of Hegel was different from that of Marx, it makes no difference to the force of this point. Engels is said to have simply counterposed the revolutionary Hegelian method to the conservative Hegelian system, rather than carried out a fully materialist critique of both method and system. But since it is precisely the conservative nature of such universal systems to which Engels' objects, it is

highly unlikely that he would have reproduced exactly this fault in his own analysis.

72   Engels, *Dialectics of Nature*, *MECW*, op cit, p515.
73   G Lichtheim, op cit, p248.
74   N Levine, op cit, p174.
75   Engels, *The German Ideology*, *MECW*, op cit, p93.
76   Marx and Engels, *Selected Correspondence*, op cit, p396.
77   Marx, *The Eighteenth Brumaire of Louis Bonaparte*, in Marx, *Surveys from Exile* (Penguin, 1973), p146.
78   Engels, *Selected Correspondence* (Moscow, 1975), p395. Virtually the same phrase—'men make their history themselves'—crops up in Engels' letter to Turati, *Selected Correspondence*, p442.
79   Engels, 'Reply to Mr. Paul Ernst', *MECW*, Vol 27 (London, 1990), p84.
80   Engels, *Selected Correspondence*, op cit, p402.
81   Ibid, p399.
82   Ibid, pp398-399.
83   Ibid.
84   Ibid, p399.
85   Ibid, p400.
86   Ibid, p400.
87   Ibid, p399.
88   Ibid, p402.
89   Engels, *Ludwig Feuerbach and the End of Classical German Philosophy*, op cit, p40.
90   Ibid, p54.
91   Ibid, p55.
92   Engels, *Selected Correspondence*, op cit, p457.
93   Ibid, p459.
94   Engels, *Ludwig Feuerbach and the End of Classical German Philosophy*, op cit, p51.
95   Marx and Engels, *Selected Correspondence*, op cit, p179. Marx repeated the same point in *Capital*, Vol III. That Engels fully understood this point is not only obvious from his own writings, but also from a revision which he made to Marx's *Wage Labour and Capital* when it was republished in 1891. Marx's original 1849 text had argued, 'The bourgeois therefore buys the workers' labour with money. They sell him their labour for money.' In that original form Marx could be read to mean that this is a just market exchange—a fair day's work for a fair day's pay. In *Capital* Marx had spelt out that this is only the *appearance* of a fair transaction because, in reality, what the worker sells is his labour *power* which can be exploited beyond the point where it has earned enough to reproduce itself and so delivers surplus value to the capitalist. Thus there is, right at the heart of the capitalist system, a fateful gap between appearance and reality. Engels amended the 1891 edition to bring out this point: 'The capitalist, it seems, therefore *buys* their labour for money. They *sell* him their labour for money. But this is merely the appearance. In reality, what they sell to the capitalist is their labour *power*.' See the excellent account of this and other questions in J D Hunley, *The Life and Thought of Frederich Engels*, op cit, pp87-88.
96   Engels, *The Condition of the Working Class in England*, *MECW*, Vol 4 (London, 1975), p507.
97   Ibid. See also H Draper, *Karl Marx's Theory of Revolution*, Vol II (New York, 1978), pp91-146.
98   Marx and Engels, *The German Ideology*, *MECW*, op cit, p53.
99   Engels, quoted in H Draper, op cit, p75. Engels later found that the people had not been as completely revolutionised as he had at first hoped. Nevertheless, as

Draper notes, 'the principle was still the measuring rod of the limitations of the March revolution: its greatest shortcoming is that it has not revolutionised the Berliners.'

100   Engels, *Selected Correspondence*, op cit, pp379-380. Also see the discussion in J D Hunley, op cit, pp116-117.

101   K Kautsky, quoted in J Larrain, *A Reconstruction of Historical Materialism*, (London, 1986), p53.

102   Engels, quoted in J D Hunley, op cit, p101.

103   Ibid, p105.

104   Engels, Introduction to K Marx, *The Class Struggles in France*, *MECW*, Vol 27 (London, 1990), p520. This is yet another striking testimony to Engels' insistence that workers themselves must be the conscious authors of their own liberation.

105   Indeed, Engels suggests that the shortcomings of barricades might mean that revolutionaries would have to go over to the offensive rather than simply build defensive street fortifications.

106   Engels, *Selected Correspondence*, op cit, p461.

107   Ibid.

108   Engels, quoted in J D Hunley, op cit, p111.

Notes to Chapter Three

1   The history of modern bourgeois philosophy has been very much a history of the polemic between the two views, although it cross cuts with other arguments, over how we gain access to knowledge, between empiricism and rationalism.

2   He never completed it, but it was later published in its incomplete form soon after his death, in the German socialist journal, *Die Neue Zeit*.

3   Utilising copious notes by Marx on Morgan's book, published as Karl Marx, *Ethnological notebooks*.

4   Gregor Mendel actually published his findings in an obscure journal published in Bruen (Brno) in 1865, but they were not rediscovered by other biologists until the turn of the century.

5   B Trigger, 'Comment' on Tobias, 'Piltdown, the Case Against Keith', in *Current Anthropology*, Vol 33, No 3, June 1992, p275.

6   For an account of all these confusions, see A Kuper, *The Chosen Primate* (London, 1994), pp33-47.

7   On the paucity of attempts to explain human evolution until the 1960s, see the introduction to R Foley (ed), *Hominid Evolution and Community Ecology* (London, 1984), p3.

8   C Stringer, 'Human evolution and biological adaptation in the Pleistocene, in ibid, p53.

9   N Roberts, 'Pleistocene environment in time and space', in ibid, p33.

10   Such a rapid change in the state of knowledge means that otherwise very useful works can be out of date in important respects. This applies, for instance, like Charles Woolfson's Marxist account of much of the material on human evolution, *The Labour Theory of Culture*, although it was only published in 1982 and although its basic argument is very close to the one I present here. While I was writing this article, reports appeared in the scientific press suggesting the famous 'Java man' fossil was a million years older than previously thought (*New Scientist*, 7 May, 1994) and that the earliest example yet of an Australopithecine had been found in Ethiopia.

11   And of one of their allegedly 'radical' followers, Chris Knight. His book *Blood Relations* (Yale, 1991) is one great big 'Just So' story—with lots of factual

material distorted in an attempt to justify his claims. See my review, 'Blood Simple', *International Socialism* 54, Spring 1992, p169.

12   Engels himself does at points in *The Origin of the Family*, but see later.

13   A separate species, *Pan paniscus*, to the common chimp (*Pan troglodytes*).

14   Although a few zoologists still argue for the Orang-utang. See, for instance, J H J Schwartz, *The Red Ape* (London, 1987), reviewed by Peter Andrews in *New Scientist*, 14 May 1987.

15   S I Washburn and R More, 'Only Once', in P B Hammond, *Physical Anthropology and Archaeology* (New York, 1976), p18.

16   R Ardrey, *African Genesis* (London, 1969), pp9-10.

17   C J Lumsden and E O Wilson, *Genes, Mind and Culture* (Cambridge, Mass, 1981), p258.

18   R Ardrey, op cit, p170.

19   C J Lumsden and E O Wilson, op cit, p354.

20   These studies have been not been easy to undertake in a scientifically controlled way. They have involved trailing dispersed bands often 40 or more strong through sometimes dense woodland and among tree tops to which humans cannot easily get access, while recognising that the human presence itself can influence ape behaviour (with chimps, for instance, fighting over food when it is handed out once a day from a single human source in a way in which they might not when eating from dispersed plant life). As a result the evidence from the studies is open to different interpretations. They do, however, all point in a very different direction to the old 'baboon' model. For discussions taking into account the wild life studies, see I S Bernstein and F O Smith (eds), *Primate Ecology and Human Origins* (New York, 1979); W C McGrew, 'Chimpanzee Material Culture', in R A Foley, *The Origins of Human Behaviour* (London, 1991), pp16-20. For accounts of original investigations, see J Goodall, *The Chimpanzees of Gombe* (Cambridge, Mass, 1986); M P Giglieri, *The Chimpanzees of Kibale Forest* (New York, 1984); A F Dixson, *The Natural History of the Gorilla* (London, 1981); B M F Galiliki and G Teleki, *Current Anthropology*, June 1981.

21   Thus aggression between males over mating is more frequent in captivity than in the wild 'because of the greater ability of the male to control the female in the cage', according to R H Nadler, 'Aggression in Common Chimps, Gorillas and Orang-utangs'; female pygmy chimps exercise choice over the males they mate with in the wild in a way in which they cannot while caged, according to J F Dahl, 'Sexual Aggression in Captive Pygmy Chimps'. Abstracts of both papers appear in *International Journal of Primatology*, 1987, p451.

22   For a summary of the evidence on this, see N M Tanner, *Becoming Human* (Cambridge, 1981), pp87-89.

23   R Leakey and R Lewin, *Origins* (London, 1977), p64.

24   N M Tanner, *Becoming Human*, op cit, pp95-96. See also Dixson, op cit, p148.

25   A F Dixson, op cit, p128. Amazingly, Ardrey admits that the gorilla is not aggressive or driven by a 'territorial imperative'—and then concludes it has lost 'vital instincts', that 'universal primate compulsions' have faded because the species is 'doomed'! R Ardrey, as above, pp126-127.

26   This makes sense. Vegetarian foodstuffs are relatively bulky and found on dispersed trees and bushes. There is no advantage for the individual or the troop either in all eating at the same place. By contrast, meat can only be obtained if several chimps co-operate to kill a single, animal—and that is unlikely to happen unless the prey is shared between them.

27   See the drawings of Lokelema, a 25-35 year old female, and Bosondro, a 5.5 to 7.5 year old male, in N M Tanner, *On Becoming Human*, op cit, pp124-125.

28   A L Zihlman, 'Common Ancestors and Uncommon Apes', in J R Durrant, *Human Origins* (Oxford,1989), p98.

29   Ibid, p98. See also J Kingdon, *Self Made Man* (London, 1993), p25. Cronin
      suggests that molecular evidence points to *pan paniscus* being the 'relic stock'
      from which gorillas, the common chimpanzee and humans all descended, quoted
      in N M Tanner, *On Becoming Human*, op cit, p58.
30   The Australopithecines are usually divided into three or four species. One,
      Australopithecus afaresis (of which there exists a full skeleton, nicknamed 'Lucy'),
      is seen as a direct ancestor of modern human beings; the others are usually seen as
      evolutionary dead ends, as creatures that adapted to certain ecological niches but
      which could not make the transition to new niches when the terrain changed.
31   Dart, the discoverer of the first Australopithecine skeletons, saw animals bones
      found with them as evidence of hunting by Australopithecines. But this claim has
      been challenged since, and the bones are usually thought to have been gathered by
      hyenas.
32   There is no universally accepted account of where the ape line ends and the
      human line begins, nor or how the human line is be distinguished into different
      species. However, most present day accounts put Australopithecus with the apes
      and accept the 2 million year old skull 1470 as being from the earliest known
      human species, *homo habilis*. See, for instance, R Leakey and R Lewin, *Origins
      Revisited* (London, 1993), p117.
33   P V Tobias, 'The brain of *homo habilis*', *Journal of Human Evolution*, 1987,
      p741; R Leakey, 'Recent fossil finds in Africa', in J R Durant, ed, *Human Origins*
      (Oxford, 1989); N M Tanner, *On Becoming Human*, op cit, p254.
34   It is claimed that skeletal remains at Omo in Ethiopia and Klasies River and
      Border Cave in South Africa are of modern humans living 130,000, and 80,000 to
      100,000 years ago. But this evidence is challenged by people like Milford Wolpoff
      and Alan Thorne, see, for example, their article, 'The case against Eve', *New
      Scientist*, 22 June 1991, and the brief summary of critical comments at the 1987
      Cambridge conference on human origins in S McBrearty, 'The origins of modern
      humans', *Man* 25, 1989, p131. It is also claimed that remains of anatomically
      modern humans found at Qafzeh in Palestine are 80,000 to 100,000 years old see,
      for instance, McBrearty, p131,who notes, 'this is consistent with either an African
      or a south west Asian origin for modern people'.
35   There is much controversy about the age of various early human remains in the
      Americas. For one summary of the arguments, see Gordon R Willey, 'The Earliest
      Americans', in P B Hammond (ed), *Physical Anthropology and Archaeology*, op cit.
36   A point made by Graves, 'New Models and Metaphors for the Neanderthal
      Debate', *Current Anthropology*, Vol 32, No 5, December 1991, p513. For an
      account of the discussion from more than half a century ago, see V G Childe,
      What happened In History (Harmondsworth, 1954), p30.
37   This alternative view sometimes called the 'multi-regionalist view' and its best
      known proponent is Milford Wohlpoff.
38   There are doubts about the full 'Out of Africa thesis' from people like Roger
      Leakey who do not ascribe to the full multi-regionalist position either. See, for
      instance, Leakey, 'Recent fossil finds in Africa', in J R Durant, op cit, p55: 'I
      believe the world of 100,000 years ago was populated by regionally distinct
      groups of the same species; I do not favour the idea that the modern form of our
      species had a single geographic origin…The fossil evidence from widely
      separated parts of the world indicates to me that '*homo sapiens* in its modern form
      arose from a population of a more archaic form wherever its was established.' His
      tone is much more measured in his 1993 book, *Origins Reconsidered*, but this
      book was written jointly with Roger Lewin, who favours the single origins view.
      The joint authorship probably explains why the book gives such an excellent
      overview of the debate, see R Leakey and R Lewin, *Origins Reconsidered*, 1993,
      pp211-235. For other accounts of the controversy see: Roger Lewin, 'DNA

evidence strengthens Eve hypothesis', *New Scientist*, 19 October 1991; J Poulton, 'All about Eve', *New Scientist*, 14 May 1987; C Stringer, 'The Asian Connection', *New Scientist*, 17 November 1990; 'Scientists Fight It Out and It's All about Eve', *Observer*, 16 February 1992; M Wohlpoff and A Thorne, 'The Case Against Eve', *New Scientist*, 22 July 1991; S McBrearty, 'The Origin of Modern Humans', *Man* 25, pp129-143; R Leakey, 'Recent Fossil Finds in Africa', and C Stringers, 'Homo Sapiens: Single or Multiple Origin', both in J R Davent (ed), *Human Origins* (Oxford, 1989); P Mellors and C Stringer (eds), *The Human Revolution* (Edinburgh, 1989); P Graves, 'New Models and Metaphors for the Neanderthal Debate', *Current Anthropology*, Vol 32, No 5, December 1991; R A Foley, *The Origin of Human Behaviour* (London, 1991), p83.

39   The 'multi-regionalist' view is sometimes seen as somehow providing some justification for racism, since it argues that people in different parts of the world began to develop certain differentiating features hundreds of thousand rather than tens of thousands of years ago. But this is make an elementary logical mistake. Since it assumes a much slower rate of evolution, and therefore of the evolution of human differences, than the single origins view, it cannot be taken to prove the final differentiation was any greater.

Just as mistaken is the claim that the origin of modern humans in Africa refutes the white racists or even proves that Africans are a superior 'race' to 'whites'. A racist could easily accept an African origins for modern humans, and then insist that this shows Africans are more 'primitive' since they have 'evolved less' than 'whites', basing the claim on the argument that if modern man could evolve very quickly into a separate and superior species from the Neanderthals 100,000 or so years ago, why could not white have developed into separate and superior species to blacks 20,000 years ago? This was, in fact, the racist argument during the many decades in which Neanderthals were seen as 'primitive ape men'.

Racist arguments are wrong, not because of one or other hypothesis about human origins, but because there is no backing for them in what we know about the genetic and biological make-up of living human beings. The human species cannot be divided into distinct sub-groups, each of which is made of individuals who are distinguished from those in other subgroups by a complete set of genes and physical characteristics. At most it can be divided into groups according to variations in particular individual characteristics such as the amount of melanin in the skin, the tendency of hair to curl, eye colour, blood group, height, nose length, or whatnot. But these groups for particular characteristics are not congruent with each other. The group of people with little melanin ('whites') contains many people with brown eyes. The group of people with large noses contains people with all levels of melanin. This cross cutting nature of the groupings applies even when particular characteristics tend to be concentrated in certain parts of the world: so the geographic distribution of blood groups does not coincide at all with that for melanin (ie skin 'colour'), and neither coincides with the distribution of the sickle cell gene (which is found among Greeks, Turks, Italians, Arabs and Africans). So the common sense notion of race—a product of the slave trade and imperialist conquest—cannot be used as a valid scientific category. For a full discussion on these matters, see F B Livingstone, 'On the non-existence of human races', in *Current Anthropology*, 3 (1962), p279; see also the comment on Livingstone's argument by T Dobzhansky, in the same place.

It would be a fundamental mistake for anyone to make the argument against racism dependent upon theories about the past which might by thrown into doubt by a new discovery of archaic bones or new techniques for deciphering humanity's genetic past.

40   R Ardrey, *African Genesis* (London, 1967), p20.

41   R A Dart, 'The Predatory Transition from Ape to Man', *International Anthropological and Linguistic Review*, Vol 1, No 4, 1953.

42   This is the presentation of the argument by two of its opponents, M Wolpoff and A Thorne ('The Case Against Eves', *New Scientist*, 22 June 1991). But the same gloss is put on the hypothesis by some of those who support it.

43   I am simplifying the argument here to make it as easy to follow as possible. In fact, most characteristics are a product of many different pairs of genes. But this does not affect the validity of my point. For a fuller popular account of the most modern genetic theory, see S Jones, *The Language of Genes* (London, 1993), Ch 2.

44   Geneticists distinguish between the continuous transformation of a whole species into a new species which succeeds the old through gene selection ('anagenesis') and the branching off of one sub-population to develop into a new species alongside the old ('cladogenesis'). See the introduction to R Foley (ed), *Hominid Evolution and Community Ecology*, p15. Alexeev calls those who see whole human species developing into new species as 'lumpers', those who see one small group splitting off to form a new group 'splitters'. O Alexeev, *The Origins of the Human Race* (Moscow, nd), p101.

45   This leads them to point out the 'African Eve' and the 'multi-regionalist' hypotheses need not necessarily exclude each other: 'If genes controlling skull shape are in nuclear DNA, which seems probable, they may locally change frequency as a 'result of drift or local environmental selection pressures. Thus we so no incompatibility in the African origin of all human mitochondrial tissue and the local continuation of distinctive bone structure. The existence of both certainly strengthens of the view of the human race as one single interbreeding population', T Rowell and M C King, letter in *New Scientist*, 14 September 1991.

46   C Stringer, '*Homo sapiens*, single or multiple origin', in J R Durant, op cit, p77.

47   S McBrearty, op cit, p134.

48   See, for example, P Graves, op cit, p521, and E Zubrow, quoted in R Leakey and R Lewin, *Origins Reconsidered*, p234-5

49   N M Tanner, op cit, p155

50   For summaries of Isaacs' views, and the criticisms made of them by Binford and others, see R J Blumenschine, 'Breakfast at Olorgesalie', *Journal of Human Evolution*, Vol 21, No 4, October 1991, and J M Sept, 'Was there no place like home?', *Current Anthropology*, Vol 33, No 2, April 1992.

51   J A Gowlett, 'The Mental Abilities of Early Man', in R Foley (ed), op cit.

52   Quoted in N M Tanner, op cit, p206 See also P V Tobias, 'The brain of *homo habilis*', *Journal of Human Evolution*, 1987, p741.

53   C Woolfson, *The Labour Theory of Culture*, op cit, p3.

54   J M Sept, 'Was there no place like home?', op cit, and Binford, quoted in R J Blumenshine, 'Breakfast at Olorgesailie', p307.

55   Argument quoted by P Graves, op cit, p519.

56   Robert Cargett's view, referred to in R Leakey and R Lewin, *Origins Reconsidered*, p270; see also M C Stirner, T D White and N Toth, 'The Cultural Significance of Grotta Guaterii Reconsidered', *Current Anthropology*, Vol 32, No 2, April 1991.

57   Strangely enough, this argument is put very strongly by a would-be Marxist, Chris Knight, op cit.

58   Lieberman's arguments are contained in his Uniquely Human (Cambridge Mass, 1991).

59   See Gould and Eldridge, *Paleobiology* 3,1977; for a criticism of their views, see Cronin and others, *Nature* 292; for a summary of the debate, see C Stringer, 'Human Evolution and Biological Adaptation in the Pleistocene', in R A Foley (ed), *Hominid Ecology*, p57.

60   A Kuper, op cit, p53.

61   Ibid, p79.

62   The importance of twine or string of some sort is stressed by Jonathan Kingdon, whose knowledge of the ecology of African mammals is able to throw enormous light on the conditions in which early human found themselves, see his *Self Made Man*, op cit, p51.

63   W C McGrew, 'Chimpanzee Material Culture', in R A Foley (ed), *The Origins of Human Behaviour* (London, 1991, p19-20.

64   S T Parker and K R Gibson, 'The Importance of Theory for Reconstructing the Evolution of Language and Intelligence', in A B Chiarelli and R S Corrucinia (eds), *Advanced Primate Biology* (Berlin, 1982), p49.

65   T Wynn, 'Archaeological Evidence for Modern Intelligence', in R A Foley (ed), *The Origins*, op cit, pp56-63.

66   A Kuper, op cit, p 89.

67   P Graves, op cit, pp519-521; R A Foley, *The Origins*, op cit, p83.

68   N David, 'On upper palaeolithic society, ecology and technological change: the Noaillan case', in Colin Renfrew (ed), *Explaining Cultural Change* (London, 1973), p276.

69   B Arensburg and B Vandermeersch claim that the hyoid bone of a Neanderthal from 60,000 years ago found in the Kebara Cave at Mount Carmel in Israel indicates that 'the morphological basis for human speech capabilities appears to have been fully developed', quoted in R Leakey and R Lewin, *Origins Reconsidered*, op cit, p272. Lieberman challenges the significance of this find. For his own account of this controversy, see his *Uniquely Human*, op cit, p67.

70   Lieberman, ibid, p65.

71   C Stringer, 'Human Evolution and Biological Adaptation in the Pleistocene', in R A Foley (ed), op cit, p64.

72   Even Lieberman, with his contention that full use of language was a late development, stresses the role of labour: 'The brain mechanisms that control speech probably derive from ones that facilitated precise one-handed manual tasks.'

73   The point is very important, since one of the best refuters of sociobiology, Stephen Gould, shows some signs in his recent works of a certain 'post-modernist' slippage. In *Bully for Brontosaurus* he tends towards acceptance of the view that language arose suddenly 35,000 years ago, while in *Wonderful Life* (London, 1989) he outlines a whole philosophy of history that emphasizes its accident proneness and arbitrariness rather than its intelligibility, as when he writes: 'A historical explanation does not rest on direct deductions from laws of nature, but on an unpredictable sequence of antecedent states, where any major change in any step in the sequence would have altered the final result. This final result is therefore dependent, or contingent, upon everything that came before—the unerasable and determining signature of history' (p283). But, in fact, everything is not 'contingent'. In certain conditions, both in the biological world and in history, certain things are likely to happen—faced with mass exinctions of species, certain creatures with a certain genetic make-up are more likely to survive than others, faced with a certain change in the environment certain sorts of human labour and social organisation are more likely to be able to cope than others, faced with certain changes in society classes with certain interests are likely to react in certain ways. That is why we cannot only write history, but use it, within limits, to illuminate the present. I can't help feeling that Gould himself would have recognised this in the radical 1960s and his present stance is very much a reflection of changing intellectual fashions rather than personal conviction. It should also be added that excellent simplicity of language with which he expresses scientific ideas can disguise the fact that sometimes the views he expresses are ones which other researchers strenuously resist (as with his particular interpretation of the Burgess Shale findings in *Wonderful Life*).

74   N M Tanner, op cit, p56.

75 R J Rayner and others, *Journal of Human Evolution*, Vol 24, p219, quoted in S Bunney, 'Early Humans were Forest Dwellers', *New Scientist*, 10 April 1993.

76 See, for example, the contribution of W S Laughlin, 'Hunting, its Evolutionary Importance', in P B Hammond, op cit, p42.

77 For instance, L Binford, *Bones, Ancient Man and Modern Myths* (New York, 1981).

78 See, for example, B J King, 'Comment' on J M Sept, 'Was there no place like home?', *Current Anthropology*, Vol 33, No 2, April 1992, p197.

79 N M Tanner, op cit, p139.

80 Ibid, p149.

81 B Trigger, comment on Tobias, 'Piltdown, the Case Against Keith', in *Current Anthropology*, Vol 33, No 3, June 1992.

82 E Leacock, 'Women in Egalitarian society', in *Myths of Male Dominance* (New York, 1981), p31.

83 See B Trigger, *V Gordon Childe*.

84 E Gellner, *Plough, Sword and Book* (London, 1991), p16.

85 C Ward Gailey, *From Kinship to Kingship* (Austin), p16.

86 This has been true of some of the Stalinist interpretations. But it has also been true of some people from the genuine left. Thus Evelyn Reed's account in *Women's Evolution*, although often very good at criticising the old anti-evolutionist orthodoxy, goes astray by seriously misinterpreting anthropological data so as to fit it in with things said by Engels at certain points in *The Origin*. This is true, for instance, of her assertions about bitter 'competition' between early human males, about the alleged role cannibalism in 'primitive' societies and about the alleged connection between inheritance along the male line and recognition of paternity. For a thorough critique of Reed's work, see the review by Eleanor Leacock in *Myths of Male Dominance* (New York, 1981), pp183-194.

87 F Engels, *The Origin of the Family, Private Property and the State* (Moscow, nd), p6.

88 Although in Morgan's case this materialist insight was mixed with an idealist view, arguing that 'social and civil institutions, in virtue of their connection with perpetual human wants, have been developed from a few primary germs of thought', L H Morgan, *Ancient Society*, p5. Morgan was also, it should be added, not a revolutionary. He believed the bourgeois democracy was the highest form of human society to which all others were striving.

89 Ibid, p24.

90 Ibid, p18.

91 Engels, *The Origin of the Family*, op cit, pp42-43.

92 In fact, modern archaeologists extend the definition a little to include certain societies in which cities do not play the major part, like early Ancient Egypt and the Maya culture of Central America, because they contained most of the other features usually associated with urban societies—separate groups of artisans and administrators, the widespread use of metals, literacy etc. In the same way they usually include societies like those of the Incas or of pre-Islamic West Africa, in which there were cities and states but no alphabet.

93 Although one of the gurus of Thatcherism, Hayek, dissented, arguing that thousands of years of primitive communism had produced what he regarded as very dangerous 'innate instincts', leading the mass of people today to want 'a just distribution, in which organised power is used to allocated to each what he deserves', to 'pursue perceived desirable common objects' and 'to do good to known people'.

94 Engels, *The Origin of the Family*, op cit, pp157-159.

95 E Friedl, *Women and Men, the Anthropologist's View* (New York, 1975).

96   E Leacock, 'Women's Status in Egalitarian Societies', *Myths of Male Dominance*, op cit, pp139-140.
97   R Lee, *The !Kung San* (Cambridge, 1979), p118.
98   The '!' at the beginning of !Kung denotes a 'click' sound which does not exist in Indo-European languages.
99   R Lee, op cit, p244
100   Guago, quoted in Richard Lee, op cit, p244
101   Le P P Lejeune (1834), quoted in M Sahlins, *Stone Age Economics* (London, 1974), p14.
102   Colin Turnbull, *The Forest People*, (New York, 1962), pp107, 110 and124-5.
103   R Lee, op cit, pp343-345.
104   E Friedl, *Women and Men*, op cit, p15.
105   R Lee, op cit, p336-338.
106   All the quoted phrases are from R Ardrey, op cit, pp300, 30 and 399.
107   W Lloyd Warner, *A Black Civilisation* (New York, 1964), quoted in Sahlin, *Stone Age Economics*, op cit, p12
108   E Friedl, *Women and Men*, op cit, p14
109   See R Lee, op cit, p55, see also C Turnbull, *The Forest People*, op cit, p127; M Sahlins, *Stone Age Economics*, op cit, p123.
110   As M Sahlens has noted, 'The surviving food collectors are displaced persons... occupying marginal haunts...untypical of the mode of production...barred from the better parts the earth, first by agricultural, later by industrial economies'. There is the 'possibility that the ethnography of hunters and gatherers is largely a record of incomplete cultures. Fragile cycles of ritual and exchange could have disappeared without trace, lost in the earliest stages of colonialism, when the intergroup relations they mediated were attacked and confounded': *Stone Age Economics*, op cit, p8 and p38. For evidence that some different principles of social organisation may have applied among the !Kung a century ago to now, see R Lee, op cit, p340. For speculation about how palaeolithic hunter-gatherer societies may have different from shriving ones, see R Foley, 'Hominids, humans and hunter-gatherers', in T Ingold, D Riches and J Woodburn, *Hunters and Gatherers*, Vol 1 (London, 1988, p207-221.
111   R Lee, 'Reflections on primitive communism', in T Ingold, D Riches and J Woodburn, *Hunters and Gatherers*, Vol 1 (New York, 1991), p262.
112   R Lee, 'Reflections on primitive communism', op cit, p268.
113   F Engels, *The Origin of the Family*, op cit, p37.
114   Ibid, p41.
115   Ibid, p87.
116   See J V S Megaw (ed), *Hunter Gatherers and the First Farmer Beyond Europe*, and the essays by M Dolukhanov, G W W Baker, C M Nelson, D R Harris and M Tosi in C Renfrew (ed), *Explaining Cultural Change*, op cit.
117   This is one of key arguments in M Sahlins' *Stone Age Economics*.
118   C Ward Gailey, *Kinship to Kingship* (Austin 1987), pp67.
119   R Lee, 'Reflections on primitive communism', as above, p262.
120   C Levi Strauss, quoted in M Sahlins, *Stone Age Economics*, op cit, p132.
121   H I Hogbin, quoted in M Sahlins, ibid, p135.
122   J F Lafitau, quoted in R Lee, 'Reflections on primitive communism', op cit, p252.
123   E Evans-Pritchard, quoted in R Lee, 'Reflections on primitive communism', op cit, p252.
124   A Richards, quoted in M Sahlins, *Stone Age Economics*, op cit, p125
125   R Firth, quoted in M Sahlins, *Stone Age Economics*, op cit, p125
126   R Firth, quoted in M Sahlins, ibid, p129

127   So M Sahlins refers to 'the domestic mode of production', *Stone Age Economics*, op cit. By contrast, K Sachs refers to 'the corporate mode of production', see *Sisters and Wives*, op cit, p109

128   K Sachs, ibid, op cit, p116-117

129   M Sahlins, op cit, p140

130   E Friedl, *Women and Men, an Anthropologist's View* (New York, 1975), p51.

131   See M Sahlins, op cit, chapter one, R Lee, *!Kung San*, op cit, and C Turnbull, *The Forest People*, op cit.

132   This is a point made A Testart, *Les chasseurs-cueilleurs ou l'origin des inegalités*, Paris 1982.

133   D O Henry, *From Foraging to Agriculture* (Philadelphia, 1989), p227.

134   D O Henry argues that the collapse of the ecological conditions for 'complex' foraging was caused from climatic changes. But the cause could have been the cumulative impact on the environment of growing numbers of foragers. The growing human population could have had a dramatic impact on the size of the wild mammalian herds it fed on, producing sudden, acute shortages. This would explain why there are repeated historical instances, in different parts of the world, of society based on complex foraging (sometimes, as in parts of Latin America with limited recourse to horticulture) suddenly either going over completely to agriculture or reverting to nomadic hunting and gathering.

135   For accounts of the transition to agriculture in the Americas see, for example, R Mc Adams, *The Evolution of Urban Society* (London, 1966), pp39-40; F Katz, *Ancient American Civilisations* (London, 1989), pp19-22; W Bray, 'From Foraging to Farming in Mexico', in J V S Megaw (ed), *Hunters, Gatherers and the First Farmers outside Europe*, p225-234.

136   According to P M Dolukhonov, 'The Neolithisation of Europe:a chronological and ecological approach', in C Renfrew (ed), *Explaining Cultural Change* op cit, p331-336. The datings here, as elsewhere, are approximate and might well be subject to revision in the light of more recent knowledge.

137   For estimates of dates, see C K Maisels, *The Emergence of Civilisation* (London, 1990); M Rice, *Egypt's Making* (London, 1990); M I Finlay, *Early Greece: the Bronze and Archaic ages* (London, 1981); F Katz, *Ancient American Civilisations*, op cit; and G Connah, *African Civilisations* (Cambridge 1987).

138   V Gordon Childe, *What Happened in History*, op cit, pp59-62.

139   Ibid, p80-81.

140   C K Maisels, *The Emergence of Civilisation:from hunting and gathering to agriculture, cities and the state in the Near East* (London, 1993), p297.

141   C K Maisels, ibid, p297.

142   V Gordon Childe, *Social Evolution* (London, 1963), pp155-6.

143   V Gordon Childe, *What Happened in History*, op cit, p88.

144   See C K Maisels, op cit, p146.

145   T B Jones, quoted in C K Maisels, op cit, p184.

146   T B Jones and J W Snyder, quoted in C K Maisels, op cit, p186.

147   See for a discussion on these pre-urban stone constructions, see C Renfrew, *Before Civilisation* (Harmondsworth, 1976).

148   Thus it is certain that developments in the Aegean were encouraged by what had happened on the Asian mainland to the south east and the African mainland to the south; it is likely that some of the developments in Egypt (the sorts of grains which were sown, some of the artifacts) were influenced, to a limited degree, by contacts with the earlier developing Mesopotamian civilisation; and it is just possible that the Latin American civilisations had had some contact with those of East and South East Asia.

149   V Gordon Childe, *Social Evolution*, op cit, pp160-161.

150   Ibid, pp160-161. Gordon Childe argues: 'No doubt in the old world plough cultivation had everywhere replaced hoe cultivation before the rise of civilisation. But the plough was unknown to the civilised Mayas, who had in fact no domestic animals at all...In Crete and temperate Europe as well as in Hither Asia wheeled vehicles were used before civilisation was achieved, but on the Nile such were unknown for 1,500 years after the rise of civilisation... In Egypt and Crete and among the Celts civilisation was preceded by the rise of chiefs to the status of divine kings who concentrate the social surplus. In Mesopotamia, on the contrary, it was the temple of a superhuman divinity that performed this function...while 'royal tombs' are recognisable only later...'

151   Marx's insights into the possibilities of a society in which a bureaucratic ruling class owned property and exploited the rest of society collectively were probably misapplied in his writings on early 19th century India, where there had been widespread private ownership of land for more than a thousand years. See R Tharpar, *Ancient Indian Social History* (Hyderabad, 1984).

152   A point made by C Gailey, op cit, p22.

153   See, for example, C K Maisels, op cit, p269.

154   R Tharpar, *Ancient Indian Social History*, op cit, p19.

155   See the discussion on this question in F Katz, *Ancient American Civilisations*, op cit, p70.

156   Estimates given in A B Lloyd, 'The late period', in B Trigger, Kemp, O'Connor and Lloyd, *Ancient Egypt, A Social History*, op cit, p310.

157   C Gailey, op cit.

158   And, to be honest, Gailey does not succeed in such explanation either.

159   E R Service, 'Classical and modern theories of the origins of government', in R Cohen and E R Service (ed), *Origin of the State*.

160   M H Fried, 'The state, the chicken and the egg, or what came first?', in R Cohen and E R Service, ibid, p35.

161   Especially in the famous Preface to *The Critique of Political Economy*.

162   C Renfrew, 'The emergence of civilisation', in C Renfrew (ed), *Explaining Cultural Change*, op cit, p421 and p424. What is more, cultivation itself could destabilise the environment—by lowering the water table level or exhausting the soil—leading to 'increased instability' in society and 'local pressures on population, provoking change'. C Renfrew, op cit, p427.

163   D R Harris, 'The prehistory of tropical agriculture', in C Renfrew (ed), *Explaining Cultural Change* , op cit, p398-9.

164   Ibid, p399.

165   F Engels, *The Origin of the Family*, op cit, p160-161.

166   Ibid, p286.

167   Ibid, p105. NB: the passage should not be misread, as it is occasionally, as saying the first class oppression *is* that of the female sex by the male sex. The key expression is 'coincides'.

168   See E Leacock, *Myths of Male Dominance*, op cit.

169   This is the argument of E Friedl, *Women and Men, an Anthropologist's View* op cit, p22.

170   Ibid, p29

171   Ibid, p25

172   M Etienne and E Leacock, 'Introduction', in M Etienne and E Leacock, *Women and Colonialism: Anthropological Perspectives*, (New York, 1980). 'Most description of Australian culture suffer from..male bias...Recent work...has discovered evidence of female autonomy the participation of women in ceremonial decision making ceremonies, the marriage of older women to younger men, the building of female solidarity among in-laws, the women's section of the camp which is off-limits to men and whose women can carry on affairs with men they wish to without any

obligation to formal marriage.' See also D Bell, 'Descent politics', in the same
work.

173   As E Leacock points out, Levi Strauss only devoted one and a half pages of his
massive *The Elementary Structures of Kinship* to matrilocal-matrilineal
societies—and makes four inaccurate statements in the course of doing so. See E
Leacock, *Myths of Male Dominance*, op cit, p235.

174   P S Nsugbe, *Ohaffia: a Matrilineal Ibo People* (Oxford, 1974), p68. The adult
women have a law making body, the Ikpirikpe, which 'is the one and only body
which can deal with offenses committed by women.' If the men were to make a
decision the women disapproved of, it would take counter-measures—for
example, it could rule that 'the village housewives leave their homes and husbands
en mass, abandoning all children temporarily, and not return unless their views
were heard'.

175   P S Nsugbe, ibid, pp82, 83, 85.

176   K Sachs, *Sisters and Wives*, op cit, p117 and 121.

177   For an elaboration of this point, see E Leacock, *Myths of Male Dominance*, op cit
p120.

178   Gailey, *Kinship to Kingship*, op cit, p12.

179   E Leacock, *Myths of Male Dominance*, op cit, p217.

180   E Friedl, *Women and Men*, op cit, p46.

181   F Engels, *The Origin of the Family*, op cit, p47.

182   For Morgan's views, see L S Morgan, *Systems of Consanguinity and Knowledge
of the Human Family* (New York, 1871) ,p487, and *Ancient Society*, op cit, p31.

183   F Engels, *The Origin of the Family*, op cit, p85.

184   See, for instance, E Terray, *Marxism and 'primitive societies'* (New York, 1973),
p139-40.

185   F Engels, *The Origin of the Family*, op cit, p84.

186   Ibid, p55.

187   Ibid, p56.

188   C Fluer Lobban notes that Marx was 'rather sarcastic about the notion of primitive
promiscuity' in his own *Ethnological Notebooks*, see C Fluer Lobban, 'Marxist
reappraisal of matriarchy', *Current Anthropology*, June 1979, p347.

189   F Engels, *The Origin of the Family*, op cit, p65-6.

190   Ibid, p88.

191   K Sachs makes exactly this point, see *Sisters and Wives*, op cit, p104.

192   This is a summary of Gailey's argument. It is possible that in summarising it, I
may have put my own gloss on an argument which, at times, I found slightly
obscure. See C Gailey, *Kinship to Kingship*, op cit, px.

193   V Gordon Childe, *What Happened in History*, op cit, p52-3.

194   Ibid, p59. Childe seems, later, to have become more sceptical about a 'matriarchy'
stage. See his *Social Evolution*, op cit, pp66-67.

195   V Gordon Childe, *What Happened in History*, op cit, p72.

196   E Friedl, *Women and Men*, op cit, p54.

197   Ibid, p9.

198   Ibid, p17.

199   Ibid, p59.

200   Due to the greater density of population.

201   A point made by Gordon Childe in *Social Evolution*, op cit, p159.

202   It has been argued, for example by Gordon Childe (*Social Evolution*, ibid, p67),
this need not, necessarily, have meant a society in which females were equal to
men—after all, modern hinduism contains a significant goddess and the Catholic
church has the cult of the Virgin Mary. But there is all the difference in the world
between an ideology in which female gods can be supreme and one in which

female figures play a mediating role between worshippers and the dominant male figure.

203   F Engels, *The Origin of the Family*, op cit.
204   Ibid, p116
205   Ibid, p 120
206   Ibid, p119
207   Ibid, p134-5
208   See L German, *Sex, Class and Socialism*, (second edition, Bookmarks, 1994).

Notes to Chapter Four

1   Quoted in preface to Engels, *The Dialetics of Nature* (Moscow, 1982), p6.
2   The notes which form *The Dialectics of Nature* were not published until 1927, many years after Engels' death.
3   H Sheehan, *Marxism and the Philosophy of Science* (New Jersey, 1993), p29. This book is a useful guide to the arguments within the Marxist tradition on science.
4   Ibid, p30.
5   For instance, far from the rigid, mechanical deterministic view Engels is often attacked for, he time and again attacks such an approach. Indeed this is so much the case that one is often forced to wonder if these critics have ever actually read Engels! Rigid determinism in natural science in the 19th century was best summed up by the French scientist Pierre Laplace. He claimed that the result of modern science was an all embracing determinism in which the past, present and future down to the smallest detail were all equally and completely determined.
        Such 'Determinism', Engels argued, 'tries to dispose of chance by denying it altogether. According to this conception only simple, direct necessity prevails in nature.' He mocks this view: 'That a particular pea-pod contains five peas and not four or six, that a particular dog's tail is five inches long and not a whit longer or shorter, that this year a particular clover flower was fertilised by a bee and another not, and indeed by precisely one particular bee and at a particular time, that a particular windblown dandelion seed has sprouted and another not, that last night I was bitten by a flea at four o'clock in the morning, and not at three or five o'clock, and on the right shoulder and not on the left calf—these are all facts which have been produced by an irrevocable concatenation of cause and effect, by an unshatterable necessity of such a nature indeed that the gaseous sphere, from which the solar system was derived, was already so constituted that these events had to happen this and not otherwise. With this kind of necessity we likewise do not get away from the theological conception of nature. Whether with Augustine and Calvin we call it the eternal decree of God, or Kismet as the Turks do, or whether we call it necessity, is all pretty much the same' (*The Dialectics of Nature*, p499).
6   H Sheehan, op cit, also defends Engels well from some of the attacks he has suffered.
7   F Engels, *The Dialectics of Nature* in *Marx, Engels, Collected Works* (*MECW*), Vol 25 (London, 1987), p319.
8   Ibid, p320.
9   His explanation, which drew on work on magnetism by Gilbert, was wrong, but the attempt was important. Until then a central belief in all explanations of nature was the sharp distinction between the Moon and the Earth and the rest of the heavens, the 'sublunary' and 'superlunary' spheres in the language of the day. This distinction was based on the authority of Aristotle, who had been adopted by the Catholic Church, the key ideological authority in feudal society, for its own purposes. In the superlunary sphere, the world of the planets and stars, everything was perfect, unblemished and unchanging, everything was supposed to move

endlessly in perfect circles. Change, decay, transformation were the preserve of the 'corrupt' sublunary sphere, ie Earth and its immediate environment. Kepler's arguments were therefore a challenge to this central doctrine of the old world view. Galileo's findings with the telecsope must also be seen in this context to appreciate their revolutionary nature.

10   Engels, *The Dialectics of Nature*, *MECW*, op cit, p465.
11   Ibid, p466.
12   Ibid, p466.
13   Ibid, p466. For one period of history Boris Hessen fulfilled Engels' hope. Hessen's account of the relationship between the development of Newton's science and social and production developments is a masterpiece. See 'The Social and Economic Roots of Newton's Principia' in *Science at the Crossroads: Papers presented to the International Congress of the History of Science and Technology*, held in London from 29 June to 3 July 1931, by the delegates of the USSR (London, 1971). Hessen disappared in the Stalinist purges in the USSR in the 1930s.
14   Ibid, p321.
15   Ibid, pp321-322.
16   Ibid, p322.
17   Ibid, p322.
18   Ibid, p322.
19   Ibid, p322. Newton's theory explained the motion of the planets once they were moving, he required a 'first impulse' (ie god) to set the whole mechanism in motion.
20   Engels, *Anti-Dühring*, *MECW*, Vol 25, op cit, p25.
21   Engels, *The Dialectics of Nature*, *MECW*, op cit, p324.
22   Ibid, p323.
23   Ibid, p324.
24   Ibid, p324.
25   Ibid, p324.
26   Ibid, p325.
27   See a description of this process by one of the key founders of thermodynamics in *Reflexions on the Motive Power of Fire* by Sadi Carnot, translated and edited (with excellent and fascinating notes) by R Fox (Manchester University Press, 1986).
28   Engels, *The Dialectics of Nature*, *MECW*, op cit, p325.
29   Ibid, p325.
30   Ibid, p326.
31   Ibid, p326.
32   Quoted in H Sheehan, op cit, p38.
33   Engels, *The Dialectics of Nature*, *MECW*, op cit, p327.
34   K Marx and F Engels, *Communist Manifesto, Marx Engels Selected Works*, Vol 1 (Moscow 1977), p111.
35   Ibid.
36   Engels, *The Dialectics of Nature*, *MECW*, op cit, p327.
37   Ibid, p327.
38   Engels, *Anti-Dühring*, *MECW*, op cit, p21.
39   Ibid, p22.
40   Ibid, p22.
41   Engels, *The Dialectics of Nature*, *MECW*, op cit, p353.
42   Ibid, p491.
43   Engels, *Anti-Dühring*, *MECW*, op cit, p22.
44   Ibid, p22.
45   Ibid, p22.
46   Ibid, pp22-23.

47   Ibid, p23.
48   Engels, *The Dialectics of Nature*, *MECW*, op cit, p495.
49   Ibid, p515.
50   Ibid, pp515-516.
51   Engels, *Anti-Dühring*, *MECW*, op cit, p23.
52   Engels, *The Dialectics of Nature*, *MECW*, op cit, p356.
53   Ibid, pp342-343. Engels tackles many arguments about what is 'scientific
      method'. In doing so he challenges many of the then fashionable arguments in a
      way that was decades in advance of his time. This is especially relevant given that
      at the time of writing Karl Popper, the famous philosopher of science, has recently
      died. Popper, especially through his *Logic of Scientific Discovery*, had been one of
      the most influential philosophers of science of the last few decades, and there is
      much in his arguments that is important.

      Few of those who study or follow Popper have probably ever bothered to
read Engels. Popper himself was a bitter—if shallow—opponent of Marxism. It is
therefore amusing that many of Popper's most original insights about science were
precisely those to which Engels had pointed. Popper attacked the traditional
empiricist view of science as the gradual accumulation of secure facts, with
theories then being developed by induction from these facts and verified through
experiment. Instead Popper argued that even the most straightforward observation
of nature contains irreducible elements of theory—all observation is 'theory
laden'. Engels makes precisely this point in a sharp attack on empiricism:
'However great one's contempt for all theoretical thought, nevertheless one cannot
bring two natural facts into relation with each other, or understand the connection
existing between them, without theoretical thought' (*The Dialectics of Nature*,
p354).

      Again Popper attacked the notion that scientific theories are constructed by
induction from empirical facts. Rather he argued that science develops through the
formation of bold conjectures, or hypotheses, which may not be based on facts but
which can be tested experimentally. Moreover, far from verifying theory, the point
of these tests was to falsify wrong theories. Scientific theories had to be open to
falsification; hypotheses were to be refuted by experience. Much of this approach
can be found in outline in Engels' work. He called induction 'a swindle'.
'According to the inductionists, induction is an infallible method. It is so little so
that its apparently surest results are every day overthrown by new discoveries'
(Engels, *The Dialectics of Nature*, p508). And he gives example after example of
how theories had been refuted by new facts. Engels also pointed out the logical
problem with induction, in precisely an example found in Popper, that 'it does not
follow from the continual rising of the sun in the morning that it will rise again
tomorrow' (Engels, *The Dialectics of Nature*, p510). And Engels draws the
conclusion, 'The form of development of natural science, in so far as it thinks, is
the *hypothesis*', and that science develops as 'observational material weeds out
these hypotheses' (*The Dialectics of Nature*, p529, emphasis in Engels' original).

      Critics of Engels often argue that dialectics denies the validity of formal
logic. This is simply not true. Dialectics is rather a critique of the limits of formal
logic. Such logic is invaluable, but is not capable of *fully* grasping a dynamic,
changing world. (It is interesting to note in this context that some logicians today
are seeking to develop new kinds of logic based upon the quantum mechanical
nature of reality—which does not easily fit the categories of traditional logic.)

      In later years Engels' ideas on dialectics were distorted out of all
recognition by official Stalinist philosophers of states like the USSR, China and
the old regimes in Eastern Europe. This has sometime led many genuine Marxists
who opposed these regimes to be suspicious of talk of 'dialectics'. This, however
understandable its motives, is mistaken. These regimes turned every aspect of

genuine Marxism on its head in a grotesque parody aimed at legitimising their own rule and exploitation of workers. Genuine Marxists have always had to rescue the real meaning of Marxism from such distortions and insist on its continued relevance. The same approach should be adopted with Engels' arguments on dialectics.

54 Engels, *The Dialectics of Nature*, *MECW*, op cit, p356.

55 Ibid, p357.

56 Ibid, p359.

57 Ibid, p359.

58 Ibid, p359.

59 Ibid, p361.

60 Ibid, p357.

61 Ibid, p492.

62 Engels, *Anti-Dühring*, *MECW*, op cit, p130.

63 Ibid, pp76-77.

64 Ibid, p130.

65 Engels, *The Dialectics of Nature*,in *MECW*, op cit, p587.

66 Engels, *Anti-Dühring*, *MECW*, op cit, p24.

67 Engels, *The Dialectics of Nature*, *MECW*, op cit, p321.

68 S Rose, R Lewontin and L Kamin, *Not In Our Genes* (Penguin, 1984); S Rose, *The Making of Memory* (London, 1992); R Lewontin, *The Doctrine of DNA* (London, 1993); R Levins and R Lewontin, *The Dialectical Biologist* (Harvard University Press, 1985). Why biologists are more inclined to a dialectical approach than most other scientists is an interesting question. I suspect it is a result of a combination of factors. One is that the scientific material itself more clearly pushes biologists towards a dialectical understanding. Secondly, political and philosophical argument is forced upon biologists in a far sharper way than in many sciences, given, for example, arguments about human nature etc. Thirdly, the fact that a number of the individual biologists concerned have at various points been connected to Marxist political traditions, and more so than in, say, physics, must play a part.

69 P Davies, *The Mind of God* (London, 1992), pp231-232. To be fair to Davies he is one of the few writers on modern physics who asks the right questions. Most of his attack on materialism is in fact a well justified refutation of mechanical materialism. The thrust of much of this is little different from Engels' own arguments. I do not know if Davies has ever read Engels. Unfortunately, whether through ignorance of this tradition or otherwise, Davies's correct rejection of mechanical materialism leads him to mistakenly reject genuine materialism.

70 P Davies and J Gribbin, *The Matter Myth* (London, 1991), p7.

71 Ibid, p8.

72 Engels, *The Dialectics of Nature*, *MECW*, op cit, p527.

73 Good discussions of the problems and interesting suggestions of possible solutions, written in a fairly non-technical fashion, can be found, for example, in P Coveney and R Highfield, *The Arrow of Time* (London, 1991), and M Gell-Mann, *The Quark and the Jaguar* (Little Brown, 1994). Some of the problems are beginning to be resolved in the most convincing way by a new generation of fascinating experiments, many centred in France under scientists like Serge Haroche. They are beginning to *demonstrate* how the transition from the strangeness of the quantum mechanical behaviour of atomic objects to the more familiar behaviour of larger scale objects takes place. (Lecture by Serge Haroche, Royal Society, London, October 1994.)

74 This was the theme of a major article in the March 1994 edition of the reputable *Scientific American* magazine, for instance.

75 Quoted in *The Arrow of Time*, op cit.

76   H Sheehan, op cit, p31.

77   Ibid, p319.

78   The whole of the October 1994 issue of the excellent *Scientific American* magazine is devoted to an overview of this whole process through its various stages. On reading through this after reading Engels one cannot help feeling that it should have been dedicated to his memory. In passing it is worth saying that the 'big bang' model has its own limitations. It is only valid up to a point. The laws of physics in their present form break down at the very high energies and densities as we try and track evolution back towards the 'bang'. No one can yet trace that development back beyond a certain point as a result. On the same theme even the fundamental principle of the conservation of energy is only strictly valid within certain limits. It is now established that it can be violated provided the time scale involved in the violation is small enough—as a consequence of the uncertainty principle of quantum mechanics.

79   It is misleading, as is often suggested, to say the butterfly alone 'causes' the hurricane. The real point is that a tiny change in the totality of causes can result in radically different outcomes.

80   One interesting aspect of chaos theory is that the old notions about dimensions have had to be radically changed. Usually one thinks of something having one (a line), two (a surface) or three (a solid) dimensions. In chaos theory this understanding is shown to be limited and insufficient to grasp reality. Objects can have fractional dimensions (eg 1.57). The beautiful pictures often seen in books on chaos are of such 'fractals'.

81   For a fuller discussion of chaos theory see my 'Order out of Chaos', *International Socialism* 48, 1990. Also see, for instance, I Stewart, *Does God Play Dice?* (Basil Blackwell, 1989); J Gleick, *Chaos: Making a New Science* (Sphere, 1988).

82   Thermodynamics and classical dynamics can be reconciled (via statistical mechanics) for systems at, or near, equilibrium. But this reconciliation breaks down for systems far from thermodynamic equilibrium. Engels' discussion of mathematics, of which he had a good knowledge and keen interest, is another important aspect of his work. His attitude is refreshing compared to much modern philosophical discussion on mathematics. All too often such discussion sees mathematical concepts as either simply the free creation of the human mind, completely divorced from the real world, or as existing independently of the material world or human thought in some 'timeless, etherial sense'. This is the view of the leading mathematician Roger Penrose (see R Penrose, *The Emperor's New Mind*, London, 1990). In this view, known as Platonism, as the notion has much in common with arguments advanced by the ancient Greek philosopher, these eternal concepts exist 'out there' as much as 'Mount Everest' (Penrose, pxv) and are 'discovered' when mathematicians succeed in breaking through to this 'Platonic' world by an act of insight or when they 'have stumbled across the "works of God" ' (Penrose, p126).

        In contrast to such approaches, Engels insists that mathematical concepts are rooted in the material world. 'The concepts of number and figure have not been derived from any source other than the world of reality' (*Anti-Dühring*, op cit, p36). For instance, 'Counting requires not only objects that can be counted, but also the ability to exclude all properties of the objects considered except their number—and this ability is the product of a long historical development based on experience. Like the idea of number, so the idea of figure is borrowed exclusively from the external world and does not arise in the mind out of pure thought. There must have been things which had shape and whose shapes were compared before anyone could arrive at the idea of figure.

        'Pure mathematics deals with the space forms and quantity relations of the real world—that is with material which is very real indeed. The fact that this material appears in an extremely abstract form can only superficially conceal its origin from the external world' (*Anti-Dühring*, op cit, pp36-37). Though Engels insists mathematics is in this way rooted in the real world, it is not simply a reflection of it but rather an abstraction from it: 'In order to make it possible to investigate these forms and relations in their pure state, it is necessary to separate them entirely from their content, to put the content aside as irrelevant, thus we get points without dimensions, lines without breadth and thickness, a and b, x and y, constants and variables; and only at the very end do we reach the free creations and imaginations of the mind itself, that is to say imaginary magnitudes.' Engels was certainly not arguing that mathematical concepts did not soar far away from their material origins as they were developed. He attacked, for instance, those who were unhappy with the idea of what mathematicians call imaginary numbers—like i, the square root of -1.

Engels went on to comment on the problem of why it is that 'pure' mathematics can be 'applied' to the real world—a problem which has long exercised philosophers of mathematics. 'Like all other sciences, mathematics arose out of the needs of men...but, as in every department of thought, at a certain stage of development the laws, which were abstracted from the real world, become divorced from the real world, and are set up against it as something independent, as laws coming from the outside, to which the world has to conform.

'In this way...pure mathematics was subsequently applied to the world, although it is borrowed from this same world and represents only one part of its forms of interconnection—and it is only just because of this that it can be applied at all' (*Anti-Dühring*, op cit, p37). Engels' comments are certainly a long way short of a fully worked out philosophy of mathematics but they contain much that provides a useful starting point in any serious attempt to construct such an understanding.

83 See for a discussion of all these points, for example: *The Arrow of Time*, op cit, M Mitchell Waldrop, *Complexity* (Viking, 1993), and I Prigogine and I Stengers, *Order Out of Chaos* (Flamingo, 1985).

84 Quoted in M Mitchell Waldrop, op cit, p82. Anderson won his Nobel Prize in 1977 for his detailed explanation of a marvellously dialectical process in nature. Metals are either conductors or insulators of electricity. But it was then found that certain metals could undergo a transition from being a conductor into an insulator. Anderson explained how this startling transformation happened.

85 In fundamental particle physics many of the theories put forward today to overcome some of the difficulties with existing explanations combine two elements. On the one hand they often seem to contain genuine insights which will one day have to be incorporated into any new understanding. But on the other they are often riddled with fanciful notions and wild flights of speculation which are far removed from any meaningful contact with any aspect of the world open to us at present—and very often even the advocates of these theories are not sure what they are really talking about.

A good example is the latest attempt to reconcile quantum theory with gravity—string theory. This seems to have genuine insight. All previous attempts have been plagued by infinite quantities which occur in the mathematical descriptions and which make a nonsense of them. The easiest way to *picture* why these arise is to recall that in, for example, gravity the force changes in inverse proportion to the square of the distance—$1/r^2$. In established explanations particles like, for instance, electrons are pictured as being point-like, having no extension. Think what happens to an expression like $1/r^2$ when r becomes zero. In a more complicated but analogous manner many of the fundamental problems in modern science are rooted in the very notion of point-like particles which dominates physics. String theory gets rid of these infinities and for the first time seems to point to a genuine reconciliation of quantum theory and gravity. The key element is that it sees particles not as point-like objects but rather as two dimensional 'strings', with energies and masses of different particles being analogous to various 'harmonics' on a guitar string. The problem, however, is that the whole theory only makes sense in a 'space' of ten dimensions which somehow is structured in such a way that we only see the three dimensions of everyday experience. The theory seems to be saying the essence of reality is a ten dimensional space, but the appearance is three dimensions of everyday experience. There are severe problems with this notion. One, for instance, is that some key mathematical structures vital to explaining the world are *only* valid in a space of three dimensions. In consequence no one, including its inventors, is sure what string theory means, or how real the extra dimensions are supposed to be. And as yet no one has found a way to extract from it testable consequences. Is it the starting point of a new understanding or a flight of speculation that will turn out to have no connection with the way the world really is? (For a discussion of string theory see F David Pleat, *Superstrings*, Cardinal, 1988).

86   V I Lenin, *Materialism and Empirio-Criticism* (Peking, 1972), p311.
87   I Prigogine and I Stengers, *Order out of Chaos* (London, 1988), p252.
88   R Levins and R Lewontin, *The Dialectical Biologist* (Harvard University Press, 1985).
89   S Hawking, *A Brief History of Time* (Bantam, 1989), p175.
90   I Prigogine and I Stengers, op cit, p313.
91   For a more detailed discussion of the ideas of modern science covered in this section the following references are a good starting point. One of the best is undoubtedly P Coveney and R Highfield, *The Arrow of Time*, which covers almost all the ground discussed here. Also useful are M Mitchell Waldrop, *Complexity*, I Prigogine and I Stengers, *Order out of Chaos*, and M Gell-Mann, *The Quark and the Jaguar*. Those interested can find further references in these works. All require effort but none require a formal mathematical or scientific training to understand. Anyone wanting to go into the arguments in a more detailed fashion could try the fairly comprehensive collection of essays, P Davies (ed), *The New Physics* (Cambridge University Press, 1989)—many, but not all, of these require a fairly good knowledge of mathematics.
92   Engels, *Anti-Dühring*, *MECW*, op cit, p106.

Index

S